THE SEX FILES: Forbidden Zone

Steve was trembling with excitement as he got undressed. Everything was happening just as he had imagined it. There was the bed with the covers drawn back, and there was Tanya in her French lingerie kneeling down in front of him. He climbed up behind her and she gasped. Then she called, 'OK, Tracey, you can come in now.'

The girl entered and sat on the edge of the bed. She gazed at Tanya kneeling there and Steve, naked, going into her from behind. Then she took off her top to show him her big breasts, displayed to perfection in an intricate brassiere of black lace that emphasised the deep cleavage between.

It was what he'd always dreamed of . . .

THE SEX FILES
FILE 2

Forbidden Zone

Nick Li

HEADLINE
DELTA

First published in 1997
by HEADLINE BOOK PUBLISHING

A HEADLINE DELTA paperback

10 9 8 7 6 5 4 3 2 1

ISBN 0 7472 5726 4

Typeset by
Letterpart Limited, Reigate, Surrey

Printed and bound in Great Britain by
Mackays of Chatham plc, Chatham, Kent

HEADLINE BOOK PUBLISHING
A division of Hodder Headline PLC
338 Euston Road
London NW1 3BH

Forbidden Zone

ONE

Tom Kaukonen had been teaching math at Trumperton County High for upwards of fifteen years now, and for the past five he had been head of department. The extra commitment meant he could no longer afford the time to assist with the football coaching program but his knee – damaged in a tackle by an Ohio State linebacker twenty years ago – had been playing him up worse as time went by and, in a sense, it was a relief no longer having to spend two evenings a week and every Saturday bellowing instructions from the sideline.

Tom stood a whisper over six one and was respected throughout the town as man of probity – chairman of the Elks, treasurer and committee member of the local history society, devoted father of Candice (13), Helena (11) and Hartley (9) and husband of Margaret (37). He owned a white four-door Pontiac and a partly restored '63 T-bird that needed a lot of work still. He had a ranch-style home out on Chippewawa Avenue that was too small for his needs but was close to the school.

In his fifteen years at Trumperton County High he had seen a lot of kids pass through his math class. Some of them had done real well. Marty Dryden (whom he'd taught from 1978 to 1982) was now a full professor at Massachusetts Institute of Technology, and Tom

1

secretly envied him. Then there was Laura Wilshire, always one of his favourites. Everyone expected her to sail through applied mathematics at Harvard, but in her second year there (1990-1) she had surprised everyone by changing to computer science. Now she was the youngest Vice-President in the history of Apple Corporation but she still remembered to send Tom and Margaret an affectionate Christmas card each year.

The biggest mystery of all, though, was Neil Casady (1993-5). Tom watched him through the window of his white Pontiac, parked along with hundreds of similarly anonymous vehicles in serried ranks outside the Q-Mart, loading groceries into the trunks of waiting cars. Jesus, thought Tom, looking at Casady's maroon bellboy cap and cheap nylon jacket. Neil Casady had a mathematical brain on him that could have made him a chess genius to rival Fischer or Spassky. He could so easily have been another Marty Dryden but instead he'd chosen to pack groceries at Q-Mart and to play in some rock band that did gigs at beer joints out of town and hadn't a snowball's chance in hell of picking up a contract. Still, that was what he said he wanted to do, but the loss made Tom feel sad. He was a good-looking boy too – no one's idea of a nerd.

The boy put the last of the bags inside the lady's car. Tom recognised her – Annie Palowitz, wife of Jerry, last-year-but-one's Elks secretary. Neil waved away the proffered tip – the staff at Q-Mart weren't allowed to accept gratuities – and the woman in the beige station wagon with the Nothing Could Be Finer Than To Be In Carolina sticker drove away.

The conveyer was empty, at least for the moment. Even though Neil wasn't supposed to smoke while on duty, he pulled out a pack of Luckies and lit up, glancing round from time to time to check that the supervisor was still on his lunch break.

So many kids smoking nowadays, thought Tom. He could smell it on them in class – far more than ever there used to have been. Whatever could have happened to all that expensive health education, he wondered. He'd never smoked himself, even when it seemed the natural thing for a guy to do. But Tom had never really thought of himself as a regular guy, one of the jocks. If anything, the feeling was growing with advancing years.

He got out of the car, remembering to pick up the list that Margaret had given him. He liked doing the grocery shopping. It was only a five-minute drive from Trumperton County High down to the Q-Mart and it saved Margaret the trouble. Her office – she worked as an attorney with Klein Bogdanovich – was downtown and it wasn't easy for her to slip away. Besides, the once-weekly shop got him out of the place and away from all the departmental politics that were forever flying around. Other days he'd retreat to the library or the computer suite rather than face the endless wrangling and bickering. Twenty years ago it was all about the theory and practice of teaching. Today department heads half his age bitched about their budgets.

'Hi, Mr Kaukonen,' said Neil as he approached. He smiled, showing even white teeth and at the same time he ground out the cigarette he'd been smoking. Tom Kaukonen, to him, was still an authority figure, even though he was a good two or three inches taller than his old math teacher. Neil had been a useful centre but his heart wasn't really in basketball.

'Hi, Neil,' Tom responded. 'How's it going?'

'Pretty good, you know.'

'That's good. How's that band of yours?'

'Pretty good.'

'Did you read that book on calculus I lent you yet? I thought you might find it interesting.'

'Which book was that?' Neil suddenly looked puzzled, guilty, confused – the various emotions flickering quickly across his handsome, clean-chiselled features. He'd evidently forgotten – or, more likely, just wasn't interested.

3

Tom Kaukonen had done what he could to try and nurture the boy's prodigious mathematical talents after he'd left school but it was beginning to look obvious that he was fighting a losing battle.

'Oh,' Tom said, feigning a look of puzzlement. 'Maybe it was someone else I lent it to.'

Neil didn't say anything. What could he say? He just looked at him levelly. The cigarette smoke still hung around in the air.

'Just doing the shopping, you know,' Tom ventured.

'Sure,' said Neil. 'On your lunch hour, huh?'

'That's right. It's either that, or listen to old Jock Partridge bellyaching for an hour and a quarter.'

Neil laughed. Jock Partridge enjoyed the respect of neither staff nor students, which was probably why he had been principal of Trumperton County High for these past thirteen years.

Another load of groceries came humping down the conveyor. A black Honda, almost new, came nosing down to the pick-up point.

'There is one thing, though –' said Tom Kaukonen, a little hesitantly. Neil picked up the grocery box, glanced at him, that familiar knowing sideways glance. When he quit school he'd mown the Kaukonens' grass for them most weeks, done various little jobs for them. It was Tom's little scheme to try and keep an eye on him, not to break the ties. Neil was always doing little things for the Kaukonens. Sometimes, afterwards, he and Tom would share a beer and Tom would try to interest him in some mathematical problem or show him some article in one of the specialised journals. Neil would either be totally indifferent or else he'd get to the heart of the matter faster than a Kray-2 with afterburners.

'Sure,' said Neil, smiling. 'What is it?'

Now it was Tom's turn to smile, a little less certainly.

'Neil,' he said, after glancing around the parking lot. 'Neil, I'd really like to fuck that sweet butt of yours.'

4

Neil Casady didn't flinch, nor did the smile leave his handsome features, classically Aryan and symmetrical to a fault. He just stood there for a few seconds while Tom Kaukonen's heart raced. He shuffled lightly from foot to foot – Tom recalled seeing him playing ball in the school gym, how fast and light on his feet he was for a big guy. Then he hit his old math teacher so hard with his balled-up fist that Tom's nose burst and the blood sprayed all over his maroon nylon overall with the Q-Mart logo on the left breast.

The old fart at the wheel of the black Honda just sat there, amazed.

Tom took the rest of the afternoon off. He phoned the school secretary to say he'd walked straight into the revolving door at the Q-Mart and he told Margaret the same thing when she came home from work that evening.

Everyone believed him. After all, if you couldn't trust a guy like Tom Kaukonen, who in the hell could you trust?

TWO

Bernice McCracken had just driven into the parking lot
to pick up her husband Jim from outside the ice-packing
plant where he was shop foreman on the day shift. He'd
recently lost his licence for three months on account of
acquiring too many penalty points in the given period –
nothing serious, just getting caught a couple of times in
a speed trap doing ten over the limit and a little problem
with a defective rear indicator that had led to a minor
accident – but having to do the driving didn't bother
Bernice any. She'd learned to drive a tractor at age
twelve on her pappy's farm and it peed her off that she
and Jim didn't really ever have enough money to buy her
a little car of her own – nothing fancy, just a nice little
Hyundai or a Toyota would do – what with the mortgage
payments on the house and the extortionate sums that
Jim had to pay monthly to his ex-wife, a real ball-breaker
called Maybelline who worked as a waitress at Bobby's
Burlesque Bar at the corner of Vine Street and A.

   She liked driving the Olds. It had muscle and it didn't
roll the way most Detroit cars did. The sound system
that Jim had fitted was good, too. Right now she was
playing Alanis Morisette, her favourite. Besides, tonight
was their wedding anniversary and Jim would like a
drink or six, so it was as well that Bernice had the car.
She didn't drink hardly at all now, having seen what it

6

had done to her brother Bob's liver, and of course her nephew Jackie had been killed by a drunk driver a mite under three years ago. Six years old and with everything going for him, it didn't hardly make any sense. Her eyes went misty at the thought. She didn't mind Jim drinking when he had a mind to – which wasn't all that often, if truth be told – but as for herself, she could just as well live without it.

She checked her eye make-up in the mirror, fingered her hair. Pretty good, she reckoned. She wiggled her ass in time to the music, blew herself a kiss.

Gimp Waterson came by on a forklift truck, gave her a big wave. Bernice and Gimp's wife Terri went to the Jacuzzi together every Tuesday and then to this Mex eatery they knew. She looked at her watch – a quarter of six. The Alanis Morisette tape finished and she listened to REM instead.

There was no hurry. Sometimes she might have got a little pissed that Jim was late coming out of work but it didn't seem to matter none, even though they had a big night out ahead. So she was feeling pretty good when Jim came out of the side door to the machine shop. She was looking forward to the meal – they were going to McCluskey's, their favourite place, out beyond Tagholme Drive – and to what would inevitably follow when they hit the sack afterwards.

'Hi, honey,' said Jim as he got into the passenger seat beside her and kissed her. She could smell the machine oil on him and she knew he would need to shower and get a change of clothes before they went out.

She gunned the engine and drove out of the parking lot. The nearside front brake drum was binding, she noticed.

'Hey, what's this?' asked Jim after he'd got himself clipped in and dumped his lunch pail on the back seat.

She smiled at him. 'Thought I'd give you a nice surprise,' she said. They weren't going out till eight but

7

already she was dressed ready for the evening, in the tight black number that Jim liked so much. She was wearing a new perfume, too, CK1 from Calvin Klein.

Bernice was one year short of her thirtieth birthday but she could have passed easily for twenty-five or twenty-six. Jim, she knew, was real proud of her, liked to show her off to his friends. Quite a few of the guys in the machine shop had given her admiring glances as she'd waited for him in the lot but they all respected Jim and knew Bernice wouldn't play around.

Jim hunkered round in his seat to look at the woman he'd been married to for the past five years. Blonde hair that was kind of fluffy, a nice pair and a gorgeous ass – but it was her legs that were Bernice's star attraction, long and slender. The short hem of her black dress had ridden up and involuntarily he reached out a hand and began to caress her thigh.

'My, aren't we the impatient one?' she laughed, and he smiled too.

Then his fingers encountered something he'd not been expecting – a lump about halfway up Bernice's thigh. He could feel it through the soft fabric of her woollen dress.

'What's this?' he said, surprised.

'Have a look-see then, if you can't wait,' she replied, again with that smile on her lips. Her face, he noticed, carried more make-up than usual.

His hand gently eased up her skirt an inch or two. It was a good thing Bernice was driving, because if it had been Jim McCracken at the wheel he would unquestionably have ploughed into the back of the Dunkin' Donut delivery truck that was halted at the lights at the Vine Street intersection, opposite Bobby's Burlesque Bar where Jim's ex worked five nights a week.

There was a heart-stopping expanse of bare flesh between the softly rumpled hem of Bernice's dress and the top of what he now realised was a nylon stocking.

The lump he had felt through the fabric, he could now see, was the catch of one of her garters.

He let out a low whistle, could feel his heart beginning to race. He'd asked Bernice several times in a hinting kind of way if she'd ever considered wearing nylon stockings and a garter belt once in a while instead of pantihose, but she'd always seemed to ignore him. Now, it seemed, she'd taken him at his word. For the first time in his life, outside the pages of the softcore magazines that circulated on a daily basis around the machine shop, he was looking at a young woman in high heels and a black lace garter belt, not in a rented motel bedroom or posed by some Arcadian waterfall but right there on the corner of A Street and Vine, smack outside United Tire. He was running his hand feverishly over his wife's bare thigh while she sat there in the driver's seat, bold as a newly minted nickel, and smiled back at him. Her lips and tongue made that o-shaped pouting lick that, between them, was their sign that a little cock-sucking might soon be on the agenda.

Half-embarrassed but strangely excited, Jim turned round and noticed that a truck had pulled up right alongside them in the right-turn lane. The guy at the wheel must have had a clear view of his wife's cool white thighs with the black lines slashing excitingly down them like strokes of a graffiti-artist's felt-tip. But Bernice didn't seem to mind. She pulled away from the lights with her dress hiked up so high that Jim could see that she wasn't wearing any panties either.

Something went plunging down through his guts so fast it was like a lift gone out of control. His dick felt like it was going to burst clean out of his oil-spattered coveralls. He wondered just what in the hell had come over her. Even on a good day with light traffic it normally took him at least fifteen minutes to make it back to their house on Orchard Drive.

Tonight, in the evening rush, Bernice made it in twelve.

THREE

WASHINGTON, DC. JUNE 9TH. 11.13 AM.

Thomas Hannah had a hangover you could have carved slices off and served with dauphinois potatoes and a chicory salad. His eyes looked like beetles swimming in tomato soup. Something had crawled into his mouth during the night and, after making liberal use of his tongue as a latrine, had quietly died there and begun to rot.

This morning, as he tried to hide himself away from prying eyes and unwelcome memos and phone calls, his brain was functioning like an obsolete 32-bit games console. He kept reading the same paragraph over and over again but it didn't make any sense.

He sipped what must have been coffee from a Styrofoam cup but his taste buds were all shot to hell. He had buried himself deep in the Dead Files department of the Bureau library in the hope that no one would disturb him. No one ever came down to Dead Files unless they really had to. This was stuff that wasn't even on fiche, let alone CD-ROM. It was old, old information that no one ever consulted but which the department could never quite bring itself to throw away.

Checking up on Soviet activity in Afghanistan pre-1955 was hard work and it was even harder when you had Mike Tyson trying to punch his way out of your brain. There was hardly any light at the desks or in the stacks, and his senses were over-compensating. The documentation he was ploughing through was all stowed away in identical grey box files and it was obvious that a lot of it had been weeded out over the years, making it more difficult than ever to follow a lead. Hannah was barely even trying this morning, the smell of ancient paper and cardboard almost making him gag.

He had a map of the country spread out in front of him. He was trying to link names with places but wasn't having a great deal of success. Even at the best of times, it was hard to carry more than six or seven of those weird-looking words in his mind at one time. Today, he could have scanned the ones he was looking for a dozen times and not recognised them.

He stopped work, rubbed his eyes, tried deep breathing exercises to see if the extra intake of oxygen would clear his head a little, just long enough for him to get a fix on reality. Still, it had been worth it, acquiring a hangover like that one. It had been a long time since he'd scored with a casual pick-up and while there were risks – there were always risks, especially in his line of business – he knew the game well enough to play the percentages with confidence. His temples may have been throbbing but his dick hummed smoothly to itself like a 24-valve car engine, winding itself down after a long night's drive.

There was no air conditioning in this part of records, at least not the kind of air conditioning that keeps human beings warm in winter and cool in summer. Everything was at a constant 52 degrees Fahrenheit, to keep the paper intact until the millennium when, presumably, they could throw it all away. Hannah felt distinctly chilly. His stomach was rumbling ominously and he knew he should have had breakfast.

He tried the coffee again but it had got no better in the meantime, and was about three degrees colder. The files he was looking at weren't leading anywhere, either. Names, names, goddamn names, those endless lists. Some of it looked like letters arranged at random. He wondered just why the hell Stone had given him this assignment in the first place. Six months he'd been working on this case, more off than on. At first he had been quite enthusiastic about it. The Bureau had been pretty quiet back then – it always was in September and early October, as people drifted back from vacations in Europe and the Far East and other places, and slowly picked up the reins. Hannah had been to the Adironacks, the same as usual. He didn't like vacations. He preferred to stay home and watch the ball games, drunk.

The investigation gave him a focus in those quiet weeks. But, as time passed by and the expected leads failed to materialise, he had begun to lose interest. Now it was something he only took up when he had nothing better with which to fill his time. Even Stone seemed to have forgotten about it. He never asked Hannah where things were going or what kind of conclusions he might be reaching.

Hannah knew what conclusions he was reaching – this thing was a waste of time, and had been almost since the day he started work on it. His eyes scanned the yellowing pages automatically, looking for names. Mujaterran came in over and over again but that wasn't the one he was looking for. Jihot, that was the monkey. Stone hadn't even told him why he needed to know about this guy Jihot. He just wanted to know if the Bureau had any reference.

Hannah scratched and yawned, looked at his watch. It lacked a quarter of twelve. Lunch would be a half-inch slice of salt beef on pumpernickel, no mustard, a chilli and mayo, with maybe a can of cola for the energy. He sure as hell needed it.

His mind, inevitably, went back to the previous evening. A gallery opening – a friend of his, Tad

Waterson, had a hand in it – and the usual conversations with the usual people over drinks and finger food. He'd noticed the girl as soon as she'd arrived – fashionably late, of course – red-haired, in leggings and a black lycra mini, a black Moschino biker jacket. Her boobs, which were the first thing he noticed, were full and prominent. Her name, incredibly, was Clemency.

She was interesting to talk to – a photographer, she said, worked on still-lifes mostly, did some advertising work via McCann Erikson. Hannah was impressed. Tad Waterson told him that she commanded big money – more for a single shoot than Hannah made in a month. She couldn't have been more than twenty-five or twenty-six, if that.

And yet it was plain she was no breadhead. Chords were struck. They talked about pictures, walked around looking at the stuff on the walls, collages and found objects. Hannah said he had a couple of Ansel Adams 20 × 16s in his apartment, shots of Yosemite National Park. She was impressed. She liked Adams. She didn't ask how much he had paid for them, which was a significant detail. They exchanged addresses and fax numbers. He could never forget a name like that, Clemency. He never did ask her surname and she didn't ask his Christian name either. In fact, she didn't really ask him anything about himself, which was just as well, really, in the circumstances.

They had quite a lot to drink – Tad kept a good cellar and this was no struggling gallery in the west forties. He went back, alone, to his rented apartment with the two Ansel Adams prints. There were no messages on the answerphone, as usual. He opened the refrigerator but there was just a couple of bottles of a mid-range New Zealand cabernet sauvignon that was two years old and probably well past its prime, and a six-pack of cans of the black stuff from Ireland.

He drank the Guinness straight out of the can, pushing

things around the small kitchenette, the TV flickering aimlessly. He was high on good wine from the gallery opening and sexual desire for Clemency. He fixed himself a sandwich, ham and mustard.

The entryphone beeped. Oh shit, he thought. Martin again.

His friend Martin had been going through tough times lately, was on the verge of a breakdown. Several times recently he'd come round to crash with Hannah, didn't like being on his own, probably. It had always been at this time of night. Sometimes he rang first to say he was coming, sometimes he didn't. Martin was a consultant obstetrician, weighed not much more than a hundred and thirty pounds and had a habit. A lot of medics did, it transpired.

As long as he didn't leave his works in the bathroom, Hannah could tolerate his nocturnal visits, the body on the couch in the morning.

'Come on in, Martin,' he said.

'It's Clemency,' said the voice in the little black grille.

In the couple of minutes it took her to ride the elevator, Hannah did more clearing up than he had done in the nine months he'd lived in the apartment. Books and papers were swept aside, coffee cups thrust into kitchen cupboards.

She was still wearing the black biker jacket. He offered her the other can of Guinness. 'Thanks,' she said, and settled into an armchair by the window. Outside, they could see the lights of the city twinkling. Hannah never drew the drapes. There weren't any voyeurs he knew of that chartered helicopters.

'I'm sorry to come barging in on you like this,' she said hesitantly. He politely demurred – the pleasure was entirely his, he said.

'It can get a bit boring out there in the evenings,' she went on, evidently charmed by his smile.

'That's not the real reason you came here, is it?'

14

She looked at him. Her eyes were very bright. She must have done some coke, he reckoned. Having a friend like Martin gave you a lot of clues to people's behaviour.

'I went back to my loft but – oh shit, there's this guy I know. We had this scene going, you know the kind of thing. I thought that was all over but there was his car parked just down the street when I got back. I've been feeling kind of strung out lately. I couldn't face it.'

He didn't believe a word of it. He could have wagered five against twenty that the crotch of her panties was absolutely sopping wet.

'So you came to visit me?' he said, maintaining the conceit. 'For tea and sympathy?'

'As you can see –' with a sweep of her hand – 'there aren't an awful lot of places to go round here. I'm a country girl. I just work here, you know. I never did put down roots.'

Some country girl, he thought, eyeing the boots and the tight black leggings, the thousand-dollar jacket.

Sipping Guinness, they talked with a readiness that perhaps surprised both of them – about what she was doing, about her past history, about her life in general. It was easy and spontaneous. Hannah was glad she didn't ask him about his life, his work, his hang-ups. It was already past midnight and he had an itch to fuck her that was damn near killing him.

Their first kiss was as inevitable – and as pre-ordained – as her coming to his apartment. Like teenagers at a crowded party, he actually took her on his lap in the big armchair, and her tongue felt firm, strong and pointed as it played around his lips. He breathed in her perfume, soft and fruity, with a sensual hint of musk. Arabesque, he thought, or Cold Metal. He was pretty darn good on perfumes.

Once he'd got her out of her jacket, he clasped her closely, a burgeoning desire vipering through him. He

15

stroked her shoulders, the soft bare flesh of her upper arms. Her tongue roved over his face, his neck, his ears. He felt her breasts crushed heavily against him, and could feel the warmth rising from her body, bringing with it a muskier edge to her perfume.

Her hair was thick and lustrous as he played with it, their lips pressed together still, their tongues snaking and intertwining. She had, he noticed, incredibly sweet breath, though she'd been smoking cigarettes at the party, and like his own her teeth had a slightly uneven quality that he found oddly appealing.

She grunted softly and squirmed a little, as if to seat herself better. She reached for his hand and placed it on her breast. Its point was hard with desire. Through the tight lycra of her mini dress he could feel the lacy fabric of her brassiere. He took the weight of her breast as she leaned forward slightly and it seemed to spill over into the palm of his hand. He stroked, pressed, squeezed, cupping it as his tongue again sought hers. His penis was stiff and, with her body lying half on top of him, it felt horribly uncomfortable, like a spring trying desperately to uncoil itself.

She had her hand inside his shirt, running under his arms, across his chest. She raked her long, red finger-nails across his nipples and bit his earlobe. 'Come on, lover,' she breathed. 'Let's see what you've got for me.'

They stood up, went through into the bedroom. It was a bare and inhospitable room. Aware of its failings as a seduction chamber, he felt oddly unsure of what to do next – it was as though he were an impecunious university freshman, not a successful Grade Seven investigator of thirty-five who had slaked his appetites with a long and largely satisfactory menu of carnal delights. Sensing his momentary hesitation, she took the initiative.

Clemency unbuttoned his shirt, running her hands across his chest, cupping his pectorals as though they were female breasts. She was not more than five feet five or six – Hannah stood over six feet tall without shoes – so she needed only to bend her knees a fraction to be able to take his nipples in her mouth by turn. As she did so, he shucked off the shirt, tugging his hands through the cuffs, heedless of the button that sprang off – he never did find it – and tossing the garment aside.

He sat on the bed and kicked off his shoes. Clemency stood there watching him, her eyes aflame, her chest visibly panting. He was surprised, looking at her this way, how long and colt-like her legs were, accentuated by the spike-heeled ankle boots she wore.

'This is a very nice welcome for a lonesome country girl,' he heard her saying. It seemed a vacuous remark to make, but she smiled warmly and looked him straight in the eye.

'Perhaps you're a very special guest, Clemency,' he responded.

Still not shifting her gaze, she tugged the tight lycra sheath over her head. Her breasts wobbled noticeably as she did so. They were magnificent, large and full, tantalisingly separated into two luscious globes by an uplift brassiere of intricate black lace that plunged low at the front. She caught his gaze and came over and straddled him, pushing her superb bosom almost into his face.

'Fancy a little suck, Hannah?' she breathed in a husky whisper.

He reached up, slipping his fingertips inside the cups, easing those marvellous tits out into his hands. Unbounded, they were heavy and pear-shaped, the nipples a delicate raspberry pink, long and inviting. He licked each one in turn, like a wine expert tasting a new vintage. And then with an audible sigh he took as much as he could of one breast deep into his mouth.

His tongue swirled around her nipple just as Clemency's had with his, nipping and teasing, caressing and cajoling. She threw her head back, her hands steadying herself on his strong shoulders. He released the nipple from his mouth and saw it glistening and swollen to twice the size of the other one. She looked down at him through her mane of red hair and smiled encouragingly.

'Suck both my tits,' she murmured.

He repeated the exercise, licking and lapping, feeling her strong back muscles with his hands as she pushed her chest forward towards him. She seemed to be pulling him to her breast like a mother with her baby, urging him to suck, offering him not just pleasure but life itself. He unhooked the bra with ease – never a fumbler, even as a teenager, he had always rather fancied himself a natural with hooks and eyes – and cast it aside. He noticed the red marks on her skin where it had held her ample flesh in check.

They rolled over to lie side by side on the bed. She tugged at his belt, unzipped him, her tongue and lips hungrily seeking his body all the while. He took over and struggled out of his chinos, pressing his full erection against the softness of her thigh, naked now and feeling strong and proud. His hand slid under the waistband of her leggings, under the thin, wispy material beneath, and then his fingers could feel the soft, crinkly fur of her pubic mound and the lips that gaped so invitingly. He closed his eyes, alive only to the experience of touch.

She was incredibly wet even before he touched her. Her panties were soaked, just as he had anticipated. He wondered if – it wasn't beyond the bounds of possibility – she had already come. He ran a finger experimentally along the warm, slippery groove of her sex, the film of lust coating his skin. She moaned softly, and spread her legs more for him. He stroked her gently, fingers delicately exploring the sensitive folds, his knuckle brushing against the erect clitoris.

He opened his eyes and saw that she was looking at him again, willing him on. He pushed a finger deep into her vagina, and then another, and her gaze never faltered. Her tongue snaked out and sought his, one arm around his shoulder, the other lying crushed and immobile between them. His hips moved slowly and easily against hers, like a long, low, loping blues rhythm, sensuous and easy. She matched him, note for note, lick for lick. He felt good.

When she came, his fingers still wriggling inside her, it was without obvious display. She sighed, drew in her breath, held him tightly and stopped moving altogether. Her eyes, for the first time, were tightly closed. Then she let out a great, shuddering breath and flopped back on the quilt, a smile playing around her lips.

They lay together, soundlessly, for several minutes. Then he got up – acutely aware of his erect penis bobbing up and down – and pulled off first her ankle boots, and then her black leggings. Underneath she was wearing shamelessly transparent pants, so brief as to barely cover her pubic mount, whose curls showed through the gauzy black fabric like whorls of lace. He could smell her vaginal secretions, muskily bitter-sweet. She hooked her thumbs under the filmy garment, shucked it off and lay there as naked as he.

Or almost as naked. The only thing she was wearing was a jewel around her neck, a kind of necklace or talisman on a silver chain. He paused for a moment, held it between his fingers. It was pure like ice.

'What's this?' he asked.

'It's a crystal,' she said. 'Clear quartz. It makes me feel good about myself.'

'Oh yeah?' said Hannah, unconvinced.

'Sure it does. Crystals have incredible healing properties, you know. They use them a lot in oriental medicines. The Tibetans call them healing stones. They give out vibrations. They can affect how you feel if you know how to use them.'

'I'll believe you,' said Hannah, and he nuzzled her

19

neck. He didn't want to know about crystals at this precise moment.

Her pussy, when he entered her, was tight and welcoming. He felt enveloped and embraced at the same time, as though she were urging him ever deeper inside her. Clemency hiked her legs up over his own and it seemed to draw him in even further. Slowly he began to move in the primordial rhythm, swaying and sliding, an inaudible beat pulsing through his blood like the deepest of deep bass notes. She matched his every move, pushing up against him, drawing away, her hips pressing up to meet his every urgent thrust.

He drew his penis out almost to the glans and then, with deliberate slowness, slid it all the way back in again.

She cried out. 'Oh, yes,' she hissed in his ear. 'Do it like that.'

He pulled out and pushed in again, and again, each thrust like an entry into her vagina. She raked her fingers across his back, more than playfully – it inflicted a sharp and momentary pain on him that only served to heighten his awareness of the sensations that were running riot through his body.

Slowly, consciousness of everything else began to ebb away. The room, the tangled bedcovers, the bedside light, even the breeze that had played through the open window – all slowly drifted away, unheeded and forgotten, until all there was only the two of them, lost in a world of muscle and flesh, of fluid and feelings, wandering alone through the darkness of the senses.

There were no formed images now in his mind – not even of the girl beneath him, her red hair and stupendous breasts. They clung on for a while, bobbing around like drifting branches in a stream, before being swept away by a greater and more irresistible force.

Stripped of any need other than to do what he was doing, his body seemed possessed of inordinate strength. He powered himself up from his elbows, taking the full weight of his torso on to his wrists, and thrust hard into her. She squealed – audibly squealed – but he was almost heedless, driven by his own biological urgency, his senses aflame. Their rhythm built up in intensity, each in turn adding a new twist, a different way of pushing, one's tongue from time to time seeking the other's and then pulling away, trailing across cheek or shoulder, soft wet trails of saliva invisibly mingling with body sweat.

Until, finally, he threw himself forward over the edge of the precipice, gliding freely in flight as he had done so often in his dreams, aware only of the tumult in his mind, the pressing urgency, the contractions and spasms and pulsing outburst of energy that preceded that great and final stillness in his loins.

'What the fuck you doing down here?' said the man standing next to him.

Hannah started – he had been miles away, with his dick nestled high up and tranquil inside Clemency's welcoming sheath.

'Jesus Christ, Collis, you damn near gave me a heart attack.'

Collis took in the loosened tie, the beetle eyes, the general air of seediness.

'You started celebrating New Year's early, then?' the other man asked. He was forty-five, the same grade as Hannah, short and paunchy. He smoked a lot, Hannah could smell it on his Arran tweed sport jacket. A lot of people in the Bureau smoked, even Pepper allegedly. There was a government circular that said the office was supposed to be smoke-free by the end of 1995 but the deadline had passed without anyone moving a muscle. Stone said the Bureau was bigger than the government and who the fuck were they to come round telling folks what they could and couldn't do. Normally Hannah would have liked to shove a red-hot harpoon up Stone's ass but the guy had loyalty to his staff, he had to admit that, even if he had a funny way of showing it sometimes.

Hannah was still thinking about Clemency's wet pussy. It was like being wakened from a dead sleep. 'Huh?' was all he could manage.

'I said, you started celebrating New Year's early, then?' Collis repeated.

'Real funny, Collis. I don't know where you dream them one-liners up from, I really don't. You read the Katzenjammer Kids or something when you were little?'

'What you looking for down here, then? Wild Commie general orchestrates over sex orgies? CIA photographs of Eisenhower's porno dungeon?'

Since the business with Felice Cody, Hannah had acquired something of a reputation down at the office water-cooler. He was the one who got to look into all the kooks and weirdos and sex freaks, the guys with twelve-inch dicks and the women who could handle three at once. There were even rumours that a video was in circulation, all kinds of interesting things taken from the Cody case. The guys weren't supposed to talk about their work too closely with other agents but somehow news of what he and Jarvis had been working on leaked out. No one dared ask Jarvis about it but a cocksman like Hannah was fair game. It was a shame, he always felt, because it was Agent Jarvis who really knew what was going on.

'Just bug out, Collis, will ya?' he said, aware of how rudely his peace had been shattered. 'I got work to do.'

'I know. Stone sent me down here to help you.'

Oh, God. Now Hannah's head was aching worse than ever. He wished he had some aspirin to take. Collis Langley talked nineteen to the dozen even under conditions of total silence and how he ever made it to Grade Seven, Hannah would never know. If getting work done with a terminal hangover was bad enough, it would be fifty times worse with Collis there blathering about his

22

kids and his pool filtration system and just about anything else that came into his fat, bald, cigarette-smoking head.

Hannah couldn't face it. He went and sat in the records department john for the best part of half an hour and then went to lunch. When he got back, Collis had gone but the smell of cigarette smoke was everywhere. His hangover, if anything, seemed to be getting worse.

FOUR

DESOTHO, NEW MEXICO. JUNE 12TH. 9.52 PM.

It should really have been the Dreyfuses' turn to have Mike and Arlene Thomas over for supper but they'd been having their kitchen refitted, and so – seeing that they usually saw each other about once every month or so – Arlene had said they should come over to their house on Greyfriars Drive that Saturday instead.

Besides, Arlene had a big surprise in store for Bill and Chrissie because an old friend of theirs, Larry Turnbuckle, was visiting from Galveston. They hadn't seen Larry since the fall, when the weather was just about warm enough for one last barbecue and Mike had dug some big thick T-bone steaks out of the freezer.

It had been a really good evening that time, and so it was tonight. Larry had seen a shooting star pass right overhead – Larry was big on astronomy, he had a twelve-inch reflector set up permanently in his garden workroom – and everyone was happily talking about old times and generally enjoying themselves.

They stood out there on the back stoop for quite some time with drinks in their hands while Larry showed them some of the constellations, but the glare from the city lights made it kind of difficult to see much. After a while it began to get pretty chilly but everyone was having too much fun to notice and so, when they did finally come indoors, Mike reckoned it was cold enough to turn the heating up, as well as the log-effect fire. Soon they were so snug in the Thomas's ranch-style living room that they could have been holed up in a log cabin while a blizzard raged outside.

There was a lot of liquor laid on but everyone seemed in a happy enough mood anyway. Bill Dreyfus had just got a big promotion at a time of life when most guys were beginning to feel edgy about young whipper-snappers stealing in on their jobs for half the salary, and Chrissie was going to give up her job at the bank – she only worked three mornings a week there anyway, now – and go back to looking after the kids full-time. It was nice to have something to celebrate for once. These days, things seemed to be on a downward spiral for a lot of people.

On a personal level, things were going pretty well between Mike and Arlene too. They'd been through a couple of sticky periods in their twelve-year marriage but last year they'd had counselling over a six-month period and that seemed to have kicked out a lot of the snags. She felt they knew each other much better as a result.

Their sex life was better too. Sometimes, in the bad days, they didn't do it more than maybe once a month. Now it was more like four or five times a week and Arlene was looking forward to doing it tonight as well. She had that warm glow inside her that she could feel mounting up steadily until, in Mike's arms, she would find her release. She could hardly wait, and she knew he felt the same way. He'd given her butt a squeeze when he came out to get more wine.

She looked across at him. She liked his muscular arms, the strong neck, the thick black hair. She felt like she could hardly keep her hands off him. Yes, it sure was a good evening. Bill was talking to Arlene about their upcoming holiday in Aspen, Colorado – they liked to go there at least once a year – and Larry and Mike were talking to Chrissie about nothing in particular, just laughing and firing off the wisecracks and everything, the same as old times.

Arlene was feeling unusually mellow and relaxed when she went out to the kitchen to fetch some more ice and check how things were coming along in the oven. She switched on the TV that stood on top of the freezer cabinet. She flipped channels and found some English movie with an actor she liked. She'd always had the hots for him. It was some kind of costume drama and she was aware of the bulge in his breeches. She smiled to herself. It would be fine later with Mike.

She must have been out there longer than she'd thought, because when she came back to where the others were Chrissie had taken her top off and was sitting there on the sofa with her luscious melon breasts upheld by a black Wonderbra. Mike was standing over her pumping furiously on his dick and then, even as Arlene watched – and she'd only been gone to get the ice a few minutes at most – he shot a big trail of come all over her exaggerated bosom.

The sight made Arlene break out in a hot flush. The next thing was, Bill was standing next to her, up real close like he was in her personal space, and suddenly she wanted him – like she *really* wanted him. She looked across at Chrissie who smiled as if to say, yes I know, and though Arlene didn't know what the hell was happening to her, or to any of her friends for that matter, she let Bill take her in his arms there and then, right there in her living room with her husband watching.

What the hell was going on? It was like she'd stepped through an invisible door into another dimension. And not just her, everyone in the room seemed to feel the same way. It was as if all the things that were maybe going through their minds were actually happening, had been brought to life. Instead of just thinking about them, they were actually doing them.

26

The next moment Arlene saw Chrissie working Larry off. Arlene had always been given to understand by Larry's wife, Naomi – still back at home in Galveston, unfortunately, with a bad case of sciatica – that Larry was pretty well hung but nothing could have prepared her for the sight that greeted her. Larry's dick must have been a good eight or nine inches long and very thick.

'Jeez, I'd love to take a suck on that,' she heard herself murmur even as Bill pushed her face forward over the couch and pulled her dress – the new one that she'd bought only that Thursday from Valérie at Sapperton Mall – up over her hips and started tugging away at the white satin panties that Mike liked so much. She was wearing the matching brassiere as well, to get him excited later. Arlene always liked to wear nice lingerie and Mike certainly wasn't complaining.

She'd never done anything remotely like this before but it felt real good as Bill slid into her and then she saw Larry come off, all over Chrissie's 38Ds again, and she could see the come running down over the black lace bra she wore. Mike came over and lay down on the sofa and started kissing her, and then Chrissie came over too and took off her skirt and her brassiere and panties and knelt down so she could suck Mike's dick. Even though, in the natural course of events, it normally took him a good twenty minutes or so to get hard again after they'd done it, Arlene seemed to have some kind of gift when it came to blowing a guy and in the blink of an eye Mike's dick looked like a cop's night-stick once more.

Christ, she thought, this is just totally out of this world. Pinch me, someone, I'm dreaming. Better still, fuck me.

Bill was pushing into her real hard from behind and she knew he would come soon, as she bucked hard against him and felt that familiar tingling from deep in her loins. A wonderful sense of abandonment seemed to fill her and with it, a sense that this was all OK.

Sometimes she'd done things that had made her feel guilty, like when she first smoked grass or when she and Lisa Carter had had that little thing going when they were sixteen, but this just felt terrific. These were people you had supper with every few weeks, after all. It wasn't as though you were being fucked by a total stranger. She'd never even realised until now how sexually attractive she found Bill Dreyfus.

Mike and Chrissie, both of them naked now, were lying on the thick fur rug in front of the imitation log fire, their arms and hands roving every which way, and then Chrissie was straddling him, guiding his dick into herself. Larry had got his video camera out – he'd been filming them earlier, to show Naomi when he got back – and was prowling around the room shooting off footage of Chrissie fucking Mike and Bill fucking Arlene and all the while he had this big goofy grin on his face like he was really enjoying himself too. Arlene thought of that lovely big dick of his and soon she was smiling too.

Arlene was almost there when Bill came off and then Larry took over, fucking straight into another man's spunk like it was the kind of thing he did every day. Arlene's cutely pointed tits were spilling out of her brassiere and Larry was cupping them and doing wondrous things to her nipples but the best thing was that big fat dick of his stuck into her right up to the hilt. Fired up by what Bill had been doing to her, she came almost immediately Larry shoved that big thick thing up into her, and now she was going to come again. She could see Chrissie leaning forward with her big melon breasts only an inch or so from her husband's probing tongue and, with a voluptuous thrill of the forbidden, Arlene decided she'd quite like a suck of them herself later, if Chrissie was willing, which the way things were going that evening she more than likely would be.

The thought of herself tonguing one of Chrissie's gorgeous strawberry nipples while Mick licked the other brought on a shimmering wave of pleasure and then she was riding the wild surf again, away in a world of her own, free and unbound and, above all, gloriously happy. It was an evening she wished would never end, and for years afterwards – for nothing quite like it ever happened again – she would wonder how on earth it could have started.

When it was all over she and Mike cleared up a little and then went to bed. They didn't say much, just got in between the sheets and then fucked each other senseless until the small hours of the morning. She could remember every little detail of what happened, it was uncanny.

In the morning, when Mike had gone to work, she found Chrissie's black brassiere underneath the chesterfield. She looked at it, the large cups, the delicate lace. She held it to her nose, inhaled Chrissie's familiar perfume. She'd love it, licking Chrissie's tits while Chrissie licked hers and the guys spunked all over the two of them.

On an impulse, she picked up the phone, dialled the bank where Chrissie worked.

'Mrs Dreyfus isn't in today,' said a voice she didn't recognise. 'She called in sick.'

Arlene thanked the man and hung up, a smile on her lips. Called in sick, eh? She dialled Chrissie's home number.

'Chrissie?'

'Huh?'

'Chrissie, it's Arlene.'

'Arlene? How are you?'

'Fine. How are you?'

'I'm fine too.' She was aware of a faint embarrassment in the other woman's voice.

'Some party, huh?'

'Jesus, are you kidding? Bill and Larry have just left to go fishing.'

'Listen, Chrissie, I just found something of yours –
your brassiere.'

'Oh yes, sure. I was wondering where I'd left it.'

'Yes, I have it right here.' All of a sudden, she felt an
overwhelming wave of desire sweeping over her.

'Chrissie, I'm thinking about you and your boobs too.
And, you know, the things we did together.'

She could hear the other woman's breathing.

'Jesus, Chrissie, I wish you were here now. I'm longing
to kiss you, to touch your body and make you come like
you did with me last night. You know, with your tongue
right up inside me.'

'Don't say that, Arlene. It makes me feel horny all
over again.'

'And why not? Hell, whyn't you come over right now
and we can spend the morning in bed.'

'I can't. I mean, I wish I could. I have the heating
engineer coming at eleven.'

'Put him off. I want to see you, Chrissie.'

'No, I really can't, but some other time, sure. Let's do
lunch, shall we?'

'Chrissie, I've got my fingers inside me right now and
I'm smelling your perfume on your brassiere. What are
you doing?'

'I'm feeling my nipples. They're real big and hard.'

'Put your fingers inside yourself, Chrissie, let's imagine we're doing each other.'

'Sure, sure. Jesus, I hope nobody sees me. I'm in the
downstairs hallway and you can see right out in the
street.'

'It's so good, Chrissie, isn't it? I wish I was licking
your tongue.'

'Here's my tongue now, licking the phone.'

'God, I wish it was in my body.'

She could feel herself coming now, could hear the
other woman's gasps, her breathing becoming heavier all
the time. She had to put the phone down so she could

pull her skirt up and rub Chrissie's black lace Wonder-bra against her pussy even as she came and came and came.

Afterwards she picked up the phone, listening for voices at the other end but it was dead.

She wished, sometimes, as the days went by, that they might have a repeat performance one day with Chrissie and Bill or whoever. Strange, wasn't it, that Larry's video footage came out as a snowstorm – she might have liked to see it, to remind her of the good times they had that night. But still, with Mike in the running for executive vice-president of the financial section, perhaps it was as well – there was no telling what could have happened if something like that fell into the wrong hands.

And nothing much happened with Chrissie, either, besides a couple of half-embarrassed afternoons, once in her bedroom and once at Chrissie's house. It just kind of tailed off and she no longer felt like that, any more. She and Mike never did talk about it, either, after that evening. Well, not openly. With him, it was like it had never happened. She wondered if he'd been embarrassed about sucking Larry's dick, though she hadn't minded in the least when Chrissie licked her out. Men were funny like that sometimes . . .

FIVE

These days, Jarvis took her pleasures singly. Circumstances had a lot to do with it, the way things had
panned out over the past eighteen months or so, but
really, that was how she preferred it. It hadn't always
been like this.

She was alone – as usual – in her apartment. The only
other living company she had was her plants, dozens of
them, if not hundreds, on every available surface and of
every conceivable species and genus. She knew the Latin
names for all of them.

It was a jungle out there. It was a jungle inside, as
well. But plants, as a rule, didn't give you shit.

Unlike men.

She'd been eating supper, bagels and cream cheese. A
half-empty pack of green salad lay on the table before
her, and a bottle of water. Her laptop was open and she
was tapping keys.

Goddamn you, she projected at the keypad. She was
trying to open files on the Ruthglen case but she
couldn't remember the icons to use. She'd had a thing
about Ruthglen this past few weeks. It wasn't much of a
cause for concern – an environmental group that had
been pressuring for more affirmative action regarding a
Government installation in South Dakota – but Stone
had a feeling that there was more to it than just a bunch

of hair-shirted pinkoes worrying their asses off about stuff that needn't concern them.

She had a PC in her study, linked in with the Bureau but she didn't want to use that. Anything that mattered she would download to the laptop – Stone didn't know she had one, and certainly nothing so powerful. There was no way the work she was doing on the files at the moment could be traced. Hannah had introduced her to one of his females who worked in software design and who'd shown her how to get files off the service without leaving a user record.

It was pretty well the only useful thing Hannah had done for her. The guy was an infuriating asshole most of the time and she'd damn near told him so on several occasions.

At last she found what she wanted. She ate cream cheese with a spoon, hardly aware of what she was doing as the pages scrolled by. Surveillance reports, mail and phone line intercepts, background info that was near to useless – she read the whole shooting match. Jarvis had done a speed-reading course as a student and, if anything, she had just got faster as the years went by. Scrolling text on a computer screen was just made for her, enabled her to skim through a page faster than ever. Her finger idly caressed the trackball as her eyes ran smack down the middle of each page.

But there was nothing in there. She'd known that at the start. All the same, she'd felt she had to go through the files, just in case. That obsessiveness, the fear that, if she didn't do something, the world might just come to an end – that was the reason Bonny Jarvis was such a good operative.

And such a pain in the butt to a lot of people. Especially men. And especially men who were trying to get into her pants.

There was an added dimension to what she'd been doing that evening. Something that had, perhaps, taken the place of the missing erotic element in her life. She liked the illicitness of working on files that she wasn't supposed to have – or at least, that people didn't know she had. A lot of the work she did involved covert operations of one kind or another, but this kind of one-to-one secrecy she found specially exciting. She liked working on her own, not leaving a trace, like a snooper.

It was a pity it had all been a big waste of time. It she'd found something useful in there, she'd have been doubly pleased. She put the laptop to sleep, finished her salad and went to bed.

Jarvis was in early next morning. She always caught the bus into work, even though she was provided with a Ford Shitbox by the Department. The bus stopped right by her apartment and it was an easy walk from the downtown stop.

There was sometimes a guy on the same bus. He must have got on a couple of stops earlier, but no more. Beyond that was where mostly blacks and Hispanics lived and he didn't look like the type who lived with blacks and Hispanics.

He was tall, lean and had a kind of predatory look to him. He wasn't her type at all but he reminded her of a guy she had gone with years and years and years ago. He was a high school drop-out, and her mom had said he was No Good. That had been enough for sixteen-year-old Bonny Jarvis. Marty had been her first. He had called her Birdie.

It didn't last. Neither did Marty. Marty lived fast and died young, under the wheels of an oncoming White Freightliner when the torsion bar in the right-hand front fork of his Triumph Thunderbird fractured when he was out riding alone at night, doing close on ninety down Camelot Hill. His family always claimed the cops were chasing him in the prowl car, they said they had witnesses who'd swear it, but the authorities vigorously contested this and produced evidence of their own. He was riding chicken, they said, trying to take the bend. All the kids did it, tried to hit that bend at eighty. Two or three had gone through the picket fence and spilled their guts.

Jarvis had wept for a week. Marty's violent end only added to his mystique. It was the old Dead Rock Star syndrome. She never told anyone – not any of her friends and certainly not her parents – that she'd once been down Camelot Hill with him on the back of his motorcycle, just the two of them in the moonlight, and they took the bend at a hundred and five. That was the first night she'd let him do it inside her, bareback. It was his way of celebrating and her way of rewarding him.

Marty spelled Rebel and Trouble in equal measure. He wore leathers and a plain white T-shirt at all times. The guy on the bus, though, wasn't like that at all. He wore a light Aquascutum coat most days and under that a good quality linen suit. He probably drove an unobtrusive Japanese executive car, not a big English road bike that leaked oil everywhere. Marty's only luggage had been a pack of Luckies but this guy carried a very thin briefcase, discreetly chained to his wrist. Jarvis reckoned you could tell a guy's status from the thickness of his briefcase alone, with extra points for the security chain. The quality – pigskin, cowskin, kid, composite, plastic – had nothing to do with it. They said Pepper had a plastic briefcase with a cigarette burn on the handle. A thin one, of course.

Thin briefcases contained just one piece of paper because that was all that mattered. Other people could handle the rest of the documentation. It was the drudges who lugged around cases like shipping trunks, bulging with files and calculators and yesterday's *Washington Post*.

Jarvis was glad the guy was on the bus again today. He

35

reminded her of those times with Marty. She didn't like to think too often about him – too much guilt and pain locked in there, maybe.

Marty had been blond, with long hair in a ponytail. This guy was dark. It was more the shape of the face that did it for her, and the way he moved – like a predatory animal. Now he was in his usual seat just behind the driver and she could look at him from her seat a couple of rows back and on the other side of the aisle.

She reckoned he was a lawyer, maybe, or a cocaine dealer for the aristocracy of Washington society. He didn't look the government type, that was for sure. He wore dark horn-rimmed glasses, thin glass, and his eyes were constantly alert, scanning the people getting on and off the bus, watching the street go by. She had never seen him read a newspaper or a magazine, nor open that skimpy briefcase and scan some document for the last time before an important meeting on the eleventh floor.

The nose – she admired his nose. So strong and yet, with its flared nostrils, so sensual and sensitive. Just like Marty. Maybe she would have liked him to have run that nose along the crack of her vagina. Just like Marty. The thought thrilled her – she'd never really fantasised about the guy. But she fantasised about Marty.

Something stirred in her. She liked the way the dark hair just curled over his collar. She'd not noticed that before. He always wore a plain white shirt, just occasionally one with a discreet stripe. She focused her mind on that and immediately they were in bed together and she was running her fingers through those waves. How daring she was being.

He had a heavy beard, she could tell from his blue chin, even at eight in the morning. And then she noticed there was a tiny bit of bloodstained cotton wool on his right jawbone this morning where he had nicked himself. So he used an old-fashioned safety razor, not a power shaver. She liked that. There were razors in her bathroom too and she liked the element of danger they suggested.

She became fascinated by that drop of dried blood. Was it because it reminded her of Marty's tangled remains, when they pulled him out from under that eighteen-wheeler? She forgot about the guy with the briefcase chained to his wrist and thought instead about her dead lover. He carried a knife, too. The cops knew and she knew – he'd shown it to her once. Death and desire were close companions. She remembered once putting a Band-Aid on his hand when he'd cut it, dipped her head and tasted his blood. He'd laughed. He was big on vampire movies.

Somehow it aroused her, the idea of a man's vitality epitomised in his leaking body fluids. She would have been happy to have sucked his cock and swallowed his come, but things like that hadn't happened when she was going with Marty, half a lifetime ago. She had often imagined that as the vibro hummed away inside her, what it might have been like. Now she knew but it was too late, as far as Marty was concerned. She had a copy of Italian *Vogue* open on her lap but she barely registered anything beyond a blur of colour and some half-remembered names.

She would fantasise most nights when she wasn't working late or had been so long in meetings with Stone and whoever that she simply hit the pillow and fell into a black and bottomless pit. In those midnight reveries she would dream up hot scenarios for herself and her lovers. The details changed and evolved with time but always it was the other one who took control of her, never the other way round.

She couldn't resist the tide any longer. She could feel her heart beating faster the way it always did when she became aroused, could sense the tingling in her fingers and toes. She ran last night's fantasy through her imagination one more time so she could get a fix on it. She and Marty were in some motel somewhere, anywhere. There was a beach nearby, and palm trees. She stood on the verandah and she could not see her Mom's car – borrowed for the night – in the parking lot, Marty's car parked right next to it. She liked to think it was stolen, a different model each time. They had a regular rendezvous out there in anonymous dreamtime America.

She went back inside – it was coming cool, the night air blowing in from the sea – and he undressed her hungrily, with little ceremony. The motel room was like every motel room she had ever been in subsequently. It had the quality of beigeness about it. The details were irrelevant, though she thought about this room several times a week. She could almost hear the waves breaking on the shore beyond.

The bed was narrow and intimate. She couldn't remember the last time she had slept in one like it. She thought of all the couples who had fucked here before them. He entered her before she was quite ready for him but she was glad to have him inside her, to run her hands down the rope-like muscles, to catch the scent of the soap he used.

His tongue sought hers. She sucked in his lower lip and nibbled it. He seemed to like it.

Now she was feeling more aroused, despite the airless room and the cheap mattress. She pushed her hips up against him, meeting him thrust for thrust, willing him to move deeper inside her. She arched her back, surprised at her own strength as she lifted herself against the weight of his heavy body, and almost immediately he came inside her in short, rhythmic pulses.

He lay his head down on her shoulders and she ran her fingers through his tail of thick blond hair. She could feel it against her thighs when he went down on her. It tickled.

After a while she pressed her leg against her lover, 'Here,' she said. 'What about me?'

He rolled over. The sheets rustled. He kissed her on the tip of her nose – he had once said it was one of the things he liked most about her.

The bus lurched. She opened her eyes. The guy who reminded her of Marty was still there, looking hard at a man in the homburg hat who had just boarded the bus at the stop outside the post office building.

She closed her eyes again. She could feel her vagina beginning to tingle, the tiny ripples slowly spreading through her body as she became orgasmic. She turned to the favourite part of her fantasy, the one she would run and re-run, like a favourite old movie.

Now they rose from the bed and stole down to the beach. There was a horse there waiting for them, as white as a ghost, outlined against the surf. They climbed onto its back.

They rode fast, the horse's hooves drumming in the wet sand, phosphorescence in the spray of the surf. He had the reins and she was safe in his arms, laughing. The salt of the sea whipped in her face and, as she thundered along, her sarong rode higher and higher and her thighs were bared.

On and on they sped over that endless beach, past palm trees that wafted gently in the night breeze. And he was unwinding her sarong and then she was naked for him beneath the stars. He shucked off his eternal white T-shirt and she could feel his chest against her bare back. She reached behind and unzipped him, scooping his cock from out of his pants. She could hear the breaking surf louder than ever.

Jarvis opened her eyes, aware of how her heart was racing, could feel the flush on her skin despite the bus's air conditioning. Good, they were only at the Lincoln Memorial. She had another three minutes. She could do a lot in three minutes.

Closing her eyes on the morning commuters, in her mind she took hold of her lover's penis and guided it to her pussy. Leaning forward, she wrapped her arms around the horse's neck, smelling the beast-smell of its mane as Marty pushed his cock deeper and deeper inside her until it he filled her completely. It seemed her face was only inches from the sand and surf as it flashed beneath her, faster and faster. She could see the thundering hooves, could hear that fabulous rhythmic drumming and in that moment she and Marty and the stallion were one enormous rutting animal. The sensation was joyous. It seemed to go on forever, to stretch out into the vast vault of stars that lay over their heads as they sped through the surf.

The spasms of her own orgasm were still shuddering through her as Jarvis opened her eyes. She felt confused, became aware of how tightly clenched her thighs were. She could smell the city coming in through the open doors, gasoline fumes mostly. The guy with the briefcase was getting off at his usual stop.

She took a series of deep breaths to compose herself, just like a horse after a gallop. She hoped no one noticed. She would just have time to visit the restroom before her scheduled meeting with Stone and Hannah at nine-oh-six. Sometimes she wished she could just curl up and go to sleep, wake up in her apartment with her plants and maybe a man beside her.

Instead, she had a working day to get through and a tough meeting to face right off the top of the slate. She'd be at her stop in a couple of minutes. She wished the meeting had been scheduled for later but there was nothing she could do about that. It was always Stone who called the tune in her department, Stone who set the times, Stone who set the clocks.

Stone was as precise as that. Not nine, or ten-fifteen. Nine-oh-six it was.

40

SIX

Tommy Vincento was worried. The old fart had gone
into the men's room a full half-hour ago and he didn't
come out again. He was a pretty frail-looking old-timer
too, with his dusty black suit and a beat-up old snap-
brimmed hat pulled well down over his eyes. He hoped
the bastard hadn't done gone and croaked in there.
Guys like that were having seizures and heart attacks the
whole time.

Finally, when he had a moment – because the Amoco
station where he worked had been non-stop all afternoon and, with Terri off sick again, he was working the
cash register on his own – he went over to the lube bay
where, as usual, a bunch of guys was hanging out. There
was Kurt Newlove and Willy Strayhorn and Ellington
Mercer, and they were all drooling over this 1993 Dodge
Viper coupé that Vinnie Richards had just driven up in.
Vinnie was maybe getting a little old for a car that
could do 167 mph in running condition but then
Vinnie would be driving cars like that until the day
they finally nailed him in his box – and even then, the
hearse would probably take off like a rocket on its way
to the boneyard, leaving tyre tracks of burned rubber
on the blacktop.

'Hey, Kurt,' said Tommy. 'You got a minute?'

Kurt came over, running his hands through his hair.

41

Tommy could see the look of guilt in his eyes. He knew he should have been getting on with his work. Herb Cohen, the owner, was just looking for an opportunity to fire Kurt and Tommy had tried to give the guy a fair warning.

Tommy explained about the problem in the washroom. The old fart's car was still parked where he had left it, over by pump number five, an '84 Honda with one tomato-red door that was a different colour to the rest. Normally Tommy didn't like to hand over the washroom key on account of all the dopers and suchlike who'd go in there to shoot up – once he'd even caught a couple of faggots going at it behind the locked door, could hear their breathing and the noises they made – but the old guy had seemed harmless enough and didn't look like trouble. Moreover, he was hopping up and down from one foot to the other like he had urgent business to attend to.

Tentatively, Tommy and Kurt opened the washroom door. It was silent inside the men's room. Tommy's nostrils flinched – the disinfectant barely hid the shit smell that was coming out from the cubicle. Some cop had once told him that old people often crapped themselves when they died. Maybe that's what had happened to the old guy, Tommy pondered, when he felt his heart giving way and knew he couldn't restart it. He felt sick. He wished he'd not smoked that joint earlier in the afternoon. It was gold mex and strong stuff, he could feel it still running around inside his corpuscles. He'd had the Grateful Dead playing on his Walkman but he didn't think he could handle a shit-covered corpse.

Kurt, sensing his unease, took control. Tommy felt relieved. Kurt went over to the cubicle door, tapped smartly with his knuckles.

'You OK in there?' Kurt had an ugly, nasal voice.

There was no response, just as Tommy had feared.

42

What with the disinfectant in the air and the adrenaline surging through his veins, his head was beginning to clear of the dope.

'How long you say he's been in here?' asked Kurt.

'A half-hour, maybe more.'

'Think we should break the door down?'

'Maybe we should call the cops.'

Tommy didn't like the idea, but what else could they do in the circumstances? Cops were trained to handle situations like this. Tommy was just a guy who worked in a gas station.

Kurt knocked again, louder this time.

'Anyone in there?' he said, kind of commanding this time. Kurt claimed to have served in the US Army in the Gulf but it didn't ring true. Someone else said Kurt had been doing a three-stretch in Highwood while the scuds were flying around.

Kurt knocked again, harder.

'Huh?' said a voice inside the cubicle. They heard a rustling, then the toilet flushed. Tommy and Kurt stood back – the gents' washroom wasn't big enough to hold more than a couple of people – and the old fart in the dusty suit came out, still wearing his hat. He had a face that looked like it was made out of leather that had been lying around in the sun too long, eyes that didn't quite match.

'Afternoon, fellas,' he said in a cracked, old-guy voice, and ran water into the basin, washed his hands as if nothing had happened.

Kurt looked at Tommy, kind of sharp. They went out, followed by the old man. He couldn't manage the pump himself and Tommy had to help him put ten dollars' worth of gas in his shabby old Honda. He paid cash with a greasy bill, as crumpled and creased as his leather face. Three times the starter motor whirred before the engine caught. The old guy revved up to about forty thousand and then he drove off in a cloud of blue smoke. He just missed side-swiping an ice truck that was making a left into Baxendale.

Tommy asked Kurt to watch the register for a moment and went back into the washroom, just to check out a hunch. There seemed nothing amiss – everything was as it had been less than an hour ago, when he'd replaced the paper towels in the dispenser after a customer had complained it was empty. There was the mop and pail in its usual corner, the usual notices on the wall, the small mirror you needed to duck down to look into.

Cautiously he pushed open the door of the cubicle. The shit smell was pretty strong but that wasn't what disturbed him. Every wall was freshly covered in a crabbed, cramped magic-marker writing. It was all Biblical texts and suchlike, as far as Tommy could tell – he was Jewish but he didn't let anyone know. It was going on about sin and hell and damnation, over and over again, a rising tide of condemnation. It was weird. He looked at the back of the door and it was all over there as well.

So that was what the old fart had been up to all that time. His eyes scanned the thinly veiled threats, the tirade of abuse that masqueraded as holy writ. He must have had a screw loose, that guy. Tommy had never seen anything like it in his life. Fortunately all the surfaces at the Amoco were covered in a graffiti-resistant material that would just wipe clean with the right solvent, but it came as a shock nevertheless. He wondered what the hell Curtis, the cleaner, would make of it all when he came to work that evening. It would mean at least an extra hour, maybe even a couple of hours overtime to wash that lot down.

He went back to the cash office, helped Kurt process a Visa card.

'Go look in the head,' he said when the customer had departed. 'That old guy's left a little piece of advice for you.'

Anything else and he might have laughed – folks wrote some pretty ripe things on toilet walls, and not just 'For a good fuck ring 961-873-2020 and ask for Marnie.' Curtis used to store them up and recall them from memory – he knew the location of every ten-inch dick in East Texas.

But there was something creepy about this. Tommy wondered if it might be the grass, or maybe he'd been reading one too many Stephen King novels. All this condemnation and sins of the fathers and lewdness and naked harlots and stuff. What the hell was the old fart banging on about?

Soon as he could, he nipped out back and rolled himself another one. It made him feel better.

SEVEN

ARJO, NEW MEXICO. JUNE 15TH. 10.53 PM.

Cue DAVID camera 3

DAVID: And that just about wraps up the late-night news here on WCTV.

Pan to MILTON.

MILTON: But viewers on a channel in Arizona got a little more than they bargained for last night.

DAVID: They'd been tuning in to catch the weather forecast, read as usual by Gina Carmody, live to camera.

MILTON: Gina's a former Miss Flagstaff . . .

DAVID (winks to camera): And I bet there's plenty of guys out there in Arizona willing to run Gina up their flag staff. Let's see what happened next, as the man said . . .

Cue VTR. Cue sound

GINA is standing in front of a weather map. She's a blonde woman, very attractive, in her mid-twenties – everyone's idea of what a weather lady should look like.

46

For perhaps ten seconds we see and hear her reading the weather forecast much as usual.

All of a sudden Gina looks right at the camera, winks and pulls up her loose cashmere top to expose bare breasts. She cups them in each hand, proffers them to the camera, mischief in her eyes and a smile on her lips. She laughs and runs her tongue along her sparkling white teeth, winking at the camera. The screen suddenly goes blank and viewers are passed to a surprised-looking anchorman who doesn't know what to say.

Cue MILTON again on camera 2

MILTON: Well, Dave, I guess they always did like to do things a little differently in Arizona.

DAVID (laughing): They sure do. And I bet that sent the temperatures soaring out there way above the seasonal average. It's been pretty cold these past few days, eh, Milton?

Pan back. DAVID and MILTON swing round in their seats behind the news desk, joshing one another.

MILTON: And so with that little surprise ending, it's goodnight from me, Milton Berger.

DAVID: And goodnight from me, David Cathcart.

Fade to credits. Cue music. Run commercials.

EIGHT

Hannah knew he had to make the early meeting with Stone and Jarvis but Clemency had never asked him to butt-fuck her before and there was every chance he might get run over by a truck before it happened again.

They'd woken in his apartment a little after seven and he could tell she was on heat. The night before she had told him he'd been away too long, as she greeted him at the airport by sticking her tongue halfway down his throat. They made it back to his apartment in record time; it was a wonder she didn't get a ticket.

Morning light stole in through the bedroom window. Clemency still had all her make-up on from last night and her clothes were strewn all over the floor, along with his own. She got up, put on his bathrobe, and went to the bathroom. When she came back she was all over him.

They did it, first of all, on the bed. Still in the bathrobe, she lay down and drew him onto her. He felt wild and elated, curiously inflamed by the thought that he really ought to be thinking about showering and shaving and feeling a little guilty about it too. He sucked on her bared breasts, the nipples plump and raspberry-red, her hand busy with his cock, expertly manipulating it into hardness.

He wondered what Stone was doing now, probably

48

taking a crap or eating his health-food cereal in the early-morning light. And Jarvis – she'd be stuffing ice-cubes up herself, or dusting her laptop. But Clemmie was damp and luxuriant, like the dark foliage of a tropical forest, and an animal warmth seemed to permeate her whole body. When he'd first started going with her, he was acutely aware of her various scents and secretions, all the more novel for the strangeness of their circumstances and the novelty of bedding a woman he had only just met and who he would, undoubtedly, never see again after a few more nights – if this relationship panned out like all the rest.

He licked at her with a rare delicacy that soon had her writhing and tossing on the sheets.

'I want you now,' she hissed and she all but hauled him bodily into her. Hannah's cock felt massively distended; he was more excited than he realised. There was some dark mystery about Clemmie, something that aroused the inner recesses of his imagination, provided an access into aspects of his psyche that were usually well hidden.

He felt tall and powerful as he pushed into her, noting the way she smiled at him as he went in, her eyes half-closed, her eyes like dark holes amid all the make-up. She was wearing, he noticed for the first time, gold sun-and-moon earrings that glistened against her burnished red hair. She was, he knew, a genuine redhead – either that, or she knew the most phenomenally talented colourist. Even her pubic hair had something of that heavy copperish tinge.

She was strong, too, pushing up at him to meet him thrust for thrust. Something in him snapped and he found he was kissing her with wanton abandon, already wanting to pour his seed into her, his lips hard against hers, aware of her tongue and teeth and her saliva mingling with his own. Her fingernails raked his back like a cat's claws, sharp and merciless.

He raised himself up high above her, his palms spread out flat on the sheets. He wanted her to see the powerful chest muscles he had built up over many hours in the gym, the endless working out with weights that had given him pectorals that were ripe like fruit and an upper-body strength to rival many a professional athlete's. He knew, as one of his old girlfriends had said as she watched him complete fifty press-ups before climbing into bed with her, where his balling muscles were and how to keep them in trim.

For a while he screwed away. She came a couple of times but he didn't. Maybe he was uptight – maybe he was worried about the meeting. He didn't know.

Then, all of a sudden, she opened her eyes and spoke to him in a voice so quiet he could hardly hear.

'Fuck my ass,' she said. She sat up, took off the bathrobe, threw it on the floor. And then her eyes were closed once more.

Hannah stopped his rhythmic pumping and was acutely aware of how fast his heart was beating, the blood throbbing through him, a film of sweat on his upper lip amid the dark early-morning stubble. He couldn't resist. He forgot the time.

She rolled over. God, her ass was divine. Then she knelt up with her face in the pillow and her buttocks were thrust right at him.

He could see the tiny puckered rosebud, just waiting for him, pink and glistening. She was so wet down there she didn't need anything else. He came up behind her, his big tool bobbing with potency, and she took hold of him and guided him to the mark.

'Now,' she said and he pushed. She gasped and he gasped too. He only went in a little way but then she relaxed and his cock slid right up inside her. The feeling was divine, like his dick was being squeezed in a vice made out of velvet.

'Fuck me in my ass,' she repeated. 'The way you

'wanna do it to Jarvis.' He thought that was what she said, but the words were hardly audible. It excited him beyond measure and he could sense the spunk that was building up inside his balls. Kneeling behind her, his breathing harsh and ragged from their exertions, he pushed right up into her so he could feel her cheeks cool and marble-smooth against his thighs, his nostrils full of the scent of sex. He came almost immediately, his first orgasm of the day, fluid and abundant.

He lay down on the pillow beside her, stroked her hair. But Clemency's eyes were closed. She was lost in a world of her own making, unknowable even to a trained investigator like Hannah.

They lay like that for ten minutes or more. Stone would be backing his car out of the garage now but Hannah couldn't help himself. He just lay there with this wonderful woman, a poet of the flesh, and wished he could stay there forever. She opened her eyes and smiled at him, surprised and pleased, perhaps, by the suddenness with which he had climaxed. She took hold of his dick – still sticky with his sperm, and still semi-erect – and gave it a squeeze.

Hannah had an undeniable streak of vanity running through him. He was, as he had often been aware, as turned on by himself as by his partner. He would have given himself a blow-job if he could – autofellatio, the ultimate in narcissism.

'Is there anything you'd particularly like?' he asked when he'd got his breath back.

'I can think of plenty. I don't have to come, you know.'

'Whatever. It's just that I really got off then, you know.'

'I know. I also know you've got a meeting in just over an hour. You better get dressed, lover boy.'

As he made his way to the Bureau, Hannah was wondering what she had meant about Jarvis. How did she know? What had he said?

★ ★ ★

Stone's office was as uncompromisingly bare as its occupant's head. There was a desk with telephones and three computer terminals, a clutch of government-issue chairs that looked like they'd been borrowed from the commissary in the basement and never returned, and that was it. No pictures, no plants, not even a rug or anything on the floor.

The room was big enough to have held a Christmas dance in, if the Bureau went in for that kind of thing, which the Bureau didn't. It was like working in an airplane hangar without any planes, or a big-city railroad terminal on a Sunday morning. Stone didn't like distractions.

Even the window gave no kind of view, just a wall of yellow brick about ten feet away, a side-on view of the louvres on some kind of ventilation fan housing, a glimpse of sky way up above. It was the kind of room where people get their toenails torn out, in an effort to help them remember things. Hannah hated going near the place. It intimidated him. It made his own apartment seem like something from the pages of one of the glossier magazines.

Bonny Jarvis was adding about thirty degrees of frost to the general chill in the air. She was sitting on one of the commissary chairs, legs primly crossed, her auburn hair pushed back from her forehead and her blue eyes looking out at the yellow brick wall. Hannah felt an involuntary stab of desire for her, like he always did. She had been the keeper of the Sex Files for three years now and you would have thought that a steady diet of other people's fuckings and suckings might have helped thaw her a little.

Not a bit of it, though. She looked like the last time a positive sexual thought had passed through her head, Michael Jackson still had some of the bits of face he'd been born with. To him she was pure frost, but he still would have liked to shoot off all over her tits.

He sat down next to her, to one side of the desk. She sniffed, dabbed at her nose with a tissue. It wasn't the time of year when people got colds unless they had ice in their veins.

He looked around him, not that there was much to draw the eye. He could see all the computers were off, not even a screensaver. Stone didn't want to give anything away. He was tight like that.

Stone was standing by the window, gazing up at the sky. The light caught his domed head, glinted on his rimless glasses. He was like a portable brain in a protective case, a precision instrument rather than a man who bled, shat and wept.

But when he spoke it was in a voice like melting chocolate. Career politicians would kill to have a voice like that, Hannah had always felt. It was a voice you could believe in, deep and rich and sonorous, every vowel carefully enunciated, every consonant lovingly polished and placed with care. Stone invited concurrence with every word he spoke.

'I want you to leave that Afghan business for the moment,' he said to the yellow brick wall.

'Fine by me. What about Collis?'

'What about Collis?'

'Collis is helping me with the files.'

'Is he? Why is that?'

'He says you asked him to.'

'Did I? OK, let Collis carry on by himself. The guy's a dipstick anyway. There's something else I want you to look at.'

Hannah and Jarvis exchanged glances, not without a hint of mutual suspicion. Stone began polishing his glasses on the end of his tie.

'And Jarvis, put Ruthglen on hold too, will you? Nothing's going to happen there.'

'You want me to de-activate the computer search programs?'

'No, keep them running. Make a note of anything significant, but I don't want any additional input from you if you can possibly avoid it. Something else has come up. A couple of things. We need to look more closely at the media. Especially in the Deep South.'

Hannah raised an eyebrow. Stone caught his glance and hooked his glasses behind his ears, which were clean and scrubbed like a schoolboy's. Stone looked at Jarvis and Hannah in turn and in that order, and his glance was cold and penetrating.

'We don't know what's going on. We are just aware that something is stirring, like there's something in the air. For no particular reason that we can think of.'

'What kind of activity has there been?' Hannah queried. 'Anything actionable?'

'Nothing to write home to mom about. No lynchings, just a whole parcel of rape stories and orgy stories and AIDS-scare stories, all that kind of shit. Every time you open a newspaper or turn on your TV, that's what you get. Cops raid gay bar, you know the score.'

'So what's up?'

'We don't know that anything is up. So far, agents have reported nothing we can get a handle on. But there is just a feeling – and I had this passed down from Pepper, it's nothing of my own making – that maybe we should give these things a closer look.'

Hannah and Jarvis looked at each other again, affirmatively.

'You said there was something else.' Jarvis's voice wasn't as clear and bell-like as usual. It was kind of croaky, like her throat was sore. Hannah liked the husky edge it gave her. It was sexy.

'Did I? Oh, sure. Does the name of Hubert Sleep mean anything to you?'

'Don't you mean *Eugene* Sleep? Owns newspapers in the South and West.'

'Buying into television.'

'That's the man. Set up the Tru-Flo Corporation in 1962. Made his pile in peanuts, subsequently diversified heavily. Likes to think of himself as a family man and something of a fundamentalist too, we hear.'

'Are you saying he's connected with these stories?'

'Not at all. I never gave it a moment's thought. It just so happens that most of them happen to be coming out in Sleep newspapers and on Sleep-owned TV channels. Let me show you something.'

Two of the computer screens booted themselves into life. One was filled with newsprint, the other with television footage.

'This is all Sleep's product,' said Stone. 'He owns a whole string of papers right across the South, Texas, Arizona and a couple of other Western states. The message is coming across louder and louder each time. It's like he's on some kind of a personal morality crusade.'

Hannah was looking at the Bible Channel. The sound wasn't on but he got the message. A couple of clean-cut guys who looked like the mannequins you saw in charity-shop windows, too wholesome to be true, were working a studio audience like a couple of carnival barkers. Most of the folks looked old or learning-impaired, like they didn't go in much for fun, still less gay bikers on acid or whatever they were condemning that week.

Stone moved a mouse around, brought up another channel. This was gospel, a bit more life to it. And then a news channel. He pulled the sound up. It was just like the regular news except that everything was from the same religious perspective. Hannah had seen the same kind of thing when he worked as an agent in Iraq after the war. It gave him a creepy feeling.

Stone flipped a remote and killed the sound.

'What I'm going to tell you now is from the top, right? And I don't want it to go any further – at least not until

I get the word from Pepper. You got me?'

Hannah and Jarvis nodded in almost perfect synchronisation.

'It appears our friend, the sanctimonious Mr Sleep, has ideas of getting himself elected to Congress on a Jesus ticket. It's time for Jimmy Swaggart meets Ross Perot, you know what I'm saying? We need to look at him more closely.'

'You mean he's intending to get elected on the back of all these stories that he's putting about?' said Hannah. 'He pushes the stories, maybe even makes them up and then he rides in on a white horse, like he's the Lone Ranger, the guy who's going to clean the town up? Jesus, what a crock of shit.'

Stone didn't answer directly. The conversation was probably being taped. But his expression said all that needed to be said. 'This guy is expanding so fast you wouldn't believe it,' he said quietly. 'It is like he is taking over the media down there.'

'Who's funding him?' asked Jarvis.

Stone shrugged. 'We can't tell. He has other interests, of course. Everything from manufacturing to leisure. But the files we have from the IRS don't suggest he has the kind of money to launch TV stations and newspapers, still less to think about running for Congress.'

'So that's why we need to take a look-see?'

'Right. We have a lot of stuff on file already, you can access it right away. But then I want you to go down there, get a feel for this guy, see what's firing him up.'

'And the stories?'

'Look into them as well. Run the two things together. Maybe there's some kind of cover there for you.'

'Can we run intercepts?'

'Sure. Pepper has given blanket clearance.'

'Do we really need to investigate in person? Maybe we could use the database here.' Jarvis seemed able to do everything via a computer screen, and had little need to go out and waste shoe leather.

'Whatever you think best. Report back to me in a week's time.'

He looked at his watch.

'I have another meeting at 9.20,' he said absently, gazing out of the blind window again. Stone's schedule was timed like his thoughts – with absolute precision.

Hannah and Jarvis left the room. They had been in there for all of six minutes. The corridor seemed like a riot of colour.

Hannah punched keys on the coffee machine. 'What do you make of that?' he said. Jarvis was plainly intent on being somewhere else in the shortest possible space of time but she condescended, Stone-like, to give him forty seconds of her time.

'We look. We do a scan. We monitor. The same as usual.'

'What about going there? Putting in some footwork.'

'We should do that too, eventually.'

'Maybe we should fly down there first off, build up some kind of dossier. Get a feel for the place, that kind of thing.'

'Suit yourself.'

'I'm not busy – I've been down in the archive all week and I need the fresh air. It's warmer down there, for a start. Maybe we might see something.'

'You think a bunch of wife-swappers and porno freaks are going to be walking around Mississippi in broad daylight? Swaggering along the levee in leather? Wise up, Hannah.'

'You sound like you have a cold coming on. Maybe you should stay here and I'll see what I can find.'

'I'm fine.'

'You should go home, go to bed, take a powder. Want me to run you back to your apartment?'

'Drop dead, Hannah.'

'No, don't take a powder. I got a new girlfriend, says

she can cure things like that with crystals. You stick a lump of rock salt or something under your pillow and in the morning you feel like a million bucks.'

'Don't make me say something I'll regret, Hannah.'

'No, I'm serious. There are even crystals healers you can contact. They're in the telephone directory, some of them are even on-line.'

'What is this? Have you been eating acid?'

'Not for a couple of weeks – it was just a thought, really. But this Sleep business. Reckon there's anything to it?'

'I don't know. Pepper seems to think so.'

'How do you want to work it? Run some search programmes?'

'Something like that. I can't think too clearly right now. I don't feel good.'

'Go home then, like I said. I'll get Marnie to fix plane tickets for tomorrow afternoon. I got something I have to finish off first.'

He stooped to pick up what might have been coffee or might, just as easily, have been Mississippi mud. As usual he burned his fingers on the rim of the plastic cup. By the time he'd finished cursing and licking his scorched fingertips, Jarvis had vanished.

NINE

'Hey,' said Tanya McCullough to the woman she was talking to at the party, a thirty-year-old and very attractive single parent called Tracey Kelley. 'Want to come back to our place afterwards and watch Steve and I ball?'

'Sure,' said Tracey, and reached for the bowl of potato chips.

Steve McCullough had had fantasies about Tracey for a long time now. He and Tanya enjoyed talking about the things that turned them on. Steve liked all the usual things such as women in garter belts and watching lesbian videos, while Tanya went for lifeguard types and would masturbate openly in front of Steve while watching endless re-runs of *Baywatch* on TV. But getting it off while Tracey looked on was a new one.

Sometimes, at night, Steve had talked about all the things he'd like to do to Tracey. He imagined his come running all over her generous breasts – she was a size sixteen, while Tanya was straight size twelve – and he badly wanted her to fondle his cock. But his favourite fuck-time fantasy was to screw his wife while Tracey watched.

All this had been in his mind for a long time and

Tanya had gone along with it. Besides, she and Tracey were good friends and there didn't seem any real danger to their marriage in letting Steve talk about these things. It kind of turned her on in a way, made her feel a little shocked. She always got a tingle when she told Steve about some guy she'd seen at the supermarket, or even just driving by in his car, that she'd wanted to go down on or something.

But this time it seemed they'd gone one step beyond. Tanya didn't really know why she'd asked. She'd just been in that kind of mood, maybe. Everyone at the party seemed to be acting a little looser than usual.

As soon as she could, she got Steve over to one side.

'I asked Tracey,' she said, real quiet.

'Asked Tracey what?'

'If she'd like to come in the bedroom with us.'

'Jesus fucking Christ, you didn't?' He looked at her in astonishment.

She nodded, gave him a sideways smile. 'Just as soon as you're ready,' she said, and went to get herself another drink.

Later, back at the McCulloughs' house, Steve was trembling with excitement as he got undressed. Everything was happening just as he had imagined it. There was the bed with the covers drawn back, and there was Tanya in her lemon-coloured French lingerie, kneeling down with her butt towards him.

He climbed up behind her, got his cock into her. She was still wearing her pants and garter belt and everything, best polyester satin. She felt warm and wet as he slid into her. Watching her strip, he had been aware of the damp patch between her legs.

Tanya gasped. 'OK, Tracey, you can come in now,' she called when she'd gotten herself comfortable.

The door opened and Tracey came in. She had a drink in her hand and a smile on her face. She came and sat on the edge of the McCulloughs' big queen-sized bed.

60

Her eyes took in Tanya, kneeling there with her tits almost spilling out of her brassiere, and Steve going into her from behind, naked so she could see his powerful back muscles and his tight butt. Steve had a good figure, worked out every day. He liked to show it off.

For a while Steve worked his dick in and out of his wife's pussy. Then, when he was sure Tracey was watching closely, he pulled it almost the whole way out so she could see how long and thick it was. He felt real good doing that, leaning back so he was almost sitting on his ankles, with his cock pulled out almost as far as it would go. Tracey was sitting right beside him and she could see every last impressive inch of him.

He was surprised he hadn't had an orgasm the moment Tracey came into the room, he felt so worked up about it all. When he was sure she'd seen enough, he leaned forward again and began working Tanya's pussy once more, his hands on her hips to steady himself, feeling the soft sheen of the fabric of her pants and garter belt.

'Take your top off, if you like,' he said to Tracey.

She smiled and stood up. She was wearing a loose T-shirt with leggings underneath.

Her breasts, as he had envisaged so many times, were magnificent. She was wearing an intricate brassiere of black lace and it held them up to perfection, emphasising the deep cleavage between them.

He could feel his balls beginning to tighten. He pushed his cock deep inside Tanya's pussy and then withdrew it completely. It stood jutting forward from his abdomen, red and kind of angry-looking, glistening with Tanya's secretions. Steve felt immensely powerful and potent, very sure of himself.

It was as if Tracey had read the script. Even as Steve stood up, she pressed herself forward and took hold of his dick, guiding it towards her tits. She frigged it only a couple of times and then Steve's spunk came flying out,

61

all over her black lace brassiere and into the deep channel between her breasts. After the initial rush of elation, Steve felt like a million-ton weight had been lifted from his shoulders.

TEN

Forty minutes before flight time, Jarvis cried off with a
fever. Hannah's phone beeped while he was hanging
around the departure lounge. She sure sounded rough,
even above the airport noise and a lot of on-line interfer-
ence. She said her thermometer was reading 102 and the
doctor was on his way. That was unusually informative
of her.

'I told you you should have tried the crystal therapy,'
Hannah said. 'The Dalai Lama swears by it.'

She put the phone down on him. He smiled. Personally, he didn't give a spit either for some of Clemency's
ideas but it was a good way to wind Jarvis up. Anything
like that – from rebirthing to aromatherapy – and his
esteemed colleague's shutters came down like closing
time at the bank.

So he was on his own for this one. Well, she hadn't
been sure about making the trip now, so maybe it was
better that way. Though the trip might have offered an
opportunity to get into Jarvis's pants, there was the rest
of her to put up with as well. He found her prissy,
officious, over-conscientious. She made him feel like a
slob.

Hannah divided his flight time between the last-but-
one issue of *Scientific American* – he had subscribed since

63

college days and still felt he had to read each issue from cover to cover – and the briefing notes that Stone had provided.

Hannah was used to dealing with strange people but Eugene Sleep sounded stranger than most. He had made his money in peanuts, had been on the fringes of Deep South politics for quite some while. There had been a suspicion of some funny money – when wasn't there, where Carolina senators and Arkansas governors were concerned? – but the IRS hadn't been able to find any of it, however hard they looked. Sleep's operations – and he wasn't just involved in peanuts, he had a finger in an airline, a printing operation, a warehousing network and interstate trucking – seemed to be totally above the line. They weren't squeaky clean to a suspicious degree – there was the odd scam and evidence here and there of adroit accountancy – but nothing that a trained IRS investigator wouldn't have sniffed out.

Things weren't looking too good, on the whole, for Sleep's Tru-Flo corporation. The recession was biting deep. So where did the money come from to run his television stations and the newspaper syndicate? And why would he choose an asshole place like Wink, Texas as the centre of his operations? It was a hard one to puzzle together, especially given the intelligence – as reasonably certain as such things could ever be – that he was intending running for Congress next time around.

Hannah had no line on this one. That was why he was flying down to Texas, to see just what might give. Even then, he didn't have much of a lead beyond an intro to the advertising manager at one of Sleep's TV stations.

He put Stone's notes back in his briefcase and resumed skimming through his copy of *Scientific American*. There was some stuff on synthetic analog systems that was way above his head so he skipped to an analysis of new uses of quartz crystals in advanced timing mechanisms. He'd been getting more than enough on mystical crystals from Clemency but, for once, this was something he could get his head round – and not a Californian fruitcake in sight.

It amazed him, as he scanned the article, the way that a seemingly inert piece of rock could vibrate at a specific frequency, with enough consistency to make it the basis of super-reliable instrumentation as well as the kind of watch you got with ten gallons of gas. So much of the sense of wonder seemed to have been booted out of science in the last twenty years but this was the kind of thing that always fired his imagination. He made a note to show the article to Clemency – it might encourage her to see things from a different angle. At least the article might help put things on a scientific footing – or perhaps it might not. He'd only known her a couple of weeks but already he could tell Clemency was a woman with a mind of her own.

When he stepped out of the airplane, the heat hit him like a wall. He checked into a Holiday Inn near the airport, rented a car and a little before three was in the reception area at the Salvation Channel.

Thurston Carpenter came down to greet him person-ally. He wore a white shirt and black pants and had a narrow face with gold-rimmed glasses. His handshake was brief and dry and Hannah wondered if he'd ever had a day's fun in his life. He was the kind who looked as though his dick was strictly for pissing through.

Hannah apologised for his colleague's absence but Carpenter took it in his stride. He got the feeling the guy didn't like women too much.

Apart from the occasional crucifix on the wall and a general sense of tidiness and restraint, Hannah could have been in any kind of office. Carpenter, he noticed, wore a tie-clip in the form of a fish and many of the other Salvation employees wore lapel pins that doubtless had some kind of spiritual significance. It made Hannah feel kind of dirty, as if he wasn't on the same plateau as them. He kind of liked that feeling, of knowing he was unquestionably the only guy in the building who'd spent the previous evening clit-munching his girlfriend.

There didn't seem to be many females working here, he noticed, as they made their way through the open-plan offices. The ones that did seemed to have secretarial jobs, and he only saw a couple of women working behind computer terminals.

Thurston Carpenter offered him a chair, which he accepted, and a cup of tea, which he declined. After an uncomfortable flight in an ageing 737 he would have preferred to relax with a cold beer or better still, a double Gibson, but he didn't think this was the place to ask.

'OK, Mr Hannah,' Carpenter said, opening up a folder on his laptop computer. It was a new-model Powerbook from Apple, much better equipment than the Bureau gave its operatives. 'Just let me get your file up on screen and we'll see how best we can help you.'

He scrolled the pages for a half-minute or so, then looked up. 'So you're interested in buying advertising space for your agency, is that right?'

'That's right, Mr Carpenter. We have a number of clients who we feel could benefit from exposure on your kind of channel.'

'Our kind of channel? I like that. Seems like you've already got a clear idea of what we're about.'

'I hope so. But I'm sure I'd like to know more, so I can brief my clients better when I get back. We're talking about quite an investment here.'

'Well, maybe we can talk for a while and then we can go and talk to some of our people. The timing of your visit's a little unfortunate in that a lot of the guys are away at AARB—'

'AARB?' Hannah looked puzzled.

'American Association of Religious Broadcasters. It's their annual conference right now in Memphis but Tom

Nulty, who's our deputy head of programming, is here in the building and I've arranged for us to go see him, if that's OK with you. We have a live news broadcast hour starting at five, so maybe you'd like to sit in on that too, see our operation at work.'

Hannah spread his palms. That would be fine, he said. He would be interested in anything Thurston Carpenter could tell him.

They talked for a while about the kind of clients Hannah's agency supposedly represented – a publisher of family-oriented CD-ROM information packages, a multi-national healthcare operation, a well-known manufacturer of patent laxatives, and several others in similar vein, all of whom had no connection whatever with Hannah and his spurious agency. He apologised for not bringing a showreel of the agency's work – some kind of secretarial mix-up, he said – but one would, he assured Carpenter, be sent to the station in a matter of days. Instead he had a big pile of brochures that Stone had been able to fit him out with.

'These are the clients that our marketing people have profiled so far,' he said. 'We've not really spoken formally to them but we have gained an understanding that they would be very positive towards advertising on the Salvation Channel.'

'That's good,' said Carpenter, rubbing his hands. 'Those are the kinds of brand names we would be happy to be associated with. Did I send you a rate card?'

Hannah nodded his assent.

'They're negotiable, of course. We have some very exciting packages we could put together. Multi-media especially.'

'That's one good reason why we came to you, to have that option. You can't separate out TV and press advertising.'

'I think we could put some very competitive rates on the table if that's the way you want to go.'

Hannah nodded again. For a man so Christian as to have a picture of the Lord on his office wall, Carpenter sure spoke a lot of hard-headed business sense. But Jesus, he had to remember, was also a carpenter.

All the while a TV set flickered silently in the corner, tuned to the Salvation Channel. The clips that Stone had sent him on video were remarkably consistent with the real thing, an endless stream of talking heads – you didn't need to be able to lip-read to guess what they were saying – leavened by Bible stories given a fictional gloss. This was, after all, late afternoon here in Texas, the peak viewing period for the very young and the very old, the time of day that was of no interest whatever to any advertiser, even for patent remedies and rupture trusses.

They spoke about time-scales, scheduling, day-rates and night-rates, networking clusters, all kinds of things that taxed to the limits Hannah's ability to bluff. Fortunately he had a friend who worked in Madison Avenue so he at least knew the language. And Clemency, she knew the ropes as well. He wondered idly what a guy like Carpenter would make of a gal like Clemency. He thought of her sweet butt and fought hard to stop a smile cracking his features.

Later they went to see Nulty in his office. Nulty was every inch the television man but Hannah could see the mission written there in his eyes in letters of fire. Surrounded by all this wholesomeness, he ached to get himself drunk in a downtown burlesque bar, to fuck some broad up against a wall in an alleyway. They talked more percentages and more viewer profiles and in the end Hannah was saying yes to whatever the guy threw at him.

'You're part of Eugene Sleep's operation, aren't you?' said Hannah as casually as he could, during a lull in the statistical throughput. 'I was wondering what kind of guy he is.'

'Well,' said Nulty, glancing sideways at Carpenter. 'I don't really know Mr Sleep all that well on a personal basis – I've only been here a little over eight weeks – but I know that he's a very committed man and that he feels the public have a right to be given the kind of television service they demand.'

'He listens to what people want,' Carpenter interjected. 'He is responding to customer demand, like any businessman.'

'That's good,' said Hannah. 'We need people like that to show the way.'

'I'd say Amen to that.'

'Someone even told me he might be thinking of running for Congress.' Hannah got the words out as slowly and casually as he could, but it was an effort.

The two television men looked at each other.

'I'd be right behind him there, if it were true,' Hannah went on. 'And so would most of middle America.'

'Well,' said Nulty in a surprisingly decisive way, 'I sure don't know anything about that. But Mr Sleep has a lot of interests, as you know. Why d'you ask?'

'Oh, I'm just curious, is all. Maybe I read it somewhere, or maybe someone at the agency said something. I was just thinking in terms of our own clients, what they might think, what their affiliations might be, how that might affect things.'

'Well,' said Carpenter, 'I'm sure that any leanings Mr Sleep might have in that direction would be fully in accordance with corporate policy.'

'I don't see that that's going to affect anything,' Nulty interjected.

'No, you're probably right,' said Hannah. 'It doesn't mean anything. Forget I ever mentioned it.'

'Hey, Thurston,' said Nulty, pointing at the big clock on his office wall. 'Weren't you guys going down to studio B to catch the main news?'

He was right. The hands said it was nearly five to five.

Hannah and Carpenter made a hasty exit. Hannah had the impression Nulty was glad to see the back of them as soon as he'd brought Eugene Sleep's political ambitions into the conversation. He made a mental note of the reaction it had provoked.

The cameras had already started rolling by the time they reached the control room. Apart from the cross above the desk, they could have been in any news studio at any TV station in any state in the union. The guy with the deskful of yellow paper was pretty average too. A caption card said his name was Bob Darrow.

But this news wasn't like the news on normal TV stations. A 727 had come down over Panama that morning, but there was no mention of it. Nor were the viewers told about the two per cent climb in the Dow Jones, a threatened strike by AMTRAK service engineers or the ten-foot python that was loose in west Los Angeles. Instead the news broadcast had an obsessively Christian slant – every item had some kind of spiritual significance, but aroused little interest in Hannah. There were rallies, exhortations, a blanket condemnation of some fool rock singer's recent utterances, this being the thirtieth anniversary or something of John Lennon's assertion that the Beatles were bigger than Jesus Christ. Some guy who had been in a heavy metal band but had now found the Lord came on and testified. Hannah remembered that guy when he was good, played some smoking guitar. Now he looked like an insurance salesman and talked like one as well.

By the time Carpenter had shown him out through the lobby, Hannah had had more than enough of Salvation TV. And yet, sitting in his hotel room later that evening with a club sandwich and a cold beer, he flipped through the channels until he found it again.

They seemed to be showing some kind of live outside broadcast. At least they were in some suburban street somewhere – the caption flash identified it as Walker,

Texas, wherever that was on the map. And there on screen was Darrow, the guy he'd seen earlier reading the news. He was talking to camera and wearing a cream-coloured belted raincoat, just like TV presenters do when they're talking to camera.

The sound was down too low for Hannah to catch what Darrow was saying. By the time he'd hit the remote the camera had panned away and they were looking at the street again. There was nothing special about it, just the usual anonymous-looking suburban homes that could have been found anywhere south of the Mason-Dixon line. Lights were on in almost all of them but the street looked deserted.

There were cars parked on driveways, the usual models. A red Ford was parked outside one of the houses and the camera came right up close on it, so you could read all the Lone Star State legend on the licence plate. Hannah wondered, for no good reason, if licence plates were still made by cons in jail.

The camera pulled back abruptly. A side door had opened in one of the houses and a man came out. He walked briskly down the drive, buttoning his quilted jacket against the chill night air. He seemed to be heading for the red Ford.

He was just an ordinary guy, as far as Hannah could tell. He stood a little above average height, had sandy hair – it was difficult to tell in the street lights, which leached out all colours apart from yellow and black – and an athletic build. There was a pronounced spring in his step, like he kept himself in shape.

All of a sudden, lights came on all over the place, until it was like daylight out there. The guy froze, like a racoon caught in car headlights.

'Earle Jackson?' said Darrow and then he was standing right up next to him, holding a microphone.

Jackson – if that was who he was – looked puzzled, almost to the point of alarm. You could tell he wanted to

71

make it to the sanctuary of his red Ford but that was twenty feet away.

'Are you Earle Jackson?' Darrow repeated.

'Yeah?' The guy looked confused, like he didn't really know. He stared round wildly at the lights, as if worried that this might be some novel kind of stick-up.

There were other people now around Earle Jackson but they were all on Darrow's side. Someone shoved a microphone like a dirty sheep into Jackson's face.

'Mr Jackson, you have a wife and three children, is that right?'

'What is this?' The guy was beginning to find his feet at last.

'Mr Jackson, can you confirm you have a wife and three children.'

For a moment Jackson seemed panic-stricken, as though something might have happened to his family.

'Yeah, sure, I mean – look, would you mind telling me what is going on? What are all these lights?'

'Mr Jackson, would you tell us what you have been doing in this house?'

The camera panned back to show the house Earle Jackson had just come out of.

'Get out of here,' Jackson hissed, but the guy with the microphone blocked his way.

'Mr Jackson, we believe you've been conducting an affair with a married lady who lives in that house. Her name, as we understand, is Mrs Lena Masters.'

The camera came in real close on Earle Jackson's face as Darrow spoke. It registered fear, anger, outrage, surprise, all in quick succession.

'Who in hell are you?' he hissed.

'Salvation Television, Mr Jackson. Your wife, Marlene, is watching our channel right now.'

'You guys are the pits.'

'Would you deny you are having an affair with Mrs Masters, Mr Jackson? We understand you are the

72

manager of Riverside Auto Parts on Barndale Avenue, is that right? And that you're a committee member of the Texas Federation of Civil War Societies? You helped restage the Battle of Bull Run a couple of years back.'

Jesus, thought Hannah, they're skinning the guy alive. He'd just been out porking his mistress and all of a sudden he's a national celebrity. They're telling everyone who he is, where he works, what kind of shoes he likes to wear on a weekend – and most of all they're branding him as an adulterer.

'You keep my wife and kids out of this,' Jackson shouted, the veins standing out red and angry on his forehead.

'So you don't deny anything?'

'I'll get an attorney on to you.'

'We have been filming you for weeks, Mr Jackson. We know all about your dalliance with Lena Masters.'

They really had it in for him. Hannah wondered why they didn't just brand him with a big letter A for adulterer, like they did to Hester Prynne in *The Scarlet Letter*.

All the while Jackson kept forcing his way towards his car, but the cameraman and the guys with the hand lights and microphones were trying to bar his way. Ruin was staring him in the face. In an upright town like Walker, it didn't take much to bring disgrace on a guy. Hannah didn't know where Walker was but it couldn't have been all that far from Waco, home of another bunch of religious nuts.

People had come out of the houses now, disturbed by the lights and the commotion outside. The camera just caught a curtain moving in Lena Masters' house, and then snapping closed again.

Earle Jackson got the door of the red Ford open but all the while Darrow was talking at him in a high, sing-song kind of voice. It was a weird mix of straight

73

investigative journo-speak and Old Testament. He was giving him both barrels now, the sins of the fathers and all that, and then Jackson got the car started and slewed off across the road, causing one of the cameramen to leap hurriedly out of the way.

Darrow, meanwhile, was unhurriedly dusting himself down while another camera lingered on him.

'Well,' he said, a nervous smile playing about his wholesome features. 'That was certainly a surprise Mr Earle Jackson wasn't expecting this evening. Let's go see what Mrs Lena Masters might have to say.'

He marched up the drive of the house, a guy with a steadycam running ahead of him, tracking his every step.

'Lena Masters is thirty-six,' he intoned, scarcely pausing for breath. 'She has two children and her husband Lou is the night foreman at the Desoto carbide plant right here in Walker. Two days a week, Mrs Walker helps run the nursery class at the local grade school.'

So they were going to stab her to death as well, Hannah thought. He felt sick at heart but the story, he had to admit, made compelling television. He wondered how long it would be before it was networked across the States.

Darrow was pounding on the side door of the house but was plainly getting no reply.

'We know you're there, Mrs Masters,' he called, but the door stayed resolutely shut. She wouldn't open it, he knew. She'd be upstairs in her room, terrified out of her life, maybe even sitting on the side of the bed where she'd so lately been lying with Earle Jackson, wondering what the fuck she was going to do now the world had imploded on her.

Darrow was still pounding on the door but Hannah had had enough. He flipped off the TV and got himself a drink from the mini-bar.

This was nothing like any of the stuff he'd seen at the studio, or that Stone had shown him back in DC. He

74

wished he had a videotape to send back to Washington – a call to Carpenter would fix that.

He drank bourbon and ginger ale. Neither was a brand he liked. He looked at his watch. It was a little after ten. All of a sudden he felt tired and a little lonesome. The job got to him sometimes, like that. It drew so much out of you that, by the time you had an hour or so to yourself, there was nothing left. You were like an empty box of Cheerios. Sometimes, after working late, he would sit at home in his bare apartment and stare at the wall for an hour at a time.

He made another drink, but that wasn't the answer. He figured he'd go out and see what kind of night life a town like Wink could offer. If it was anything like Walker, it should be a night to remember.

ELEVEN

Jarvis felt so bad, lying there cocooned in bed, that she couldn't have felt any worse if she'd gone with Hannah after all. There wasn't really all that much the doctor could do for her, just recommend she take aspirin to bring the fever down and drink plenty of liquid. A big jug of juice stood by the bed.

Her temperature was down to 100 but every bone in her body seemed to ache. She tried to read but her mind couldn't focus on the words. And yet as soon as she tossed the book aside and lay down on the pillows, her thoughts seemed to go wild, swirling around in her head. Most of them related to the Sex Files.

She was just about comfortable when the phone rang. She reached out, flipped up the aerial. It was Hannah.

'This had better be good,' she said to him. 'I'm in bed.'

'Anyone we know?'

'Cut the MCP shit, will you? I feel lousy.'

'Sure, I know. I'm sorry. I had a cold once. I guess I know how you feel.'

What Jarvis felt was irritation. Why did the powers that be have to give her this guy for a partner?

'OK, why are you ringing me?' she asked. Hannah could hear the tightness in her voice over the congestion. He got to the point pretty quickly, by his standards.

76

'Well,' he said, 'it seems they still lynch people down here, only they do it on live television.'

Then he told her about what he'd seen that evening.

'Those guys are weird,' Jarvis said when he'd done. 'They must enjoy it, or they wouldn't do it.'

'The pleasure principle?'

'Something like that.'

'What's my next move, do you think? There's not a lot I can do here on my own.'

'Don't try and make me feel guilty for not being there, Hannah. You're a big boy now, you don't need me to hold your hand.'

'I'll just carry on looking around, then. I might stay down here for a few days.'

'You do that.'

'You got any idea when you're going to be back at work?'

'Not this week, that's for certain. But I should be OK by Monday. The doctor's prescribed me antibiotics.'

'They can mess you up, you know. They screw around with your immune system. I know someone who sets a lot of store by homeopathic remedies.'

'You know I don't approve of things like that.'

'Aren't you aware that antibiotics aren't good for you, long term?'

'Look, I've got a job to do, so I take a shot.'

'Sure, I understand. Oh, there's one thing more, I just remembered.'

'What's that?'

'Are you wearing anything in bed? Or are you naked?'

She hung up on him – it was getting to be a habit.

TWELVE

Hannah was feeling pretty frustrated that evening, not really knowing where things were going. He tried ringing Clemency's number back in DC but got no reply. It had been only a little more than twenty-four hours since he'd seen her yet his pecker was beginning to stir already.

He needed company and he was on expenses. The bar he ended up in turned out to be a singles bar, the only one in town. He'd seen some other beer halls along the main drag that looked like places where guys would stick a knife in your ribs as soon as tell you the time of day. He wasn't normally the type to cruise bars but he was a stranger in a strange town and, besides, people might want to talk to him about life in Wink, Texas. He could ring this one up, charge for a few luxuries, maybe take someone out for an Italian, ease her legs apart a little. If he was supposed to be checking into why people were acting horny, he'd need some first-hand experience. The joint he'd found at least looked halfway reasonable.

He ended up going home with a girl called Phoebe. Phoebe was twenty-three, a bit-part movie actress (so she said) and a sometime singer (so she said). She had been out of work for three months and had just finished with her boyfriend of two years, through her choice rather than his. Now she was just out to enjoy herself,

78

she had said, accepting his offer of another Moscow Mule.

'Girls just wanna have fun, right?' she said as she worked the door lock. She lived in a frame house not far from the centre of town. He couldn't believe it had been so easy. She had great tits, that was what had attracted him to her.

He'd talked to her for a while first, as he'd talked to a few other people in the bar – very generally of course, not giving the game away, the way he'd been trained. Sure, they were aware of this feeling of suspicion in the air. Folks were getting real churchy, not in a friendly, down-home kind of way but mean and disapproving. The only gay bar in town, Buddies, had closed down a couple of months back. Some of them wondered if it might be the television stations and the newspapers that caused it. Everything was getting real preachy and sermonising. Phoebe didn't watch Salvation TV herself but a lot of people did. 'They even busted a kids' eighteenth birthday party,' she said. It seemed there were kids necking and fumbling, doing things like kids always do and then, all of a sudden, there were lights and cameras everywhere and that guy Darrow proselytising. It was like the Salem witch-hunts all over again.

'Sounds weird,' Hannah said, and decided she'd be the one to work on tonight. After a couple more Moscow Mules, she was his for the asking.

A porch light flicked on automatically as they went up the path to her home. She rummaged in her bag, couldn't find the key she was looking for, tipped its contents out and located the key by the metallic chink it made as it hit the step. Hannah handed her her purse and cigarette lighter.

'Do you mind going in first?' she said as she turned the lock. 'I don't like going into a dark house on my own.'

He stepped inside, found a switch, flipped on lights.

79

The place was cheaply and anonymously furnished but it was tidy and the chairs looked comfortable. Hannah decided he'd stay. After his session at the TV station, he felt he needed to talk dirty to someone.

He didn't really want another drink but felt it would be churlish to refuse her when she offered him one. As he followed her out to the kitchen, he was aware of the slinky way she swung her backside as she walked. All of a sudden, and without him realising quite how or why, they were kissing passionately, her tongue inside his mouth, those stupendous breasts against his chest. *You are fucking insane*, he told himself, but he couldn't stop himself. He was supposed to be here on Bureau duty, gathering information, and here he was, about to hit the sack with some broad he'd only just met.

Their first coupling was quick and uncompromising, hands slithering on thighs, a dress pulled up, a zipper pulled down. He fucked her against the refrigerator door, could hear the bottles and things rattling around inside. It was all over inside a minute.

'Let's go back to the lounge, shall we?' she said when they finally disengaged. The voice of Hannah the professional operative said he ought to go right now, before he got too much into deep water. But the voice of Hannah the cocksman was louder and more persuasive and he was powerless to resist. He did as he was bid. He didn't think about Clemency.

Phoebe put a couple of glasses and an open bottle of Muscadet down on the coffee table. 'It'd be a shame to waste this,' she said. 'I had some before I came out. It won't keep.' She poured him a glass.

As he reached for it, he noticed a videotape lying under the table. It was evidently hardcore, the high-booted woman on the cover dressed in studs and leather. He picked it up, intrigued. Phoebe laughed.

'Oh, that,' she said, half-embarrassed. 'Kurt – that's my old boyfriend, remember – he got it from one of the guys at work. It's really wild.'

'It looks it,' said Hannah, studying the cover as he sipped his wine. '*Kiss the Lash* – sounds like a laugh a minute. I didn't know you were into this stuff.'

There was a pause, perhaps a hint of embarrassment in her smile. 'Do you wanna see some of it?' asked Phoebe.

Hannah got to see stuff like that most days of his working life but he didn't want to let on. He was supposed to be in advertising, that was his cover story. He looked at his watch. It was half-past midnight. What the hell? He had nothing to do the following day except poke around and ask questions and he could do that with a hangover and a sore dick well enough.

'OK,' he said. 'Looks weird, right? Pretty heavy, huh?'

He hated having to play the country cousin. Some of the things Jarvis had stashed away in the Sex Files, like the enema lesbian clips and the Chilean snuff movies, would have turned a cop's stomach. A little boots and bondage might be daring in Wink, Texas, but it was as tame as a lapdog in DC. He could watch this kind of stuff while eating breakfast – and not infrequently did.

Phoebe slipped the cassette into the video recorder and flicked the remote. An image of a man chatting to two women in a bar came on the screen.

'We've started in the middle,' she said, 'but it doesn't really matter. The storyline is a bit vague.'

She snuggled up closer to him on the sofa, her legs drawn up under her. She lifted up her head and kissed him, took his hand and put it on her breast. The Wonderbra – Hannah could recognise a Wonderbra at forty paces – felt hard and creaky, but her breasts were warm and full.

'You've wanted to do that for a long time, haven't you?' she breathed. 'I could see you looking at me in the bar.'

They sipped their drinks. She was right about the

story. It didn't make a lot of sense. So he gave his attention to Phoebe for a while.

When he turned his eyes back to the video, the action had moved to a bedroom. One of the women had taken a chiffon scarf from a drawer and was draping it over the bedside lamp, bathing the room in a sultry, sexy glow. She turned round and blew a kiss at her partner, the blonde one with the big hair. Then she walked across the room and kissed her full on the lips.

Despite his cynical dismissal, Hannah felt increasingly aroused. *Kiss the Lash* looked pretty raw on a purely technical level but it had an undeniable energy to it and besides, the women were stacked the way he liked them. He watched as the guy in the film sat on the edge of the bed and the two women disappeared off-screen, evidently into a bathroom or something. Were they in a hotel or somewhere? It didn't matter.

When they came back, the dark one caught Hannah's eye first. Her make-up was newly applied, elaborate and whorish, but what really got him going was her black leather thigh boots with the excruciating, six-inch heels. Her hair was back-combed into a smoky cloud, her eyes kohl-rimmed in a face of ghostly paleness. Her lips were painted an uncompromising red, like the gash of a wound. Around her neck she wore a spiked collar of black leather.

The camera lingered over her outfit, a skin-tight black leather corset – he was reminded of Clemency and some of the things he knew she wore – which left her breasts exposed, the nipples rouged into redness. Her sex was exposed too, the sparse black pubic hair standing out against white flesh, the lips clearly visible in close-up.

Hannah wanted to laugh but the guy in the film was starting to look alarmed. The dark-haired one was starting to get aggressive with him, telling him what to do, shaking her balled-up fist at him in a way that looked pretty uncompromising. He couldn't catch what they were saying, the sound was turned down low. The guy took off his clothes and climbed onto the bed, kneeling down, awaiting orders. His penis, Hannah noted, was hugely erect.

When the blonde one came in Hannah was even more startled. Her hair was wild and loose, her lips were curled into a sulky pout and she too wore a new outfit – a catsuit of white lace, transparent as gauze, through which her breasts and buttocks, to say nothing of her labia, were plainly visible. The reason why was not hard to fathom. When she stood in her white patent-leather ankle boots with her legs wide apart, he could see that not only was the catsuit open at the crotch, but the woman's pubic hair had been completely shaved off, leaving her sex bare and visible.

'This is getting interesting,' he said to Phoebe. She didn't reply.

The blonde one walked across the room, opened a cabinet and took out two pairs of handcuffs, with which she fastened the guy, still kneeling, to the bedposts by his ankles. Then the other one took hold of a whip but she didn't use it on his naked ass. Instead, she delicately stroked its wicked-looking tip against the white lace of her friend's catsuit, drawing it with tantalising slowness up the inside of her thigh until it touched the lips of her exposed sex. At the same time she began to play with her own pussy, easing one, then two, fingers into herself, and then a third, expertly massaging her clitoris with her thumb.

Even by the standards of the Sex Files, this seemed to stand up well – and so did his cock. The movie seemed to be trawling things from the very back of Hannah's imagination, going into areas he had never reached before. He wasn't altogether sure the feeling was a pleasurable one, but from the way she was staring at the screen and the inches-long ash on the cigarette in her hand, Phoebe seemed to be even more excited than he was.

The blonde woman then lay on the bed and arranged herself so her bare pussy was only inches away from the man's face. It was pretty unambiguous what the dark one was saying now. Even as the first stroke of the lash cut into his buttocks, he began to lick at those close-shaven lips, his tongue lapping them as though he were eating an ice-cream cone. There seemed to be a good deal of shouting going on, as the whip came down again and again and things really began to move on-screen. His penis seemed even more distended than ever. Could it be, Hannah thought, that the guy was actually beginning to enjoy himself? These weren't the usual blue-movie stars, he decided, hamming it up for money to feed their expensive powder habits. These people were in it for real, and the thought gave him a thrill.

The way the blonde woman came, with the camera close up on her face, was plainly not acting either. Hannah wondered where it was all going to end. Phoebe seemed to be holding her breath as if waiting for something and then the camera panned back to the dark-haired woman, who'd been out of shot for some time.

When the camera next caught up with her, she had kitted herself out with a huge strap-on dildo, which bulged out from her groin like some obscene travesty of a penis. She stood there in her black shiny boots, a wicked look on her face, the heavy eye make-up only emphasising the leer in her eyes. She ran her hand up and down the huge length of the dildo, caressing it longingly, maybe even swaggering a little. Christ, thought Hannah, as the camera caught the look of alarm on the man's face. Something like that, right up his goddamn ass?

But that wasn't what the script demanded. Instead, he saw the blonde woman spread-eagled over the antique brass bed frame, her creamy white buttocks high in the air, her legs stretched far apart. Again the whip tickled her thighs, her buttocks, her pink exposed sex, again it came down, harder and harder, the dominatrix with her scarlet lips and nipples the very picture of fury, the dildo bobbing up and down with every savage stroke. And then she was pressing it against her friend's soft cheeks, demanding admission.

Hannah watched in awe-struck fascination as the camera revealed every detail of that bizarre coupling. The blonde girl's clean-shaven pussy seemed to suck that monstrous girth into itself until he began to wonder just how much the woman could take. And then the rhythmic thrusting that seemed to go on indefinitely, the cutaways to ecstatic faces, the bobbing nipples, the dark woman's tongue endlessly licking her lover's neck, the hands cupping breasts, the tight black straps cutting cruelly into flesh, until he could see, could actually see in full, close-up detail the trembling that seemed to course through their bodies, the labia in motion, freeze-framed at last at the very moment of triumph.

'Did you recognise the dark-haired one?' asked Phoebe, as she fast-forwarded the video.

'I don't think so, no. Should I? Is she some famous porno queen?'

She stopped the tape, rewound it, let it roll on to the scene with the dildo.

'There, look at her face. Don't you remember her? She was in the bar. She's a good friend of mine.'

Hannah wondered how he could have missed her. But then, most women look different in bondage gear and with a huge dildo strapped to their abdomen.

'Another friend of mine made the video. Does it turn you on?' said Phoebe, as she fast-forwarded once more.

'It's pretty, how can I put it, uncompromising, isn't it?' he said.

'But did it turn you on?'

Her hand was perilously close to his groin. The question was fairly redundant in the circumstances.

'Yes, it did. I've never seen anything like that before.'

'Would you like to do something like that?'

'What?'

'I mean, would you like to play some of those games?'

He realised how incredibly tired he felt, now the effect of the drinks had all but worn off. It had been one hell of a long day. The flight, the meetings at the TV station – he felt close to exhaustion.

'Sure,' he said automatically. Some other part of his brain could take over now. The rest of him was going to get some sleep.

'Just lie there,' said Phoebe. Hannah was glad she said that. His mind was racing, over-stimulated like he'd taken a handful of uppers. It was raw lust that was doing that to him.

She hiked up her dress, unclipped her nylon stockings. Then, with practised ease, she used the gauzy nylons to tie first one of Hannah's wrists to the wooden frame of the sofa, and then the other, until he was spread-eagled on the cushions in a parody of a crucifixion. He was half-expecting Darrow to come bursting in through the window.

'Don't worry,' she said. 'I'm not going to whip you. Not today, anyway.'

She lay down next to him, half on top of him, kissed his face, his neck, his shoulders. Hannah unconsciously tried to reach out and put his arms around her but was restrained by her stockings.

'It's weird,' he said. 'I can't move.'

'You don't have to move, lover. I'll do all the work.'

She slowly unbuttoned his shirt, ran her hands through the soft hair on his chest.

'I like hairy men,' she breathed. 'But not too hairy. You're just about right.' She smiled up at him. Then she began to trace her tongue across his torso, around his pectorals, across his nipples. Despite the amount of alcohol he'd got through, and the quickie in the kitchen, his cock was already rock-hard and straining against the denim of his jeans. He closed his eyes and surrendered himself to the sensations she induced in his body.

She used her lips, tongue and teeth with practised skill. A long, slow lick would be followed by a sharp bite and then a caress. Her hands stroked his ribs, played with his navel, and then he arched his back for her as she took off his shirt completely and cast it to the floor.

His groin came next. She stroked him over his conspicuous bump, lay her head on his chest, kissed the sensitive flesh of his stomach. Butterfly fingers danced across him, this way and that, to be followed by slowly raking nails that gave him goose bumps. Pleasure and pain, pleasure and pain – she seemed to be setting up a rhythm for them to dance to, except that his duty was to lie still and wait for whatever was to follow.

She pulled down his pants and there was his cock, lying engorged and ready, against his upper thigh. He felt oddly proud of himself. She touched it for the first time with a feather-like delicacy. He wanted her to suck it hard, bring him to orgasm quickly and viciously.

She sat up, took a sip of wine, fingers all the while running up and down his body. He wished she'd get on with it. She'd very cleverly made him want her – but what did she want from him? The film had made him feel distinctly uneasy.

He smiled at her when she asked how he was enjoying himself. It seemed the best kind of answer to give. He wanted to get back to something he knew more about. It was a bit like having one toke too many.

'Take your dress off,' he murmured.

'You'd like that, would you? Say please.'

'Please.'

She raked her fingernails down his ribs. It made him wince. 'I can't hear you,' she said.

'Please,' he said, louder.

She stood up, tugged at the zip, and the dress fell in

87

soft black folds at her feet. She took off her underwear and stood gloriously naked in front of him. Her breasts were magnificent. Her pubic hair was thick and abundant, and her labia were fully visible, deeply pink and glistening.

'Do you like me naked?' she asked.

'I think you've got a wonderful body. I thought so when I first saw you in the bar.'

'I don't always do it naked, though,' she went on. 'I've got all the leather stuff, you know. Maybe I'll wear it for you one day.'

'What's it like?' he asked. Darrow could wait.

'I love it. Imagine what my pussy is like when I've been wearing leather pants all evening.'

'Nice and licky.'

'Nice and licky. Would you like to lick me now? Down there, I mean?'

'I'd love to. I've wanted to lick your pussy all evening.'

She straddled over his chest as he lay there on the sofa, until her sex was just above his face. He was excited by her musky, vaginal aroma, and the sight of the engorged labia that seemed to invite his questing tongue. He licked her tentatively, drawing just the tip of his tongue across the outer labia, exploring the manifold ridges and furrows that seemed to open out like a purse before him.

He heard her moan. His nose was buried in the muff of her pubic hair – it really was extraordinarily luxuriant – and he inhaled deeply the unmistakable smell of a woman on heat. And then his tongue began again its probing of her inner recesses until, finally, he opened his mouth wide and took in as much of this anemone as he could.

She gasped. 'Suck me, lover,' he heard her breathe. 'Tongue me out.'

He licked her again, this time his tongue pushing deeper into her vagina. She squatted down on him and his nose was engulfed by her liquid folds, threatening to asphyxiate him. Somehow he was able to wriggle his head to one side and breathe more easily, his tongue all the while continuing to flicker and probe.

After two or three minutes of this his jaws were beginning to ache but he kept on at his work, aware of how much she seemed to enjoy what he was doing to her. He found her clitoris and teased it so very gently with just the tip of his tongue – she winced, shivered a little, and then pressed her thighs more firmly against the side of his head, urging him on like a rider on horseback.

He licked and played with her, wondering what she looked like in her leather gear, aware too of her perfume mingled with the scent of her secretions. He sensed she was very near her climax. He gently nipped the soft flesh at the tops of her thighs with his teeth and it seemed to drive her wild. She ground her pussy against his face and he thrust his tongue, hard and stiff, as far as he could inside her. He sensed rather than felt directly a faint trembling running through her genital area and then she called out something incomprehensible and came right across his face, shuddering and gasping, pushing him away from her as she did so.

'Hey, that was good,' Phoebe said as she slid off him, reaching out for her glass. He was aware of her fluids drying on his face, the smell of her still strong in his nostrils. He tried to sit up but realised he was restrained, and sank back on to the sofa. He didn't want any more wine, anyway. His dick was swollen nearly fit to burst.

She looked at him. 'I don't want you to come inside me again,' she said. 'I'm not really into penetrative sex, not much, anyway. You want me to do you by hand? Blow you? Fuck your ass? Let's watch another video, shall we?'

THIRTEEN

DELMAR, NEW MEXICO. JUNE 17TH. 11.06 PM.

Sam Grissom had been getting hornier and hornier all
evening, ever since he'd gone out into the back yard to
smoke his nine p.m. cigarette. His wife Annabella didn't
like him smoking in the house and he respected her
wishes, even though tonight she'd be out at her usual
Tuesday evening bridge club. She worked hard all week
selling real estate and this night off was the one little
indulgence she allowed herself.

The night sky had been exceptionally bright. Sam
looked up at the stars and wished he knew more about
them. Some of them seemed red and some of them were
blue and some seemed to twinkle more than others.

Sam thought a lot of sexy thoughts and not just about
Annabella. But this night they seemed to be coming
thick and fast. He could feel a tightness in his chest and
his mouth felt dry and it was all he could to stop himself
going upstairs and beating off. He was going to save
himself for Annabella, maybe fuck her in front of the big
mirror in the bedroom, the one in front of the dressing
table. They both of them liked to watch. He wondered if
maybe they should get a video camera, or was that just
too tacky?

He shaved, used mouthwash to get rid of the cigarette
taste and smell, put on a clean polo shirt that showed off
the muscles on his arms. A lot of women didn't seem to

be all that interested in a guy's physique – despite what the magazines said – but Annabella sure as hell was. Sam worked out a lot, and not just for the sake of his own physical fitness. Annabella liked to look at his body-builder magazines, she said it turned her on. The new issue of *Muscle Sport* had arrived that morning and it was lying casually on the bed, just waiting for her to pick it up.

He looked at his watch – a little after eleven. She'd be home any minute. Suddenly, on an impulse, he stripped off all his clothes and stood naked in the hallway. He stroked his cock a couple of times. It stood to attention. Sam knew he was well hung. He liked the feeling of having a big dick, though he still felt embarrassed using the shower at the gym. Most of the guys he knew would have killed to have a whanger like that one. In high school they'd called him King Dong.

He heard Annabella's car crunching up the driveway. His dick felt like it was going to burst, he had so much come in there. Maybe Annabella would blow him there and then in the hallway, and then they could go upstairs and fuck some more. He had plenty of options. Anna-bella rarely needed any encouragement.

She pushed the door open, saw him standing there and burst out laughing.

'What's going on?' she said.

He smiled back at her, not saying anything.

She looked at his cock and at the expression in his eyes.

'Sam, can this wait? I have a couple of phone calls to make.'

'At this hour? Come on, honey. Can't you see I'm dying to get sociable?'

'Hey, hey, calm down, OK. What's got into you?'

He laughed, took her in his arms. 'What's the matter, you don't love your old man no more?'

'Sure, sure. But Betty Harmon left a message for me

91

to call her about the PTA meeting. I didn't have time to call her earlier and you know what Betty's like.'

Sam wanted to tell her to screw Betty Harmon but didn't.

'And I gotta get something to eat. I didn't have time to before I went out. Be a honey, will ya, and make me a sandwich, while I call Betty. Just cheese and mayo is fine.'

He came and stood next to her, took her in his arms. She held him for a moment and then let him go. His hand trailed across her breasts.

'Maybe later,' she said and pecked him on the cheek. 'You know I have my period.'

Oh shit, he had clean forgotten. His ardour began to dampen, giving way to a feeling of frustration. He went upstairs, put on a bathrobe, and then came down and made her a sandwich.

She was on the phone for half an hour, while he made wind-up gestures. All the while he was getting more and more impatient. She put the phone down and immediately it rang again – it was Marge Hitchcock. Annabella had given her a lift to the bridge party and Marge was worried she'd left her gloves on the back seat. Annabella said she'd check but Marge said it could wait till morning, and all the while Sam sat in his armchair and fumed.

They ended up having an argument and Annabella started getting ready to go to bed. She had to be up early, she said. And her period would probably be over tomorrow, the day after that at the latest. She said she understood but she just wasn't in the mood. They kissed and made up but there was nothing there for him, he knew.

Sam sat up for a while in his bathrobe, watching the Cosby show but taking none of it in. Then he went upstairs to the bathroom, fished a pair of Annabella's panties out of the laundry basket and brought himself off all over them. It wasn't as nice as coming in his wife's mouth or pussy but the sense of relief was palpable, all the same.

FOURTEEN

WINK, TEXAS. JUNE 18TH. 11.48 PM.

Hannah felt that, despite the rigours of his training, he was beginning to lose control of the situation. What did Phoebe want with him? What was he doing here? He found himself worrying. His instincts, normally so sure, were muddled and indistinct. He seemed powerless to resist the forces that racked his loins.

She loaded a new cassette, touched the remote and fast-forwarded. She stopped, went back a few frames, and then pressed the play button.

Two women, not the ones he had seen earlier, were in an apartment full of antiques. There was an open door leading out on to a balcony. In the distance Hannah could see tall buildings. Something told him he was looking at the Manhattan skyline.

One of the women was tall, with straight dark hair, the other had auburn hair and a full, voluptuous figure. Both were naked apart from high-heeled shoes. A man, fully clothed, sat in an armchair, sipping whisky. He was blindfolded.

Phoebe gently took hold of his penis and began to frig it. She half-turned on the sofa so she could watch too.

The women kissed each other, ran their hands over each other, touching in an exploratory way. Then the taller girl knelt down and performed oral sex on the voluptuous one, who threw her head back in a pantomime of enjoyment. The blindfolded man continued to sit and sip his whisky. For a porno movie, the technical quality was excellent. Hannah had seen plenty of these plotless epics and he had been appalled at how amateurish they had been, all shaky hand-held camerawork, bad cuts and jumpy editing. This one looked like it had been done by a top crew, and the actors and actresses performed like professionals, not porno stars. Later, Phoebe told him the movie had been made by a crew at the TV company that had subsequently been bought by Eugene Sleep and reworked into Salvation Television. Some transformation, he pondered.

From time to time Phoebe would lick his cock, suck it into her mouth, taste it. Then she would continue to move her hand up and down, stroking his sensitive glans, playing with the hole at the top with her fingernail. He wanted to reach out and touch her but knew he couldn't become involved, so he lay back and watched the screen.

Now the women changed places, the tall one sitting on the edge of a chair, the plump one lying at her feet. There was a close-up of vaginal lips and then a tongue flickering, moving expertly along those myriad folds and creases. The tall girl wrapped her long legs around her partner's shoulders. The girl at her feet was stroking and feeling her own breasts. Then an extraordinary thing happened.

The tall girl straightened up, put her legs down and opened them wide. The other girl stood up and offered her breasts. The nipples were large, succulent, plump with desire. The tall girl licked them greedily.

Amazed, Hannah saw her partner kneel again and rub her nipples against the tall girl's vaginal lips, pressing them into the puffy folds, her breasts between her lover's thighs. And then the nipple, seen in close-up, seemed to be actually inside the vagina, was fucking the girl, was itself being moulded and sucked and shaped by the muscles of her luscious sex.

Hannah glanced down and saw that Phoebe's nipples, too, were hard and stiff – this was evidently turning her on too. She looked up at him, smiling dreamily, and almost at the same instant the first jet of his spunk shot out and arced over her breast. She quickly pressed her tits against him, a hard nipple pressed right up against the tip of his penis, and his semen flooded out and over it, silvery-white against the subtle flesh tones of her suntanned body.

FIFTEEN

DELMAR, NEW MEXICO. JUNE 18TH. 8.08 AM.

In the morning Sam Grissom woke up with a boner on him like a copper's nightstick but Annabella was already dressed and halfway out the door. She had a business meeting with a client at eight-thirty and she didn't want to be late. She kissed him lightly on the forehead and was gone.

Sam drove to the office and spent most of the morning staring at the panty-line on his secretary's skirt. By lunchtime, though, the feeling had begun to recede. He wondered if it marked the start of the male menopause or something.

Annabella and he took a bath together that evening. Then they went to bed and fucked each other like they had done when they were first married.

He realised he had nothing to worry about. But it was weird, the intensity of it all.

SIXTEEN

Jarvis sat on her living-room chesterfield with a box of tissues – unperfumed, recycled, plain packaging – and scanned the screen of her PC. Palestrina played softly in the background, Missa Mirabilis, perfect geometrical music to help concentrate the mind, but always that little edge of passion to it.

She'd been up for two days now but hadn't felt well enough to go to the Bureau. The bug had knocked her out more than she'd thought. She'd called Stone, who understood. Besides, she could do the work as well from home as she could at the office.

She sniffed, reached for a tissue, blew her nose softly. She was in a state of cocooned innocence; her temperature was back to normal now but her body felt drained after the fever. In the afternoon she would try to sleep a while.

'Look after yourself,' Stone had said. 'Don't try to do too much.' But it was an effort for her. She had that obsessive quality that all the best operatives at the Bureau had. She couldn't leave a question unanswered. She had taken one holiday in five years – plus periods of statutory leave, sure, but not actually going away anywhere – and this was her first time off sick for almost as long.

She was scanning the usual intercepts that the Bureau

97

had gathered. Hannah hadn't filed anything on Sleep yet but she knew that, if there was anything to find, he'd find it. She had never felt, privately, that Hannah had quite the levels of diligence that she regarded as ideal but he made up for it – though she would never admit it to his face – by his powers of intuition. He could think on his feet, and was the best guy she'd ever met at putting two and two together. However, all that crystal-healing stuff was way out of line. She knew he had a girlfriend who was into that kind of nonsense and it seemed to have gone to his head. Or perhaps he was just yanking her chain.

She focused back on the screen and wondered if it was just the Sleep media empire that was drumming up all this hell-fire and damnation stuff, or whether other parties with a vested interest were getting het up as well. For most of the morning she had been looking at the small religious groups, all the groups of nuts and kooks that made the Fundamentalists and Seventh-day Adventists seem like major league players. She had no affiliations herself, the very idea made her laugh.

Right now she was looking into the files of a print works near Oklahoma City that handled close on forty per cent of all the magazines and other printed materials put out by the cults and sub-cults, the splinter groups and the groups that were splinters of splinters, ever fragmenting themselves like amoebae in an effort to find ultimate purity. Looking into their writings seemed the best way of discovering what she needed. I am the word indeed.

Standard Bureau software got her into and out of other people's on-line facilities without being noticed. Once she got in, it was quite an easy matter to find the information she wanted. She was using the search function of her PC, identifying keywords like 'behaviour' and 'morals' and 'shame' – a whole lexicon of disapproval. The Bureau's investigation programs – developed in covert association with a couple of the major software houses and kept very, very quiet (only a dozen or so departments were allowed access to them) – saved her a lot of time. She couldn't imagine actually having to read through all the endless drafts, rewrites, print-outs and discards that the files provided. It would have taken forever and Stone wanted an answer by the end of the week. They'd already been on the case nearly a fortnight and he wanted results.

Earlier that day she'd been looking into the phone and fax intercepts of three of the most vociferous splinter-group leaders. These were guys – and always it was guys, never women in cases like these – who made Jimmy Swaggart seem like a model of restraint. Really, it would have needed a linguistics analyst to do it justice but she reckoned she knew what she was looking for. Buzzwords again, those little tell-tale signs that would demonstrate what was on everyone's mind at the moment. She knew what these guys were talking about almost before they opened their mouths.

When Jarvis first joined the Bureau they did it all with wiretaps. Now they had programs that would get them into other people's programs – with State Department dispensation, of course – without them knowing. If they were on-line or networked, even if it was just one PC linked with another, the Bureau could lend an ear. If she had wanted to, she could have seen what Ford's personnel department in Detroit were sending to Ford's personnel department in England about the new head of corporate finance. She could have looked at Benazir Bhutto's personal chequeing account, studied record sales on the East Coast and seen how they tallied with the charts – they didn't, of course – and watched the sales of gasoline through each pump at the Amoco in Walker, Texas. If it made a mark on the surface of the Earth, Jarvis could access it and download it if necessary.

The name of Keiller Dickinson Stark came up with a beep. Keiller Dickinson Stark led the New Watchtower Evangelists and True Believers from a base in Terrapin, Louisiana. The New Watchtower Evangelists didn't total more than – she checked the figure automatically – 368 paid-up members but they made more noise than the five thousand must have made when Jesus came up with the loaves and fishes. Keiller Dickinson Stark had two convictions for fraud and embezzlement under different names, but this fact may or more likely may not have been known to the 368 Evangelists and True Believers who, in the last financial year April to April, had paid close to $2.5 million into various Stark accounts.

In her apartment building in Washington, DC she was looking at a fax which had been sent from Stark's bayou headquarters to the editor of the local newspaper. Though this wasn't one of Sleep's trans-national stable of titles, it was still the usual stuff – proclaiming the rising tide of moral degeneracy, the need for firm action, the reassertion of fixed values. Here we go again, she thought. The fax was signed by Stark himself. There was a reference in the text to previous letters published in the Terrapin *Sentinel* but she could find no trace of them in the office files of the New Watchtower Evangelists and True Believers.

She called up the Terrapin *Sentinel* on screen. Developing the entry program had cost the Bureau close to $150 million and Jarvis reckoned it was worth every last cent. Effortlessly she slipped through the security checks and the computer began scanning the newspaper's files. There were the letters from Stark, pretty much the same as the one she had just read. One of them was cross-referenced to another folder. She opened that up. It was news stories that had been filed but never used, items about sewing bees and petty thefts and wedding anniversaries, just general newspaper-office junk that no one could find a use for. There was another folder within

100

that. For a moment or two she wondered whether it would be worth the trouble, but went ahead anyway.

For a second she could hardly believe what she saw. It was as if she'd gotten stuck into a loop and had wound up back with the Sex Files. Here were all the familiar accounts of pornography rings, under-age sex and indecency charges, but so many of them, and all filed within the last six months or so. She looked at the same period in the previous years and the numbers bore no comparison. One file in particular caught her eye. It was rough copy, unsubbed, just the way the stringer had sent it in via his modem.

Police were called last night, she read, *to an empty grain store near Buffalo Springs after complaints about noise. Inside they found anything up to four hundred teenagers – some from as far away as Rupert County – dancing to wild, repetitive music. Many of them were naked and apparently high on drugs. A search revealed a small quantity of marijuana and LSD.*

The storage site is owned by the Hardy Grain Company based in Jacksdale, Louisiana, but has not been used for some years after the company concentrated its operations on its site at Lemonhead.

From his home, the Vice-President in Hardy Grain, A P Hardy (56) of Burlington, LA, said he had allowed his son Matthew to use the grain store as the venue for a party to celebrate his high school graduation. He said he was shocked by what he had been told. His son had been hospitalised the previous week following a riding accident but the party appears to have gone ahead without him. None of the apparent organisers or arrested parties were known to the Hardy family.

The Sentinel was unable to speak to Matthew Hardy, who is believed to be recovering from his accident in a private clinic. No charges have been preferred.

Why wasn't the story used? Jarvis wondered. It had all the right elements – wild teenagers, nakedness, a prominent local family, an air of mystery. And yet it had been spiked. She couldn't understand it.

She found more stories in similar vein. Some of them she could understand as being not entirely fit for a family newspaper, but she got the clear impression that the people of Terrapin, Louisiana, weren't being told everything that was happening on their back porch.

She decided to go for a digital walk around the place. First off, she studied pay-per-view TV. Late night baby-blue movies seemed very popular, but the figures were episodic. There'd be one week when practically the whole place seemed to be watching *The Orchid Room* and yet the next week, when the channel screened the altogether raunchier *Naked Desire*, the figures were way down. She checked magazine sales – the same kind of imbalance. The local distributor had had to reorder the June *Playboy*, but the previous month's returns of unsold copies had been far higher than the seasonal average.

How were things with Madame Fantasie, the upmarket lingerie boutique at the Westway Mall? Christmas was their biggest time and then in April/May time for swimsuits but in early July, at a time when they'd normally be at their quietest, they had had a big rush on garter belts, thongs and suchlike. It didn't make any sense. Maybe people had seen *The Orchid Room* and got all fired up; she didn't know.

Sales of condoms showed similar peaks and troughs. But it was all kind of bitty, one day at a time. Nothing correlated. She could see how an average pattern might look by skimming back over previous years. Bearing in mind a depressed economy and the closure of a large engineering works in the town, she still couldn't see any boom-and-bust movement. It was like everything was happening at random, which was weird. It would be nice if she could see that one week everyone was buying black uplift brassieres and reading *Hustler* and renting raunchy videos, and the next they just weren't, but it wasn't like that at all. It was weird.

The scientist soon took over, though, as it always did with Jarvis. It was just a blip, that was all – a few weeks when things go against the grain but then gradually settle down to the long-term pattern. And yet, and yet . . . She wished there was someone she could talk to but Hannah was a thousand miles away.

She downloaded a few files into a folder she had created and then made a gracious exit from the various programs she'd been running. The editor of the Terrapin *Sentinel* and the proprietress of Madame Fantasie never even knew they had had a visitor.

SEVENTEEN

VIGO, TEXAS. JUNE 20TH. 7.07 AM.

Hannah spent a couple more days cruising around the South-west. He didn't have much to go on, just a hunch that the world was polarising into two camps, one that sided with Eugene Sleep and his pursed-lips vigilantes and the other that crystallised in women like Phoebe, who lived like there was no tomorrow and very little left of today.

He called Stone bright and early from an untraceable callbox in a rundown cow town somewhere near Austin.

'I figure maybe I'll go see Sleep,' he said.

Stone didn't react for a long time. Finally he spoke in that familiar chocolate voice.

'This guy doesn't keep open house, you know. Besides, what's the point?'

'The point is, I just want to get a handle on him.'

'The IRS have been trying to get a direct interview with Eugene Sleep for three years. What makes you think you can do it in three days? I want you in here on Friday for a meeting with Agent Jarvis. She'll be back at work then.'

And still freezing me out, thought Hannah.

'All the same, I think it's worth a shot.'

'I'm not so sure. I think maybe I should check that one out with Pepper, you know. Hold fire and I'll get back to you.'

'I'm sorry. I can't hear that. You're breaking up.'

'I said don't move till I tell you.'

'I can't hear you.'

'Give me your number and I'll call back.'

'Hello? You still there?'

'Goddamn it, Hannah, you know I'm still here. Speak to me, you son of a bitch.'

Hannah smiled and put the phone down.

EIGHTEEN

FLAGSTAFF, ARIZONA. JUNE 22ND. 7.45 AM.

Jack Gilhouley picked the mail out of the box while he left his morning eggs boiling. He liked them done for five minutes but Barbie didn't let them cook for more than three, and if there was one thing Jack Gilhouley couldn't abide it was a runny boiled egg.

There was nothing much today, just a Visa statement and a renewal for his AAA membership. The big brown envelope, though, that was more exciting. He'd taken *Guns and Ammo* on subscription for twelve years now but he always found it exciting to have the new month's issue arrive in his mailbox a good three or four days ahead of it hitting the newsstands.

He left *Guns and Ammo* unopened while he toasted a couple of muffins. Then he put the eggs and coffee and muffins on a tray and went through into his den. He always liked to eat breakfast in his den, alone, surrounded by his hunting trophies and the guns secure in their case.

Jack had always risen early. It must have been the hunter in him. He would get up each morning at six-thirty, fix himself a leisurely breakfast, wash and shave, get Barbie's breakfast – she didn't normally wake till nearly eight – and then drive to work. Jack was an accountant, a tax consultant with his own practice in the city. Outside of tourism – though even that was feeling

106

the pinch – the Arizona economy was up shit creek, but people always needed a good tax accountant and Jack was still buying a new car every couple of years, unlike most of his clients.

He sat down at the desk, pulled the tray towards him, cracked open the first egg of three. Some folks liked to slice off the top of their eggs but Jack did it by tap-tap-tapping the shell till it fractured and he could pick off the little broken fragments of shell, an action which he found curiously satisfying.

He ate some egg, munched on a muffin, drank half a cup of coffee. Chock Full O'Nuts was his favourite brand, always had been. He found it was rich but not too rich, strong but not too strong. He put down the cup and tore open the big brown envelope.

But *Guns and Ammo* wasn't inside. Instead, he found a copy of *Garter Belt* and a cheque for $100. What the hell? he thought. Was this some kind of joke? Bill Jackson, a friend from the gun club, was always doing that kind of thing, leaving a pair of panties or something in a guy's car where his wife would be sure to find them.

And then he remembered. Last summer, in a fit of unrequited lust, he'd taken some snaps of Barbie in the altogether and sent them off to the magazine, together with an accompanying letter detailing some of the things he and Barbie liked to do together. For the life of him he couldn't remember why he'd done it. They'd just felt like it, it was like this red mist of horniness had descended on them one day.

It wasn't that he bought magazines like that in the normal run of things, not even *Playboy* or *Penthouse*, let alone a cheap rag like *Garter Belt*. He had bought the magazine occasionally in his college days – there were very few magazines like it, back then in the sixties – and he would buy a copy once in a while even now, usually when he was away on a business trip, to give him something to beat off over until he could get back to

Barbie. He didn't go much for the airbrushed, big-breasted Heffner stereotype – the women in *Garter Belt* might have been hookers and harridans, but at least there were real women. Some of them were even people's wives and sweethearts. They had a whole section of them at the back of the book, Karen from Duluth, Minnesota and Sharon from Bisley, New Hampshire. Jack got off on them in a quiet sort of way. He liked the tackiness of it all. Or did.

His eggs and muffins lay unfinished on the desk in front of him. He opened the magazine, leafed slowly through it, smelling the new-paper smell but hardly noticing the naked and half-naked girls flaunting their charms in their improbable costumes. And then he was at the back of the magazine, in among the ads for dildoes and rubber nightdresses and suchlike. He scanned the pictures, the erotic testimonials of Dave from Bakersfield, California, and Mike from Euston, Rhode Island, describing who and what they and their ladies liked to lick and suck.

And there she was, Barbie, his wife of ten years. They'd given her a whole page to herself. Barbie Gilhouley was his second wife and she was fifteen years younger than he, had been his personal assistant, thirty-five but looked late twenties, gorgeous to his eyes and now, especially for the eyes of the readers of *Garter Belt*, was spread out for their delectation on the big bearskin rug in front of the fire in the lounge, wearing a garter belt in some of the shots but in the others stark naked, her legs wide open showing all she had.

Jack felt a chill run through him, could feel his guts churn. He could see the letter he had written but didn't dare read it. He saw his name at the end, let his eyes rove over the odd phrase – 'then Barbie sucks my dick in and swallows my boiling come' and 'I give her tongue which she sticks a finger up my ass'. It all came back to him now, that crazy period late last summer when, for a week or more, he and Barbie had fucked each other like teenagers, four or five times a night. Sometimes she'd even called him at the office and made him come back home, even though he might have been in the middle of a meeting, and she practically pulled his pants off before he'd even got out of his car.

Something had gotten unhinged in both of them at that time. Sure, they enjoyed a good sex life together, always had, but that was something else, more intense even than the times when they'd first started going together. That was when he was still married to Carole and Barbie was his PA. It had all happened initially when they'd gone to see a client in Oklahoma City – room 242 at the Clearwater Motel, he remembered it as if it had been yesterday – and then with mounting intensity and increasing frequency. Barbie took to wearing black lingerie and little g-string panties to work specifically to excite him and sometimes they would do it there and then in his office, usually when everyone else had gone home but not always. Once, she'd crouched under his desk and sucked him off while Bill West of ABP was in the room and Jack was trying – with increasing difficulty – to explain how he couldn't offset capital gains against his net liability.

But that week was a different thing altogether. Taking the nudie pictures of Barbie and sending them off to the magazine was nothing. They'd done all kinds of crazy things, like her putting a vibro up her pussy when they went out to dinner with the Jacksons. One time, with her encouragement, he'd worn some of her lingerie under his business suit to a meeting with Peppercorn and Gresley, one of his biggest clients.

Jack and Barbie often talked about that mad week of lust but nothing had been quite the same since and nothing could ever satisfactorily explain how they'd felt. Maybe it was something in the water, he would say, sheepishly. Or in the ether, or in the way the planets moved – Barbie was big on astrology – or whatever.

He'd not forgotten any of it but the memories had receded with time. And now he was sitting at his desk looking at those crisp, clear colour photographs of his wife, spread-eagled in a red lace garter belt, much as thousands of other readers would be doing at that very moment.

Oh, Jesus fucking Christ, he thought. It was like waking up the morning after the night before, only ten times worse, a hundred times. *Why the fuck did I do that?* he kept thinking. Would he tell Barbie? What would he say?

And what about his friends, neighbours, colleagues and business associates? Few, if any of them were the kind who would read a magazine like *Garter Belt* and yet you could have said the same about Jack Gilhouley. What if any of them saw it? What would their reaction be? A disapproving stare at the gun club, a ribald remark in the office? Next weekend he and a bunch of the guys were going to some hunting lodge up in the Ozarks and who knows what might come out at a time like that, with everyone shooting the breeze and drinking too much sour-mash bourbon.

He forced some more egg and a cold muffin down his throat, drank some coffee to help clear his head. The morning had started out with such promise but now he felt vulnerable and exposed, just like his wife as she was spread out before him in four-colour offset litho.

Life, thought Jack, sure is a bitch sometimes. He had to be at a client's office by nine and, for the first time in his life, he felt like calling in sick.

NINETEEN

Hannah had a friend, a top financial journalist on the *Post* who owed him one. A guy like Sleep would listen up good, he figured, if the *Post* came sniffing around him. Guys like that couldn't resist publicity in the newspapers, especially if it had Bill Halberson's by-line on it. If they couldn't get it, they bought their own.

Hannah's friend Bill leaned on Sleep's office and Sleep's office said they'd call back. They didn't do so until twenty-four hours before Hannah was due to leave for DC. They wanted to know all about Bill Halberson, had the paper fax some of his stories. There was another long pause, during which time Bill's editor wanted to know why he was so keen on Sleep all of a sudden, when he was supposed to be looking into junk-bond sharking.

Bill said it was just a hunch, Sleep was a happening name and none of the other papers had done anything on him for more than a year. Besides, he told his editor, he'd heard a flier that Sleep wanted to run for Congress. He wanted to be in there before the big story broke.

'OK, you do the interview,' said Bill's editor. The guy was close to retirement and didn't need a hard time. He even agreed to Bill's suggestion that he take a rookie photographer with him, instead of a *Post* staffer.

Sleep's office faxed them back. They liked the stories they saw but weren't keen on the photographer. They

111

said they would prefer to use their own library pix. The *Post* said they never used library pix, they prized themselves on their stable of freelances. Sleep's office said they'd call back.

Another few hours went by. OK, said Sleep's office, they'd agree to the interview and the photographer but they wanted to vet the pictures the *Post* was going to use. And they insisted that no flash units were to be allowed in the Sleep mansion, and that only the left profile be used.

'Who does this guy think he is – Tom Cruise?' said Bill's editor.

At eight the following morning a helicopter bearing a Tru-Flo logo took off from an outlying field at Dallas-Fort Worth and headed west. In the rear seats were Bill Halberson and his photographer, a thirty-six-year-old named Ed Witherspoon who bore an uncanny resemblance to Tom Hannah. One of Sleep's PRs was in the front beside the pilot and she was feeding a steady stream of b.s. into Bill's Sony portable. She was blonde, wearing a navy business suit with a cream blouse open at the neck, and Hannah/Witherspoon was trying hard not to look down her cleavage, which was a refreshingly generous one.

Thirty minutes later they landed at a private airfield in the middle of nowhere. A brand-new BMW whisked them along what might just as well have been a private road – for there was no traffic on it – and pulled up outside a set of gates that wouldn't have disgraced a prison the size of Sing-Sing. A guy in an insignia-less uniform ran a metal detector over Halberson and Hannah, another checked their bags and accreditation. And all the time the blonde with the cleavage – her name was Trudy – fed them a steady drip-drip-drip of tabloid drivel, about what a fine citizen Mr Sleep was and how well his enterprises were shaping up. She gave Bill an exclusive on a new Sleep leisure-site development that

Hannah had known about – through Jarvis, admittedly – over a month ago.

Sleep's mansion, when it finally came into view, wasn't worth sending Stone a postcard of. It was big and it was impressive in a show-colonial kind of way but Hannah had seen a lot better. What was a guy like Sleep doing in a place that looked like it was owned by a guy who ran the biggest plumbing supply business in Arkansas? It reminded him of *Dallas* – he could never understand why a family with the size and financial muscle of the Ewings should want to live in a house that must have had six bedrooms at most. But there had been a lot of things about *Dallas* he couldn't understand, like why they always ate breakfast together and took their meals in the parking lot. And why Sue Ellen, a woman who made a lot of dramatic entrances and exits, should wear jackets with shoulders so wide she'd have to go through doors sideways.

They were ushered into some kind of anteroom. Trudy gave the impression she'd been there a hundred times before. The place gave nothing away. Everything was beige and bland. If you were recovering from open-heart surgery you might find it kind of restful but as a feast for the senses, the Sleep pile was like looking deep into a bowl of oatmeal.

Trudy, like the good PR lady she was, stuck with them the whole time. She was the only woman they saw. There was a lot of muscular-looking guys around the place who didn't appear to have much to tax their bodies and brains with, but everything seemed to run like a well-oiled machine.

Hannah snapped open his camera case and ran his hands over the controls of the Nikon F-401 he'd rented in Austin. The guy in the pro shop where he'd rented it had given him a quick rundown of its features but with the controls set on auto he didn't need to worry too much. He only had it with him for verification. People might look a little askance at a shutterbug who didn't have a camera with him. He felt he had to have the best.

One of the muscular aides came by and spoke with Trudy. She nodded.

'All right,' she said, 'we can go in and see Mr Sleep now.'

TWENTY

Jarvis sat in her breakfast nook spooning in bran and nuts, taken with organic yoghurt straight from the pot. She drank English tea straight, no milk. She'd just run out Hannah's report, filed last night from a motel room in Texas before he caught the late evening flight back to Washington. As with anything Hannah wrote, it was messy and ungrammatical:

Eugene Sleep is in his late fifties, grey hair, hard face. He made it plain right from the start that Salvation TV is only the beginning. He is buying into digital television in a big way. He isn't going for the main open markets because Murdoch has already cornered it. Instead he has targeted the Bible Belt. Soon Sleep will be on line in your very own home. He has a deal with a manufacturer in South Korea to provide all the hardware, decoders and everything.

Sleep wants to change the way we think. He likes to think he's expanding into the millennium but in fact he's going back a hundred years. This guy has a fixation on some golden age when people did what they were told and kids did not speak back to Pop. He really believes in the Second Coming. He thinks the world needs to be prepared and that, in his book, means kicking out all the womanisers, adulterers, whores, HIV positives, dope dealers, pinkoes, liberals – in fact anyone who doesn't think and act exactly like Eugene Sleep. He didn't exactly say that one of his subsidiaries in Macao or

115

the Philippines is currently manufacturing gas chambers, but that's his line of thought on this one.

Jarvis poured her second cup of tea, checked the time. It was 7:15. Her morning routine was as exact and reliable as the digital clock on the wall above her. Jarvis was a woman who never had to rush. It took her exactly fifteen minutes to make up her face to look like she was wearing no make-up at all. She went back to the report.

A lot of this was said off the record (heh-heh) and between the lines. Mostly the information he relayed was concerned with his business strategy – after all, this was the ostensible reason for the interview. Bill Halberson tried to get him going on his political aspirations but he wasn't going to be drawn on that one.

But Sleep is certainly using his papers and his TV access to run a one-man hate campaign. Personally I think he's nuts. I guess he's also a fruiter, all those guys around the place with big muscles and tight buns? A pity, Agent Jarvis, you couldn't have been with me.

She winced at that one.

There are plenty of guys like Sleep around, from Billy Graham down to Swaggart and guys like him. The questions is, what's firing him up? Why is he acting like this? What is he reacting to? What is going on down there that Eugene Sleep feels is worth $1.5 billion a year – his figure – to try and drive out?

That's what you were meant to find out, asshole, Jarvis said to herself.

TWENTY-ONE

WASHINGTON, DC. JUNE 24TH. 11.21 AM.

Bureau – authorised telephone intercept. Confidential. Copies of recording available on request.

FIRST FEMALE VOICE: You wanna talk about it?

SECOND FEMALE VOICE: I gotta talk to someone.

FFV: You don't have to.

SFV: Well, I just wanna get it off my chest.

FFV: How'd it start?

SFV: We were just standing around, you know. Everyone was having a good time, there was a nice feel to it.

FFV: There usually is at these things. I really used to enjoy the PTA evenings when Rebecca was at the school. Things aren't the same at the high school.

SFV: It was getting pretty hot out there so I went out to get some fresh air. And that was when I saw them –

FFV: Who'd you see?

SFV: Kirsten and Jack. They were necking like teenagers, over where the cars were parked.

FFV: And then what happened?

SFV: They got into Jack's car and I could see they were making love. I went back inside. I guess I must have been pretty confused because I went into the wrong room, not the one where we were having the drinks party, and that's where I found Terri and Mike.

FFV: Where were they?

SFV: In the principal's office. It wasn't locked. I just went in by mistake. The lights were off but I could see everything. She was lying on the desk and Mike was on top of her (SOBS).

FFV: It's all right honey, take your time.

SFV: I mean, right there in the school. It was like everyone was doing it (MORE SOBS).

FFV: I know, I know.

SFV: How can you know? You find your husband with another woman. How can you possible know how it feels inside?

FFV: I'm sorry, I really am. It must feel real bad.

SFV: Look, I don't want to talk about it any more, OK?

FFV: That's OK, honey. Just try not to let it get to you, all right?

Stone turned the player off and rewound the cassette

back to the starting point. He was methodical about things like that. Hannah was the type who didn't put albums back in their sleeves and left the caps off toothpaste tubes.

He'd made the meeting with seconds to spare. Jarvis gave him an icy look but then, incredibly, Stone himself didn't show up for another ten minutes. He came in looking ashen, said he'd been speaking to Pepper. He stared at the yellow wall outside his office for a good thirty seconds and Hannah could see his shoulders rising and falling as he did his breathing exercises. When he turned round he was Stone again. He put the tape on straight away, without preamble.

'Well, what do you make of it?' he asked Hannah.

'Where'd you get it?'

'Jarvis got it. Yesterday afternoon.'

He looked at Jarvis. She was all cool poise. You could never have guessed she'd just had a week off work with a fever.

He turned back to Stone. 'One woman's telling another woman she caught her husband with his pants down. Sounds like a wild party.'

'Local PTA meeting.' It was the first time Jarvis had spoken.

'Where?'

'Near Denver, Colorado.'

'I know where Denver is. How'd you get the tape?'

'Intercept. We'd picked up three calls that morning.'

'Why were you listening to two women in Denver, Colorado?'

'Because the second woman you hear on the tape is Eugene Sleep's sister. The first call she made was to big brother.'

'I get it,' said Hannah. But he didn't, not really. He soon learned why.

'Jarvis figures someone may want to use that information to blackmail him – or her,' said Stone.

119

Lights came on in Hannah's head.

'Or to discredit Sleep. I mean, he can't go around exposing adulterers if his own brother-in-law is putting it about too.'

'You've got a dirty mind, Hannah.'

'I know. That's why I work for this department. I started out in Insurance Fraud, you know.'

Stone and Jarvis exchanged glances. It was obvious to Hannah that they had been talking this one through earlier. Both of them had the upper hand over him, at least for the moment, even though he was the one who'd met Sleep.

'I wish you hadn't gone to see him without my OK,' Stone said.

'It was fine,' said Hannah. 'Read the *Post* the day after tomorrow.'

'Just as long as Pepper doesn't find out. I should have checked, you know. But I couldn't get hold of him and you had a dead phone or something.'

Stone seemed strangely vulnerable for once, like he was trying to protect something.

'I was working within my remit, you know. I did nothing that transgressed against protocol.'

'What do you make of the guy?' asked Stone, ignoring what he'd just said. 'Would something like this stick to him?'

'I doubt it, in the normal run of things. That guy is surrounded by lawyers and sharpers. No one touches Eugene Sleep.'

'What would happen if, say, the *Enquirer* ran a story like that?'

'Sleep would buy up the *Enquirer*. And then destroy it.'

'Last year a Texas Congressman tried to block Sleep's nomination to the Board of Governors of Texas State University,' Jarvis broke in. 'Sleep made sure every one of his papers ran a stream of negative stories on this guy.

There was nothing indictable, but just the right amount of counter-steering. Sleep's nomination went through. The Congressman decided not to run for another term. That's the mark of the man.'

Stone looked grave. 'Who else knows about what went on at the PTA party?'

'As far as we know, just the people who were there, and their immediate circle. It's a small town, though. People might suspect something.'

Hannah took a big leap in the dark. 'Are you suggesting that the Bureau feels it is its bounden duty to protect Sleep in some way?' he ventured. He was careful to talk about the Bureau generally, not to say *you* or *we* or anything. He was casting a net.

'I don't know,' said Stone, his face a blank. 'I can't really answer that.'

Jarvis stared at the floor. She had clammed up as surely as the automatic cash dispenser had done the night before last with Hannah's card inside and Clemmie wanting to be taken out somewhere grand to eat. But Hannah persevered.

'Is the world going to be any worse off with a creep like Sleep out of the way? Hell, we did for Pinochet. Why not lose Sleep as well?'

Stone didn't like this line of questioning. It was putting him on the spot, as if it were his decision, his policy. Hannah knew he knew this.

'It's just an idea Pepper has,' he said at length. So that was it. Hannah might have known Pepper was behind it.

'What idea's that?' Sometimes, Hannah had to act dumb.

'Pepper thinks we should keep Sleep in circulation, at least for now. But ease off him ourselves, not get too close.'

'I didn't know Pepper was a born-again believer.'

'I doubt it.'

But that was as much information as Hannah needed. And he didn't have to work too hard to get it. So it was Pepper who was interested in Sleep, not Stone.

That was the significant detail.

TWENTY-TWO

HASTIE, COLORADO. JUNE 25TH. 10.23 AM.

TRANSCRIPT OF INTERVIEW BETWEEN AGENT
JARVIS AND KAREN DOE

Jarvis: Can you tell me what the mood was at the party?

Doe: It was kind of happy. Everyone felt good.

Jarvis: Was there a lot to drink?

Doe: No more than usual. I don't hardly drink at all, myself. But I don't mind other people drinking.

Jarvis: So what happened?

Doe: Oh, people just kind of got a little loosened-up, you know.

Jarvis: Tell me more. What do you mean, loosened-up?

Doe: Well, they were talking in a more intimate kind of way. More kind of friendly, you know what I mean?

Jarvis: Was there any kind of sexual element in this?

Doe: No, not at that stage. That came later. I'll tell you one thing that happened –

Jarvis: Confine yourself to the questions please, Miss Doe.

Doe: I'm sorry. I guess I got carried away.

Jarvis: So people were just being more open, right? How did that manifest itself?

Doe: Oh, I was talking to Jim Brownlee and he was standing, like, real close to me. Now, normally I wouldn't have liked him to stand so close – Jim's a nice guy, don't get me wrong, but I would normally have wanted him to respect my personal space a little more, you know what I mean?

Jarvis: Can you recall how other people were being more open, as you put it?

Doe: Well, Barb Kettle was talking about something that had happened when she and Bob – that's her husband, Bob – were up at their trailer home by the lake. The story was that Barb had lost her bikini top or something – I didn't hear much of it because I was talking to Jim, but everyone was laughing and normally Barb is, well, kind of prissy about things like that. But she was laughing too.

Jarvis: Did you see Mike O'Neil?

Doe: Sure, he was with Jaqui and a bunch of others. I could tell she was, like, coming on real strong to him and he was kind of flirting back at her.

Jarvis: Did you feel there was anything wrong with that?

124

With the way Mike O'Neil and the others were acting?

Doe: Well, no, not really. That's the funny thing. I guess that right now I feel real embarrassed about it, you know, but then – it just seemed OK, you know.

Jarvis: You knew what was happening?

Doe: Oh, sure.

Jarvis: Miss Doe, have you ever taken hallucinogenic drugs of any kind?

Doe: No, I haven't. And I don't see that it's any of your business to ask.

Jarvis: I'm sorry, Miss Doe. It's purely a routine question. You were telling me about how you felt.

Doe: Was I? Oh yes, sure. Well. It all seemed fine, like I said. I was feeling pretty good, you know.

Jarvis: This man you were talking to –

Doe: You mean Jim Brownlee?

Jarvis: Jim Brownlee, right. Have you ever felt attracted to him?

Doe: Yes and no.

Jarvis: How do you mean? Please be honest. The Bureau will respect your confidence.

Doe: Well, he's kind of good-looking and he's a nice guy and everything. But he's married to Helena, and Helena and I have been best friends since high school.

Jarvis: And you respected them? Is that a true reflection of your feelings?

Doe: Yes, that's it. Respect, I guess.

Jarvis: But later you went to the science lab with Jim Brownlee and had sex with him. Why was that?

Doe: It just seemed the right thing to do, at the time. You know, all of a sudden the chemistry was there.

Jarvis: And what happened in the lab?

Doe: I had sex with Jim Brownlee. It sounds kind of cold like that, but that wasn't how it felt at the time.

Jarvis: Did he penetrate you?

Doe: Sure. We did it a couple of times, actually.

Jarvis: With your consent?

Doe: Sure. The Second time I climbed on top of him and we did it right there on one of the benches. We did it twice in about fifteen minutes. It was real good, you know. Jesus, I was coming so much I nearly fell off the bench. You ever get that feeling?

Jarvis: Please confine yourself to the questions, Miss Doe.

TRANSCRIPT OF INTERVIEW BETWEEN AGENT HANNAH AND WILLIAM ('BILLY') KEYES

Hannah: Did you notice the way Mike O'Neil was acting?

Keyes: No, no. I didn't even know Mike was there.

Hannah: How about some of the others? Karen Doe, for instance, or Jim Brownlee?

Keyes: No, no, I told you, I was too busy trying to get into Kimberley Dyson's pants.

Hannah: You went there with that intention?

Keyes: Yes. No.

Hannah: What do you mean? Either you did or you didn't. Which one?

Keyes: Well, I'd been trying to get off with Kimberley for a long time. And I guess she kind of liked the look of me too.

Hannah: She married?

Keyes: Yeah, but her husband's away a lot. Kimberley kind of puts it about a bit. I was after a piece of the action. You know how it is.

Hannah: A PTA party is a kind of strange situation to make a move, isn't it?

Keyes: Maybe so, but when the sap starts to rise—

Hannah: So what happened?

Keyes: Like I said, we were sticking pretty close together. We had a few glasses of wine and then Kimberley says she wants to go out for a smoke.

Hannah: You can't smoke in the school, is that right?

Keyes: Right. Not many places a guy can, now. Can you smoke where you work?

Hannah: We aren't supposed to, but everyone does. Even the Big Chief.

Keyes: You're lucky, fella.

Hannah: Tell me about you and Kimberley. She sounds like quite a gal.

Keyes: Well, we're out there round by the parking lot and the next thing is, I'm necking with her and one thing leads to another and I'm in her car with her.

Hannah: Front seat or back seat?

Keyes: Back.

Hannah: Could anyone see you?

Keyes: Man, I was so fucking fired up, I wouldn't have cared if the whole of the school football team had been out there watching me.

Hannah: How long were you there? In her car?

Keyes: I don't know. Half an hour maybe.

Hannah: And what did you do?

Keyes: She was pretty wired up and I got my hand up her skirt and, man, she was soaking. I got my fingers in there and I was working them around, you know, like I was trying to drive her wild. And she was opening her legs wider and wider for me. You know how it is?

Hannah: Sure. Go on.

Keyes: Well, she's kind of got my shirt unbuttoned and

then she unzips my pants and goes down on me. Man, she sure knows how to blow a guy. It was all I could do to stop myself coming off in her mouth. She could suck a golf ball through a sixty-foot garden hose, you know what I mean.

Hannah: Tell me more.

Keyes: The next thing is I got her top up and got her bra unhooked and Jesus, those tits. Man, they're perfect, you know.

Hannah: They big?

Keyes: Pretty big, yeah.

Hannah: She likes to wiggle them about a bit, right? Shake them in your face, that kind of thing?

Keyes: Man, I couldn't keep my hands off of them, and then I'm licking her and sucking her nipples and she's kind of moaning and playing with my dick. So I got on top of her there in the back seat of her car and she's got her skirt hiked up around her waist. I kind of got into her right away and then – oh yeah, another thing is she's wearing these tiny little thong panties, you know, that don't hardly cover her snatch, and she didn't bother taking them off, we just did it like that, both of us half-dressed.

Hannah: She was a willing participant?

Keyes: Willing? Listen, that girl was begging for it. You ever get it when a woman's so wound up she's got her tongue halfway down your throat and she's kind of growling at you, all at the same time?

Hannah: Uh-huh. I think I know what you mean. Go on.

129

Keyes: Well, we're writhing around there in the back seat and it was obvious this little party wasn't going to last long. I could tell she was starting to come and my balls were feeling like they were going to explode, and the next thing is she's got her legs wrapped right around me and she's pushing up like she's working out at a gym. Man, was I giving it to her –

Hannah: She was enjoying it too? It sounds like it, right?

Keyes: You bet. To look at her, you'd think butter wouldn't melt in her mouth but she's telling me to fuck her slit, all that kind of thing.

Hannah: Really? You don't think anyone heard you, or saw you? You must have been making a hell of a noise.

Keyes: I dunno. I didn't notice anything. Maybe you ought to go see Kimberley. Maybe she did.

Hannah: Maybe I should.

Keyes: Yeah, I think that's a good idea.

Hannah: So that was how it ended, that night? You did it in the back of the car – and then what?

Keyes: Yeah, well, I was pretty bushed by then so afterwards we went back inside but the party was almost over.

Hannah: End of story?

Keyes: No. I've seen her a couple of times since. Hey, the second time, we was over at her place and—

Hannah: It's really just that one particular night I'm interested in.

Keyes: Oh yes, sure, I understand. But I just wanted to tell you that the second time, when I went over to her place, she was waiting for me in this baby-doll outfit, you know, the high-heel shoes and all the works like something out of a magazine. You wanna hear about that?

Hannah: It may not relate directly to my inquiries but tell me anyway. Maybe there might be some kind of lead there. (TAPE RECORDER IS SWITCHED OFF, PRESUMABLY BY AGENT HANNAH).

TWENTY-THREE

'What do you think about it?' asked Hannah.

'What do I think about what?' queried Jarvis, looking petulant.

They were sitting in the Chicken Lickin'. Jarvis had wanted to go someplace where she could get a decent salad. Hannah lobbied for Steak City. Permissible expenses at the Bureau kept them just above the welfare level when it came to finding a place to eat, so they settled on Chicken Lickin'. Outside, in the rain, the lights inside a gigantic yellow plastic rooster pulsed on and off in an attempt to captivate passing motorists. But at six-thirty in the evening, they had the place pretty much to themselves.

'About all this weird shit that's been going on.'

Jarvis speared a piece of limp lettuce. She'd wanted radiccio and they gave her week-old cos. The salad dressing tasted like it had been drained out of a sump. She wasn't in a very good mood. Hannah wondered if she ever was. A good fucking should see to that, but . . .

'I don't think anyone's going to make a move to blackmail Sleep, or to discredit him, or anything like that. I think it's just about blown over.'

'Stone doesn't think that, even if Pepper maybe does. He thinks we still need to keep following this line up.'

Jarvis shook her head. 'The trail's going cold,' she

said. 'If anyone was going to do something, they would have done it by now. And yet—'

'And yet what?'

'I don't know.' She toyed with a piece of Kiev.

'You know something.'

'I don't.' She looked hard at him. 'And that's the truth. But there's something I can't get a handle on.'

'You mean, there's something in the air.'

'I don't run on hunches.' That was the understatement of the year. Jarvis needed hard scientific evidence from at least three incontrovertible sources before she could even be reasonably certain what day of the week it was. This was a Tuesday.

'But there's something bothering you.'

'Yeah. I can't figure it, though.'

'Want to talk about it?'

'I don't know. I don't even know what there is to talk about.'

'Shall I tell you what I think you're thinking, then?'

She looked at him again, went back to picking at her food. She didn't approve of the potato salad either.

'Go ahead,' she may or may not have said.

Hannah chewed hard. This chicken was tough. It must have been an old yard rooster, the kind you needed to boil for twenty-four hours before you could fry it.

'You're thinking this guy Sleep is really starting to stir things up down here. That a lot of people are getting a guilty conscience or something, and he's working on that, so he can come sweeping in on his white horse and shoot the bad guys. But there are other buttwipes rattling their cages too.'

She blanched at his phraseology. Not while I'm eating, her expression said.

'I'm thinking of the guys with the Bibles in their hands way out in right field. They're getting itchy feet too. There are some pretty strange people in these backwater places we've been hearing about everywhere from here to the Carolinas. They don't just not like liberals, they out-and-out *hate* them, does that thought strike you?'

'You think Sleep is responsible for that, too?'

'I don't know. Stone doesn't know. Pepper doesn't know. All I know is there's a hell of a lot of fundamentalist shit being pumped out all over the place and it's not coming from Sleep. There's this air of righteousness going around the whole area and yet—'

Jarvis had stopped eating, her fork poised in mid-air. She ate like an English person, deft little movements of her knife and fork in perfect syncopation. Hannah ate like a slob, cut all his food up first and then shovelled it in with his fork. If he'd smoked, he'd have been hauling on a cigarette at the same time.

Hannah knew he was right. He had read her mind. 'You tell me the rest,' he said quietly.

'Some people are acting totally the other way,' she said. 'They're not in the least bothered by conscience or religious scruples.'

'Exactly. You get the guy like I saw on TV the other week, his life is probably ruined by whatever happened to him. And yet we get people acting like they can't help themselves. We're getting wedding showers that are practically turning into Roman orgies at the same time as the churches are packing them in. It doesn't make sense. And all these stories that are coming in to the newspapers, but only a selected amount is coming out, just as much as Sleep thinks is necessary makes it into print. It's like two sides of the same coin.'

'Maybe it's cause and effect.'

'Maybe. Or chicken and egg. Who can tell which came first?'

A waiter came up to take their plates away. He wore a hat with a chicken head on it, and on top of that a red plastic coxcomb. Jarvis didn't want dessert. Hannah had pumpkin pie with a double order of tin roof ripple ice-cream.

TWENTY-FOUR

Hannah had one more call to make that night. Carmen Fisher was one of the teachers who had been at the PTA meeting. She had been away on a course for the last few days, had only just resumed teaching the previous day. She would have had little chance to discuss the events of that night with any of the others, even if she had had a mind to.

Hannah and Jarvis were too busy to see her on Monday. Tuesday evening she stayed late at the school – she ran the art club, which didn't finish till six, and after that she held a community class for adults who wanted to learn to paint. Hannah was apologetic but insistent. She consented to see him at her home at nine.

'We should both go along,' he said. 'That way we know better what's going on, what each of us sees. Different perspectives, you know what I mean?'

But Jarvis didn't want to. He wondered if she felt that eating supper with him was more than enough for one day. Besides, she said, she needed to work on her computer. There were files she'd brought with her she hadn't even looked at, and there were records to complete. She particularly wanted to check out some newspaper files. She could do it all from her laptop. Hannah wondered just what the hell she had with her inside that cool grey casing.

So Hannah went on his own. He parked his rented car outside the small wood-frame house in a quiet residential street and rang the bell. Carmen Fisher answered almost immediately, a tall, good-looking woman with a mass of reddish hair, somewhere in her mid-forties he guessed. She looked like an older version of Clemency.

They went inside. The house was full of art. Hannah knew it was good, even though there was nothing that he recognised, no Edward Hoppers or Andrew Wyeths, the kind of paintings that only the very richest collectors could afford nowadays, not art teachers from Colorado. But what she had was just as good – not just paintings but pottery, furniture, Navajo rugs and all kinds of things like that. Most of these painters and potters, it turned out, were friends of hers.

There were plants everywhere, too, green and luxuriant. All of them, he noticed, had crystals set into their pots. Hannah studied them while Carmen made coffee that he didn't really want. He was keen to get this interview over with. He was tired of talking, he just wanted to get back to the motel and find out what Jarvis had trawled up from the newspaper files, and then sleep and fly out of there in the morning, back to Clemmie.

'I see you're into crystals and all those things,' he said when she came back carrying the coffee. She set the tray down on an old Shaker table, the real thing, maybe eighty years old and worth a good three or four grand.

She looked slightly taken aback, brushed the reddish curls from her face. 'I didn't know you agents were interested in things like that,' she said with a quizzical smile.

'I have a girlfriend who is,' he replied. 'All her plants have crystals next to them. She says it helps them grow.'

'It certainly does,' replied Carmen. 'Crystals have such energy, you know. And plants are all about energy, their own energy, the energy of the sun, earth energy. They are very powerful living things, plants. And crystals, too, if you know how to use them. The native Americans did, of course. They understand crystals. But we trust everything to nitrates and fertilisers and bio-this and eco-that, and really it's just our native wisdom that we should be using.'

Her hand reached out and languidly caressed a maidenhair fern, soft and delicate against her long fingers. Hannah wondered how soon he could cut through this crap and start the interview.

She was surprisingly responsive to his questioning, however. She wasn't the least bit embarrassed about it. Gradually he felt himself start to relax. She described the sequence of events much as she might have described witnessing a robbery, pausing every now and then to throw a log on the fire.

She had nothing new to add, he could tell that after only ten minutes of systematic questioning. But still he lingered on in that warm room full of antique furniture and old wisdom. There were only a couple of table lamps to shed light and the fire cast a coppery glow onto her hair. Gradually they left the subject of the PTA meeting behind and talked about other things – not about his work, for he was too reticent for that, but about the things they liked – they seemed to have a surprising amount in common – and what they both wanted out of life. For an interviewee, she was very comfortable to talk to. It didn't faze her in the slightest that she was being interrogated by a government agent trained in the art of coaxing information out of people, with their consent or otherwise. Carmen Fisher needed no coaxing. She told him everything she knew. Looking at her, with her legs tucked under her and her oversize denim shirt just about managing to conceal the swell of a fine bosom, Hannah felt how like Clemency she was, only more grown up. But Clemmie was in New York today, and Carmen was ageless.

He felt himself relax, becoming more and more

mellow. And with the mellowness came desire, a feeling so palpable within him that it was as if he had turned on a tap. An hour after Hannah rang the bell, Carmen was lying naked on the big old brass-framed bed upstairs while he was down between her legs, eating her out.

'No, don't stop,' she whispered when he made a move to do something different. 'Just keep it like that, OK? Jesus, that feels good.'

She was bucking and writhing around so much, she almost threw Hannah off the bed. One thing was for sure – she didn't get this kind of treatment too often.

He broke free for a moment, gulping in great lungfuls of air that were tinged with her heavy perfume and the strong, musky scent of her sex.

'What's happening?' she said, her voice soft and husky. 'Get back down there and eat me out good. I was just about there when you stopped.'

He brought her off quickly and expertly. Her appreciation of his oral skills was gratifying, for Hannah had got the feeling that a lot of Southern women didn't know much about eating out and blow-jobs. Women who were like a wild thing with a dick inside them suddenly became all coy when he tried to get a little lick-action going. Perhaps it was different out here in the West, if Carmen was anything to go by.

He climbed on top of her, conscious of his cock bobbing there in front of her eyes, of his balls hanging down heavy and full. He would have got her to suck him off there and then but Carmen wasn't ready for that yet. Later on, maybe, after he'd balled her.

He slipped inside her nice and easy. She was loose and wet and just about dying to be fucked. What the hell if he was supposed to be on duty? She didn't seem to mind any and she sure knew how to move her hips around and boogie. She was lying back on the pillows with her eyes closed and her mouth half-open, naked as the day she was born.

Hannah had been surprised how quickly she'd gotten her clothes off. Some women, especially the older ones, were kind of reluctant the first time they went with someone new. Maybe they were bothered about the stretch marks and the sagging tits, all that kind of thing. But Carmen, she'd stepped out of her shirt and leggings just like that, and then out of her brassiere, and then out of her panties. Standing beside her in the big, rug-strewn bedroom, he'd hardly got his shirt cuffs unbuttoned before she was standing there next to him, stark naked and feeling his cock. He knew she'd been waiting for him, building herself up to a peak of anticipation. He liked to know a woman had the hots for him.

So now he was moving back and forth, back and forth, building up the rhythm, using the strength in his arms and legs, feeling her spreading her own legs wider and wider to draw him in until she brought her knees up and then wrapped her legs around him, twisting and turning. They rolled over, still locked together, and then it was her turn to be on top of him, her hair wild and loose, the coppery muff almost exactly the same colour. She had generous pear-shaped tits and her nipples stood out big and proud and hard. He rolled them between his teeth, nipping and making her gasp as she flaunted herself above him. She was, he knew, entirely at ease with her own body. She didn't have a bikini line around her ass, he noticed. Which meant, he suddenly realised, she must sunbathe naked. In a place like Hastie, now, that really was daring, PTA or no PTA.

He grabbed hold of that firm, forty-something-year-old ass and squeezed the cheeks. She moaned and, leaning forward, bit him hard on the neck, so hard it hurt. Hell, he suddenly thought, I hope that didn't leave a mark. Shocked, he pulled her ass down onto him, feeling his cock burying itself right up inside almost to the end of her vagina, and then he could feel it coming, that irresistible urge deep inside himself. He carried on

139

thrusting, sharp, vicious stabs now, but he was well on his way. With one last effort he pushed up at her, lifting her whole body clean off the bed and up into the air, and then he was shooting his seed into her.

He must have dozed off – bad manners, Agent Hannah, he told himself when he came round. He could hear the distant sound of traffic along the avenues, tyres slick on wet night-time leaves.

She had lit a cigarette after, which surprised him, and now lay back on the bed smoking. Hannah half-thought about taking one for himself. He had one hand resting on her thigh, brushing those auburn curls, wet and matted now from his sperm and her juices. Feeling confident, the way he usually did when he'd taken a woman for the first time, he slipped a finger inside her, then two. She made no move to stop him, just lay back on the pillows, blowing out smoke. After a few minutes she stubbed out her cigarette and turned her head to face him.

'You really are one hell of a persuasive investigator, you know,' she said to him.

Hannah, flattered, made gee-whiz noises. 'Oh, yeah?' he said. 'What makes you say that?'

'Just the way you do it, that's all. Kind of understand-ing. Cops and people can be so brutish, sometimes. You're different, Agent Hannah. What kind of work you do? Besides bedding the women you're supposed to be interviewing?'

'That's classified information, Miss Fisher.'

'But I bet you appreciate good cock-sucking, isn't that right?' she asked, real casual.

'That's private information too, I'm afraid.'

'Let's just see if I'm right, shall we?'

Carmen slid down the bed. Propped up on the pillows, Hannah looked on in fascination as her pink tongue flickered for a moment before she began to lick the tip of his cock, probing the little oval hole in the end.

140

She was holding the shaft in her fist, gently pumping it up and down as she did so. Then she sank her mouth down onto him, wide open, and took all of him in, her tongue swirling around him.

He moved as best he could so he could reach down and run his fingers through her hair and along the smooth skin of her shoulders.

'That's good,' he breathed, aware of little other than the sensations of his body. Lying there on her bed, Jarvis at the other end of town, he hardly had a care in the world.

Her mouth fitted him like a velvet glove. Something about the way she blew him told him she didn't do it that often, but what she lacked in finesse she made up for in her evident relish. After a while, it got like she was eating him. He was sure her jaws must have been aching by now but she kept on with her lips and her tongue, teasing and tormenting him, licking him up and down his full length before taking all of him back down deep in her throat.

She had a rhythm going now, hypnotic and powerful, and Hannah surrendered to it. Images of sex began to fill his mind, various women he had known, tits, hair, lips – all the women began to blur into one and the focus of that desire was Carmen Fisher. When he knew he was coming he grunted and touched her shoulder but she paid him no mind, just carried on sucking away at him. Even when he got past the point of no return, when she must have known from the way he twisted and moaned what was going on, she still continued to do him. Now he was fucking her in her mouth the way he'd fucked her earlier in her pussy, strong and sure. And then he couldn't hold back any longer and his stuff came boiling up out of him again.

He was excited by coming in her willing mouth and his orgasm was big and prolonged, the spasms amplified, the desire out of control. All he was aware of was that

141

powerful ejection from his body and the feeling of her mouth enclosing him, welcoming him into her, drinking his fluids down, milking him dry, until his body stopped twitching and that tremendous tension was at last stilled.

Hannah got back to the motel about a half after midnight. He was about ready to hit the sack when there was a tap on the door.

He checked that his gun was still in its holster.

'Who is it?' he said, his voice low and even.

'It's me, Jarvis. I've got to see you.'

So the moment had come at last, he said to himself with a grin. The trouble was, most of his bodily fluids were swimming around inside Miss Carmen Fisher right now, and he didn't know if he had any left for his colleague. Still, he could always try . . .

He unlocked the door, still in his shirtsleeves. She looked tired and worried, not at all the picture of desire that he had so fondly imagined.

She came in, sat down on the edge of the bed. 'You got a drink?' she said. 'I could use one.'

Hannah had a fifth of Johnnie Walker Red on the dresser. He poured some for her in a tooth mug, then took a shot for himself. She drained hers quickly.

'Those files we've been looking at—' she began.

'Which files?'

'The newspaper files.'

'Right. Got you. You have a problem?'

'They're not there any more.'

'What do you mean?'

'I can't locate them.'

'Maybe the software's faulty.'

'The software is fine. I ran a check through it.'

'Maybe they've installed new security systems that prevent us getting access.'

'Nothing's changed. I can get into all their other files.'

'Which papers are we talking about?'

142

'The ones that Sleep owns. All of them. Every single one I've looked at.'

'And the files aren't there?'

'They've simply been trashed, without leaving a trace. I couldn't find a thing.'

She looked close to tears.

'Maybe I should try.'

'You? You know how to work Scarab-3?'

'What's that?'

'That's the access software.'

'I never heard of it.'

'Then there's no point you trying, is there? Believe me, Hannah, I tried.'

'So what are you saying? Surely those files must be somewhere?'

'What I'm saying is, someone must have got there and blown the lot.'

'Right after we were there?'

'Right afterwards.'

'How did they know?'

'I don't know. Scarab-3 doesn't leave a trace. No one could have known. Unless they've got something that could run rings round our system.'

Hannah didn't know what to say. He wondered about putting his arms around his colleague but thought better of it.

'Where does that leave us?' he asked. 'Did you copy any of it?'

'Some. But not enough. Just recent stuff. Some of those files went back a long way. Two, three years even.'

'What will happen when they find out? The newspapers, I mean.'

'Maybe they won't. I mean, those files are just one step up from the trash basket. No one hardly ever opens them – I checked, looked through the user records. All they do is dump things there, the stories that have been spiked. And once a story's been spiked, that's the end of it. The names of the files still exist, but there's nothing in there. If you try and enter a new file, it just self-destructs. But it doesn't tell you that. People could go on dumping new stuff in there for years and not realise they'll never get it back.'

'Haven't you got enough to go on?'

'No. I've barely even begun.'

To Hannah's regret, she went back to her room, still looking ashen. By morning she had got it figured. They would have to find a newspaper that didn't keep its files on computer. Won't that, said Hannah, be a little like trying to locate a community that didn't use cars?

What about the Amish? asked Jarvis. He had to concede she was right. She got going on her laptop. By nine-fifteen she had found three small-town newspapers that had not licensed software from any of the major houses. If they didn't have any software, they couldn't be running computers.

TWENTY-FIVE

GARFORTH, ALABAMA. JUNE 26TH. 4.17 PM.

Sam Pasciznyk ran the kind of newspaper office Jarvis and Hannah thought had vanished with the last remake of *The Front Page*. A door at street level led up a flight of uncarpeted wooden stairs to the first-floor offices of the Conington County *Advertiser*. A glass door stood ajar. Beyond it they could hear the clack-clack-clack of a manual typewriter.

Hannah pushed open the door. A woman who looked like someone out of a Norman Rockwell painting looked up from behind a desk. 'Yes?' she said, peering over rimless glasses. She had her hair up in a bun and looked like she hadn't cracked a smile in six months.

Hannah and Jarvis flashed their IDs. She wasn't impressed. She took the trouble to study them with great care, like she was checking all the words for spelling.

'We're here to see Mr Pasciznyk,' Hannah said.

'He's busy right now, but he'll see you if you wouldn't mind waiting a moment,' she said.

She nodded at a couple of steel-framed chairs against the wall, the kind of chairs you might find stacked up outside the functions room of a union local. Hannah hoped the wait wouldn't be long. The chairs didn't look any too comfortable.

Just when he was beginning to wonder whether these people were operating on a different time scale, a door beyond the desk opened and an enormous head peered round the edge.

'Hi!' said the disembodied head. 'I'm Sam Pasciznyk. Come through.'

Hannah and Jarvis followed the editor of the Conington County *Advertiser* along a corridor so labyrinthine they could have been negotiating the inner organs of a wartime U-boat. The walls were lined with shelves stacked with files and folders. Everything was covered in dust.

They went up a narrow flight of stairs that doubled back on itself before reaching an attic landing. Instinctively Hannah looked up Jarvis's skirt. She was wearing black pantihose and white briefs, just as he'd suspected. He felt a tingle of arousal.

'This is our nerve centre,' said Pasciznyk, ushering them into a large office of unbelievable untidiness. Every available space in every dimension was stacked with paper in one form or another. There were newspaper cuttings, books, folders, loose-leaf files, envelopes stuffed with paper, curling piles of black and white photographs, heaps of notebooks and torn galleys. A gleaming Canon photocopier stood in one corner, surrounded by billowing packages of paper.

Pasciznyk swept a whole sheaf of documents off a chair and offered it to Jarvis. He gave Hannah a canvas director's chair that looked none too stable. As for himself, he sat on the edge of his big, muddled desk and folded his arms across his vast, barrel-shaped chest.

'Now,' he began, 'what exactly can I do for you?'

The voice was soft, with an unmistakable Southern twang. Big guys usually spoke loudly, especially if they were newspaper editors. Pasciznyk didn't. His words were almost drowned out by the coffee that was percolating on top of the only filing cabinet in the room.

He nodded in its direction. 'Coffee'll be ready in a minute,' he said, half-apologetically.

'Well, Mr Pasciznyk—' Jarvis began.

'Siz,' he said. 'Everyone round here calls me Siz.'

'OK,' she said. Hannah knew she didn't like to be checked even before she'd gotten into her stride.

'We understand you have been collecting some information that we would be very interested in verifying for our own records.'

'You mean my Steamy Files, right? Sure, that's no problem. You just have to wade through it, is all.'

'We would need to look back over the past two years, maybe three, if that's possible.'

'It certainly would be. But they go back a lot further, you know. Some of it dates back to the 1950s.'

'You're kidding,' said Jarvis, astonishment registering on her face.

'No, that's the way it is,' said the editor. 'Why do you sound so surprised?'

'I just had no idea the records would go back so far.'

'What kind of information is it?' asked Hannah, who was equally taken aback. 'You didn't tell us much on the phone.'

'Press reports, mostly,' said Siz. 'Clippings, that kind of thing. A lot of material that was spiked, for obvious reasons. Even pages torn from reporters' notebooks – dates, phone numbers, that kind of thing.'

'Is any of this on computer?' asked Jarvis. 'CD ROM, perhaps? Even three-and-a-half-inch floppies would be fine if that's all you have.'

'Are you kidding? I don't even have a pocket calculator,' said Siz with a shrug and a smile. 'This place is a living museum and I want to keep it that way.'

Jarvis opened her case, took out her hand scanner.

'You know what this is?' she said.

Siz smiled back at her. 'No, but I'm sure you're going to tell me,' he said as he poured their coffee.

'It's a portable scanner,' she said to his vast back, silhouetted against the streaked window. 'You just run it

147

over a document and it records exactly what it sees.'

'Like a hand-held photocopier?' said Siz. He had two china cups in his bear-like paws. He put them down with surprising delicacy on the edge of the desk.

'That's not quite how it works, but you get the general idea.'

'Sounds interesting,' he said, and held out his hand. He played with the scanner for a couple of moments but it was obvious it meant nothing to him. This was a guy who wrote the headlines in indelible ink, not in Quark-Xpress.

He handed the scanner back. 'What do you want to do with it?' he asked.

'With your permission, we'd like to make copies of some of your documents that you have on file.'

'Sure, that's no problem. Use the photocopier if you like – it costs a fortune to rent, we ought to get some use out of it.'

'The scanner is fine, thank you.'

'When did you start collecting this information?' Hannah asked. He was anxious to get the ball rolling.

'About 1957 or 58, that kind of time. It wasn't for any particular reason, it was just a hunch.'

'What kind of a hunch?'

'Just that there might be more to this than met the eye. Why all these sex stories all of a sudden?'

'What made you think that? What kind of material were you gathering?'

'At first I wasn't gathering anything. I was just a cub reporter back then, even had a derby hat with a press card stuck in the brim, I should imagine. I covered a story one day, a guy who was arraigned for indecent exposure. Local guy, ran a roofing company. He was fined $50 or something, quite a lot of money back then.

'I just happened to notice, after a while, that there seemed to be more of these stories than usual. It wasn't like folks were becoming rapists or sex fiends, more that

148

every now and then people seemed to lose all their inhibitions.'

'Were these all legal cases?' Hannah probed.

'No, not all. The stories that got in the *Advertiser* were – or at least the ones that the editor, old Tom Davies, thought were fit to print. The rest just got spiked. But there were other things, you know. This is a small town and news travels fast, especially if you're twenty years old and keen to make it as a newshound.'

'So you're saying there were a lot of rumours and stuff?'

'That's it. Nothing more, nothing less. Well, sometimes more. Things you could maybe begin to get a handle on. A bit of wife-swapping going on, you know – one of our compositors even asked me if I'd be interested. And then there was this roadhouse out beyond Carson and they used to say all sorts of things went on there, women going round without their tops on, that kind of stuff.'

He looked at Jarvis to see if she'd taken offence, but she just sat there, stony-faced. In her lap, her little portable Sony recorded every word they said.

'Don't get me wrong,' said Siz after a while in his soft voice. 'This wasn't so-called prurient interest, like a guy might collect pin-ups or have a girlie calendar on his wall. I was just figuring I might be on to some kind of story, that this place really was a kind of Shangri-La.'

'What happened next?'

'Well, I was just thinking about maybe writing something, probing some of these stories closer, when it all dried up. All of a sudden, people were behaving themselves once more. The roadhouse closed down, people stopped fooling around – at least in public. If you had friends over, you played poker or bridge with them once more, instead of ripping your clothes off.'

'And that was the end of it?'

'We had a bad rape case in '59, or maybe it was '60, a

149

guy got hold of a girl from the high school, that was a terrible thing. But it was an isolated incident. I guess I just forgot about the files for a while, once there was nothing much to add to them. I just picked up the occasional lead but I don't think there was anything special in it. These things kind of came in clusters, is about the way I see it.'

'Tell us about it,' said Jarvis. 'Are there any particular cases that stay in your mind?'

'The one I remember best was a scoutmaster, used to sell pictures, you know what I mean?'

'Homosexual? Paedophile?'

'No, no, nothing like that. This was just girlie stuff, you know. A shot of beaver, that kind of thing. It wasn't very common back in '61 or thereabouts. But there weren't many other stories after that. Things kind of went quiet again. I worked as a sports reporter for a while, thought about maybe moving out east to work on one of the New York papers, but I never did. I been here in Conington County pretty near all my working life.'

'Did the stories come back?' said Hannah. 'How did you build up your files?'

'It must have been in the early sixties that it all started again. That was when you had the Beatles and stuff, and there was a lot of moral indignation and suchlike. Kids were starting to grow their hair long, there were all these wild parties, everyone started to get a little loose, you know what I mean.'

He sipped his coffee. The china cup was so eggshell thin, it looked as if he would crush it between his massive fingers.

'There was a backlash to it all,' he went on. 'All these kooks came crawling out of the woodwork. They were holding rallies, burning records, you must have seen the archive footage. A lot of that kind of thing was from around here. It got kind of nasty for a while. But you don't need me to tell you about all that.'

150

Jarvis and Hannah exchanged glances.

'What do you think was behind it all?' asked Hannah.

'I don't know. I don't see any one common reason, except maybe that people just want to have a good time, once in a while. And in their own way. That's the rub, though. Sure, on the one hand you're going to get kids skinny-dipping and stuff, it happens all the time. But there's ugliness as well. Some weird people out there, sure enough.'

'How do you see the things happening now? Evangelical TV stations, newspapers? What do you make of guys like Bob Darrow?'

'Flies on a pile of shit.'

'Does the name Eugene Sleep mean anything to you?'

'It should do. He tried to buy me out a couple of years back. Wanted to turn us into some kind of Biblical tract. I showed him the door.'

'Sleep came here?'

'One of his minions did. A strange guy. Didn't like much of what he saw.'

'What do you mean?'

'Anything that was different, he didn't like it. But it's good that things are different. Kids have long hair, then they have no hair at all. There's nothing weird about that. Weird is serial killers and the US military. Guys who blow up nursery schools.'

'Don't you think they're just echoing things they see in society? Maybe even on TV?'

Siz shrugged his enormous shoulders. 'Maybe, I don't know. That's a big thing, you know. As a newspaperman I see it all the time. You get things like a firebombing or someone takes a shot at the President, that sets up all kinds of echoes. These things come in cycles.'

'You mean, like copycat killers and suchlike.'

'And the rest. Press, TV, they give it so much coverage, it's no wonder some people say voices in their head are saying they should go out and do it too. But a lot of

151

what goes on, you just don't hear about it. We have a religious community not far out of town, very quiet, keep themselves to themselves and don't bother no one. As far as I'm concerned that's fine, they pay their taxes like everyone else, they can do what they like, have five wives and go round nekkid all day as the Lord intended, if that's what they want. And then there was the Waco thing, and right after that we had a guy down here tried to get in there and blow up the whole damn shebang. He'd seen them burn on TV, he wanted to see it happen right here. We didn't touch that one and neither did the TV news crews. Cops said – and I think they're right, for once – that it's only going to stir up the next fruitcake to try something similar, and then the one after that.'

'About the files—' said Jarvis. She'd switched her little tape recorder off. Hannah was just starting to get interested in what the newspaperman was saying but his colleague plainly wanted to start again in a different direction.

'Oh sure,' said Siz, looking apologetic. 'I get carried away sometimes, I don't realise how long I've been droning on. Where do you want to start?'

'The beginning?'

'That's a long way back.'

Pasciznyk got slowly to his feet, unlocked a drawer in the bottom of the filing cabinet. It was an effort for the big guy to kneel down. When he stood up, he was clutching an expanding folder of papers more than a foot thick.

'Clear me a space on the desk, will you?' he said to Hannah. 'Just dump those page proofs on the floor.'

Hannah did as he was told. A cloud of dust rose from the papers when Siz dropped them onto the hard surface of the desk. He brushed his hands against his pants.

'Goddamn dust gets everywhere,' he said. 'Old black woman who cleans around the office, she doesn't come in here. Can't say I blame her. This room hasn't been

152

cleaned out properly in ten years, to my certain know-ledge. The strange thing is, after three or four years it doesn't seem to get any dustier.'

He opened the folder that was stretched to bursting point and beyond.

'This is everything up to 1960. I've got 1960-70 in there as well, the next three drawers. Here, I'll get it for you. Everything else is at home, in my den.'

'May we see that?'

'Sure. But I'm warning you, I've got boxes and boxes of the stuff. It'd take you a month to go through each one.'

'We've got two days.'

'Then you'd better start reading,' said Siz, with a smile. 'Look, I got to run down to the print shop now but I'll be back in an hour or so. If you need anything, pick up the phone there and dial nine. That'll get you straight through without having to go through Myrtle out there.'

The room seemed a lot emptier without him. Hannah and Jarvis looked at what they'd been given, the piles of yellowing clippings and battered photographs that had been stuffed into the tattered folders. It would be like looking for a needle in a haystack.

Jarvis was peering down a deep well, into an era that had been over and done with before she was even born. She found her interest was concentrated not on the news items that had been clipped out of endless local *Sentinels* and *Bugles* and *Clarions*, but on the incidental details. Here, alongside an account of a local bum jailed for three months for importuning in a gas station lavatory, was an advertisement for hog feed pellets. Veils were the 'in thing' that year, according to the fashion page. She studied the ongoing story of a rape prosecution, felt repelled by the insensitivity of the defendant's lawyer, and at the same time found she was interested in the new model shoes that were currently in stock at Clarkson's. She read on, her nose beginning to tingle on account of the tiny dust mites that were, for the first time in decades, making a bid for freedom.

The newspaper cuttings told her little. The dates and places just seemed totally random. Soon she began to transfer her attention to other matters. Here was a police inventory following a raid on a house that had been demolished a whole quarter-century ago to make way for a supermarket that, in its turn, had been converted into a bowling alley and back into a supermarket once more. The list of items seized in the raid, typewritten on a heavy manual machine much like the one Miss Pursed Lips had been using in the front office, made for fascinating reading: handcuffs, masks, obscene photographs, a studded belt, a double-ended vibrator. And all this in what had been quite a respectable suburb in those days.

She looked at more documents. She found photographs of men and women in various states of dress and undress. She had no idea who they were. Frozen into immortality by the flash, their fixed grins reverberated through the decades. Once she found a snapshot picture of a woman kneeling, her hair in a Lana Turner wave, to suck some headless man's penis. That kind of stuff would have been sensational in 1958. There was nothing to link the picture with any of the other materials she was surveying and yet she somehow sensed there was something connecting it all, even though she could not begin to define what it was.

She found a programme for a touring burlesque review. A wholeplate glossy photograph fell out of it, an over-brazen and over made-up young woman dressed with gauzy provocation, evidently one of the dancers. For a second the two of them made eye contact across forty years. The woman would be in her sixties now, a grandmother probably, maybe with an arthritic hip.

She ploughed on. It was like speed-reading some

souped-up version of the *National Enquirer*, an endless catalogue of lust and fallibility, diligently recorded, with times and dates and places. From time to time she would run the scanner over an item of interest but there was nothing here that she had not read a thousand times before in the Sex Files. She wanted a pattern and there wasn't any. Instead, it all seemed to be so random and incomplete – as if Pasciznyk had gathered everything he could lay his hands on for a few weeks and then, just as suddenly, lost all interest. It was maddening. How could she be expected to build up a picture if she only had a mere fraction of the jigsaw puzzle to work from?

Hannah was reading what seemed to be the sex diary of an unknown white male. Well, it did mention other things, like the weather and the occasional business meeting – the guy appeared to be some kind of seedcorn salesman – but mostly it was to do with who he was fucking at that moment in time. Hannah scanned the pages with a practised eye. It had been written thirty-eight years ago, almost to the day, when he wasn't even a twinkle in his old dad's eye.

July 18, 1958

Had a real good time with Tina. Went over to her house, got her clothes off, fooling around naked in the kitchen. She put tomato ketchup all over my dick and licked it off. Said it was the best hot dog she ever ate.

July 20, 1958

Over to the drive-in with Caroline to see *The Devil Was A Woman*. C sure was a devil right enough. I was finger-fucking her all the way through the support movie. Later on, we drove down to the river and I fucked her in the back of the car. Her big melon ass looked good enough to eat there in the moonlight. She let me do it without a rubber on. Got spunk all over the car seat. C don't like to suck my come but I know her sister will.

July 21, 1958

To Tina's again. Her parents away, we were up in her room. I showed her some magazines I had. She liked to look at them naked babes, especially the ones with big tits. We smoked a little Mary Jane and I asked her if she'd like me to take some snaps like that of her. She said she would but I didn't have no camera with me. See if I can borrow one of them Polaroids off of Danny Chilton.

July 23, 1958

Got the camera but Tina's parents were around, so we went to the drive-in and saw *The Devil Was A Woman* all over again. Got Tina to give me a hand job. I wanted her to suck my spunk but she wouldn't. Shot off all over her tits instead, then we had a fuck in some country lane somewhere off the main highway. Almost got lost trying to find the way back.

July 26, 1958

Had a big party over at Hal Wynott's place near Peterville. Lots of people fucking upstairs in the bedrooms. Went off with Mary-Lou Zimmerman. Got her bra off and was playing with her tits when in came Don Schwart and Elaine Bradley. They were pretty ripped on reefer and they offered us some. Before long all four of us were naked in the bed. I licked Elaine out while I fucked Mary-Lou –

Jesus, that girl has a sweet pussy. After, Don fucked Mary-Lou and I gave it to Elaine from behind, her on all fours. Don's got the biggest whanger I ever seen, but maybe it was just the grass made it seem like that.

July 27, 1958

Tina was trying to phone me all day, wondering why I'd gone to the party without her. She sounded pretty pissed off but when I went over and made up, she was OK. We drove out to the little woods near Kempton and I took some pictures of her bare-ass naked with Dave's camera. They weren't as good as the ones in the magazines, maybe should have used flashbulbs. We did it there and then in the woods, a couple of times, then we drove home. Went to the doctor in the evening, got some kind of an itch. I wonder which of them bitches gave it to me?

He must have been quite a boy, thought Hannah, as he thumbed through the pages. He wondered how and where they all were now, in their late fifties most of them, with mortgages and kids in college.

It was a very intermittently kept diary, he realised, not without a certain regret. Sometimes the writer would keep it up (and keep *it* up) for weeks at a time and then, just as suddenly, he'd drop it, only to resume writing a month or two later.

What was the reason? Was the anonymous diarist just lazy, or wasn't he getting any? After September, there was nothing. Hannah wondered how Pasciznyk had come by such a curious chronicle.

'How're you getting on?' he said at length to Jarvis.

'Huh?' she asked, looking up from a big dusty folder of clippings.

'I was wondering if you'd joined up the dots.'

157

'No picture that I can see,' she said icily. She was looking at some pornographic photographs of teenage boys and girls without a flicker of emotion.

Hannah looked at the material for the later years. It was pretty much the same, only the papers weren't quite so yellowed and the era seemed more familiar to him, on account of him actually being alive at the time. With the other stuff, it was like looking through the wrong end of a telescope.

In the evening, they went round to Siz's place, a big old colonial home quite a way out of town. Mrs Siz – that's what he called his old lady, although her real name was Nancy – cooked crayfish and sweet potatoes for them. It was real down-home cooking. She understood all about her husband's collection. She worked part-time as a marriage counsellor, said she'd never been so busy as she was these days. But if folks could take a look at that stuff that Siz had collected, she said, maybe they would realise they weren't so unique. Maybe they could understand a little more about themselves and their needs.

'At one time,' said Siz over coffee, 'I wondered about maybe writing a book. You know, a kind of psychological study of people's sexuality. There wouldn't be a lot of me in it, though. I'd just let the diaries and the press reports do the talking. Let people draw their own conclusions.'

'Sounds like a good idea,' said Jarvis. 'Why don't you follow it up?'

'I thought about it on and off for years and by the time I'd decided maybe to do something about it, there was a whole slew of books about people's sexual fantasies on sale in every bookshop you went into. So there didn't seem a lot of point to it somehow. Besides, it would have taken time and that was when old Charlie McGraw got sick. He was the original owner of the *Advertiser* but he used to do damn near all of it. He'd write and sub and proof and he weren't averse to setting slugs himself, if the need arose. So with Charlie off sick – he died in '78 or '79, I think it was – I had to do more and more and there just didn't seem to be time to think about it any more.

'Besides, that was when you started to get this whole rash of tabloid-style sex-sheets. You know, Elvis was my secret lover, I made love to an alien, that kind of crap. And you had twenty-four-hour porno channels on cable TV and everything and all of a sudden, the world seemed to have gone nuts, you couldn't see the wood for the trees. That's when I stopped adding to the collection. It no longer seemed exceptional. But it's all there, in case anybody says they're interested. That's why I'm glad you guys are here.'

'What will you do with it?'

'When I'm gone, you mean? I don't think the University would want it. No, it'll probably get burned, along with my old bones.'

They went through to Siz's den. The ten years and more of material he had in there was just more of the same, really. Hannah made notes and Jarvis made liberal use of her scanner, but neither of them could see any way of differentiating any of it. They were looking for veins of reason, like silver in an old drift mine, and there didn't seem to be any – just an endless catalogue of people sucking and fucking with sudden and total disregard for the conventional morality that normally ruled their lives.

But what was driving them? What made people do it? What was the hidden agenda? That was what neither of them could understand, the reasons that made perfectly respectable people tear their clothes off and start balling with the nearest person – and then go back to their normal, often quite circumspect everyday lives as if nothing unusual had happened.

At least the two investigators knew now it was nothing new. For a while, it had seemed that Sleep had a monopoly on the sins of the flesh, like he was manipulating people's desires. But it didn't look like that any more.

Siz came in after a while with a fresh tray of coffee. He had a newspaper under his arm. 'Here,' he said as he put the tray down. 'I kind of figured you might find this interesting.'

He opened up the paper – over a week old as it happened – and smoothed it out on the desk. His den was, if anything, even more untidy than his office back in town.

'I'd put this paper out with the others for the recycling plant, but I remembered there was a story in it that might interest you. Here, read this. How d'you like your coffee?'

The story he showed Hannah was about a raid on a magazine distributor. More than two thousand 'violently pornographic' titles had been confiscated. The story Jarvis read was in the next column. It concerned a female attorney who had been chairman of her local bar association but who, for personal reasons, had not been re-elected. Her appeal against the committee's decision had come to the local newspaper's attention. There seemed to be a vendetta between herself and the other members of the committee.

Chords chimed in Jarvis's memory. She ran her scanner over the page.

'You recognise the name?' said Jarvis, when they got back to their motel. She had begun tapping into her laptop. The damn thing was like an extension of her arm these days.

'Lisa Cornfield? No, should I?'

'Yes, you damn well ought to.'

'How come?'

'You remember Earle Jackson? The guy you saw on TV being crucified in the street, the one who'd just come out of his mistress's house? You showed me the tapes of it, remember?'

'Sure. But that wasn't the woman's name. That was something else, McCrae or McCracken or something.'

'Lena Masters, actually.' There was just the hint of the old ice in her voice. For a fond moment, it had seemed that Jarvis was actually thawing a little towards him. 'No, it's nothing to do with that. Lisa Cornfield is the woman that Earle Jackson hired to defend him after Sleep's Salvation Television ripped him apart.'

'Really?'

'Yes,' she said, tapping further keys. 'And that's not all.'

'I had a feeling it might not be.'

'My records say that two of the committee members of the bar association belong to the Brotherhood of the Cross.'

'That makes a difference, huh?'

'The Brotherhood has close formal links with the Church of the Holy Resurrection. That's Eugene Sleep, by any other name.'

'A loaded deck, huh?'

'That how it seems.'

'You want to know why she got thrown out of the bar association?'

'Tell me. I'm all ears.'

'She's been living with two men and was clearly enjoying a sexual relationship with both of them simultaneously.'

'How do you know that?'

'It's a part of the story that the papers didn't print. I got this all off the file last week, before everything crashed.'

'So you see her name again and it sets the ball rolling, right?'

'Right.'

'Shall I tell you what I think?'

'I know. I'd better go see Lisa Cornfield. She just might have something to tell us.'

161

TWENTY-SIX

Lisa Cornfield was thirty-six years old and she had the biggest office in one of the biggest law practices in Fort Worth. She was one of the most highly respected and able lawyers in the state, strong enough not to let her disappointment over the lost committee chairmanship affect her in any material way. Her specialism was civil rights issues and something like that was just grist to her mill.

Jarvis could be pretty cool towards other women, especially if they were young, attractive, motivated and good at what they did. Lisa Cornfield was all of these things and more, and yet Jarvis could feel respect for her even as she was shown into her office.

Lisa Cornfield was tall, five nine or ten, with short, straight black hair and liquid, intense eyes. Her oval face was beautifully made up to give the impression that she wore no make-up at all, just a hint around the eyes and a deep red lip gloss. She was wearing a conservative dark grey suit and a cream silk blouse, open at the neck to reveal a string of red beads.

Her voice was soft but had an undeniable authority. Jarvis could imagine her in court, making mincemeat out of the opposition, charming even the most ferocious old showboater of a judge, getting him to eat out of her hand before laying one on him.

162

'Well, Ms Jarvis,' she said. 'How can I help you?'

'Sorry,' said Jarvis, momentarily distracted. 'I was surprised by your office. It's not how I imagine a lawyer's office to be.'

It certainly wasn't typical. The room, though large, had a domestic quality to it. The lighting was subdued and warm. There were pictures on the walls, a Ben Shahn print, some fine sculpture and pottery, Persian rugs on the floor.

'Take a look around,' said Lisa with a smile. 'It's meant to be enjoyed.'

At last they were seated on either side of Lisa Cornfield's desk.

'OK,' Jarvis said, opening up her briefcase and taking out the laptop. 'I know you are working for a particular client, Earle Jackson, and that I cannot talk to you professionally about the details of that case.'

Lisa, her long fingers together in a cradle, nodded her assent.

'But what I think I should talk to you about is very relevant to our own enquiries. As I told your secretary when I made the appointment.'

'Tell me again. I see a lot of people and Sasha doesn't always brief me too well.' She laughed, a quiet tinkling laugh. She made Jarvis feel comfortable and at ease with her.

'Your client is, or feels he is, being persecuted by a group of religious ideologues.'

'I'd call them buttheads.' Jarvis, despite herself, felt shocked at the directness of her words. She knew how discreet lawyers usually were.

'I take it you don't share their views.'

'Perish the thought. I'm a rationalist. I don't have time for any of that stuff.'

'OK. Would it surprise you to know that two of the people on your law committee are members of the Brotherhood of the Cross?'

'Don't tell me – that would be Jim McGarvey and Walter Morris, am I right?'

'You knew already?'

'I didn't. But a simple game of elimination would tell me the most likely candidates.'

'Did you know that the Brotherhood has informal links with the Church of the Holy Resurrection, which is virtually one hundred per cent funded by Eugene Sleep?'

'No. Are you suggesting that they are somehow trying to lean on me? And indirectly on my client.'

'It's difficult not to see things that way, isn't it? Eugene Sleep is a powerful man. Salvation Television is a wholly owned subsidiary of his Tru-Flo Corporation. It's difficult not to make the connection, don't you think?'

The lawyer nodded her assent. 'But you're not here just to tell me that,' she said, her eyes narrowing.

'No, I'm not. I came here to find out what kind of reason they had to justify throwing you out of the bar association committee.'

'I don't see why that's any of your business.'

'Maybe it isn't. But I'm trying to get a line on the Brotherhood and the Church of the Holy Resurrection.'

Lisa Cornfield thought again. 'OK,' she said. 'I'll level with you. But this is off the record, right? I have a relationship with a couple of guys. Their names are Bob Harmon and Nick Truit. I tell you that because you've probably got their names on file too. We kind of live together, if you know what I mean.'

'Bob and Nick are—?'

'Are they bi? Yes, they are. What of it?'

'Nothing. I'm just trying to get things clear in my mind.'

'Sure. I'm bi too, if you want to know. We live together. We share the mortgage and the grocery bills. Maybe we might have kids one day, I don't know. These are things that I feel I want to keep private, you know. Even before the Bureau—'

'Of course. I understand. But do the people in the office know that?'

'Of course they do. You can't keep secrets in an office, as you well know.'

'That's for sure. But you don't publicise the fact.'

'Damn right I don't. But McGarvey and Morris must have found out.'

'They think that kind of thing isn't becoming?'

'I guess so. But I don't see what kind of difference it makes. McGarvey is an alcoholic. He beats his wife, I'm told. But that doesn't disqualify him from serving on the committee. Or being big in the Brotherhood. He's a sidesman, is that what you called him? Morris is a lay preacher, you're telling me.'

'You think you can fight this in open court?'

'Not on its own merits, probably not. But certainly there's a case there on ethical grounds. I'm sure I can make my point without dragging Bob and Nick into it.'

'You're a brave lady.'

'There's no bravery about it. The relationship Nick and Bob and I have feels right to each of us. No crimes are being committed, no laws are being broken, no one's getting hurt. Our lives are enriched by the whole experience. It's only uptight people like McGarvey and Morris who can't see that.'

There was such a glorious openness and certainty in Lisa Cornfield's attitude. From her own viewpoint of endless duplicity and deception, Jarvis felt a strange kind of envy for the other woman and her certainties. She felt drawn to her. She would have liked someone like Lisa Cornfield as a colleague, a friend. Instead, she became her lover, if only for one afternoon.

165

TWENTY-SEVEN

WASHINGTON, DC. JUNE 27TH. 1.26 PM.

Stone couldn't have been in a worse mood if Pammy Anderson had been lying on a bed with her legs spread for him and he'd gotten the end of his foreskin – assuming he had such a thing and Pammy hadn't gnawed it off already – stuck in his zipper.

'We think we're getting a lead on Sleep,' Hannah was saying into the phone. 'We think Sleep, or one of his agents, is trying to get a lever on the attorney who's handling the Earle Jackson case.'

To his surprise, Stone didn't seem much interested. He ploughed ahead, just the same.

'Where the hell are you?' asked Stone when Hannah had finished his exposition.

'I'm in Click, Alabama.'

'Is Jarvis with you?'

'No, she's in Fort Worth, Texas.'

'She's where?'

'Fort Worth.'

'What in Christ's name is she doing there?'

'She is speaking with Earle Jackson's attorney. The guy who got mugged with his pants down on live TV.'

'She's doing *what?*'

Hannah repeated what he had just told him.

'Why the fuck is she doing that? No, don't tell me.

166

Listen, Hannah, I want you and Jarvis back in DC right now.'

'But we're just starting to make connections with Sleep.'

'Forget Sleep. Sleep isn't important any longer.'

'But you said—'

'I know what I said. Pepper says differently. Pepper says we drop Sleep as of now. Believe me, Hannah, it's news to me too.'

Hannah felt the disappointment hit him like he was in an elevator that had just dropped forty floors in ten seconds.

'But there's more to this thing. We don't know what it is yet, but Sleep seems to be involved, everywhere we look. There's something weird going down.'

'There's always something weird going down. This whole fucking nation is weird. Don't you read the papers, watch TV? People are crazy, don't you realise that? Not crazy nuts but crazy bad. They don't go and see Bambi movies any more, Hannah. I have personally seen footage of a UCLA professor of ethics dressed only in nylons and a garter belt and having a six-inch nail driven through his scrotum. There's a leather-scene restaurant in San Francisco where you can literally eat shit, for thirty-five dollars a plate, with a choice of four side-salads. Because of guys like you, Hannah, I get to eat shit every day, but at least they pay me for it. So why should this be anything special?'

'People are acting strange. There's a lot of upfront sexual activity, you know what I mean? There's a connection. I can see Jarvis's ears twitching.'

'Jarvis has watched too many porno videos, interviewed too many sex freaks. Jesus, she had some guy from New York in the interview room a couple of months back, this guy could suck his own dick in front of your eyes and charge you ten bucks to watch. The fucker was an FBI informant, too.'

167

'But there's definitely something there. I don't know if it has anything to do with Sleep, but—'

'You got a tampon shoved in your ear or something? Listen up good, Hannah. Sleep is history. Forget him. Dump him in the trash-basket. You got me? Then haul your ass up here just as fast as you can. Pepper's got some nutty millionaire up in Alaska thinks the Cold War isn't over yet and he wants to buy up Russia's decommissioned missiles and fire 'em right back where they came from – smack up the commies' assholes.'

'They aren't commies any more. But can't we just have two more days—' Hannah tried pleading with him, but the phone was already dead. Stone had hung up on him, the bastard.

If he'd had Pepper's number he would have rung him there and then. But Pepper didn't have a number. Sometimes Hannah wondered if he even had a face.

TWENTY-EIGHT

FORT WORTH, TEXAS. JUNE 27TH. 2.18 PM.

There was a penthouse apartment in the law office where Lisa Cornfield worked – a lounge, a big kitchen area and two bedrooms. Here she and Jarvis had lunch – just a simple affair of gravadlax and cornbread, with a side salad – and then they had each other, which was an altogether more elaborate business.

After lunch – no wine, just mineral water – Lisa lit a joint and blew out smoke in a thick cloud. It was a nice time of day to smoke grass, she said, to take you through the afternoon's work in a relaxed, warm glow. Jarvis – not entirely sure of her ground – reached out and took the cigarette from her, drew the smoke deep down into her lungs. Outside she could hear the noises on the street, the hum of traffic, the sound of America going about its everyday business.

As she smoked the spliff, Jarvis felt her inhibitions slowly beginning to drain away from her. It was as if she were entering some kind of exclusion zone, giving way to feelings that she could barely acknowledge in herself outside her innermost fantasies.

It was obvious, just from the way they talked and, especially, the way Lisa listened to her, what the afternoon held in store. Lisa made a phone call.

'I'm in the penthouse,' she said. 'With Miss Jarvis. I don't want any calls. We have some important business to discuss, relating to the Peters case. We may be here most of the afternoon.'

When they'd smoked the joint Jarvis stood up and took off her dress. Lisa did the same, without a word. They stood there, at the entrance to one of the bedrooms, their arms around one another, their nipples almost touching, one pair pink and firm, the other small and brown. Slowly, almost imperceptibly, their mouths and tongues met. The first kiss was slow and long, a gentle indication of pleasures to come. Jarvis had removed her panties along with her dress. She pressed her vulva against Lisa and was aware of the soft white lace that brushed against her naked skin.

She took Lisa's hand and pulled her gently into the bedroom, then knelt down, hooked her thumbs around Lisa's pants and pulled them down far enough to insinuate her tongue into the gap between her legs. Lisa sighed and ran her fingers through Jarvis's hair. She always came when anyone – male or female – licked her pussy.

Jarvis eased the pants down and off, tossed them to one side. How clean and fresh Lisa smelt down there. Now both women were completely naked together there in the bedroom as, five floors down, lawyers studied torts, invoiced clients and consulted legal textbooks. There was no hurry. Both of them felt calm and relaxed, though Jarvis's heart was fluttering with anticipation. She used her hands to part Lisa's legs and then ran her tongue experimentally around the other girl's lips. She tasted as clean as she smelled, and slightly tart.

Still crouching, with her face barely leaving Lisa's vulva, Jarvis moved around until she found the edge of the bed. She sat down on it and pulled Lisa onto her lap until the two girls were face to face, Lisa sitting with her legs around her, her pussy already damp against Jarvis's thighs.

Jarvis reached up and put her arms around the lawyer's neck, pulling her face down to meet her probing lips. Their tongues played together, and breast touched breast as Lisa gently rubbed herself against Jarvis's lap. Jarvis broke off their kiss and applied her lips instead to Lisa's breasts, circling the areolae with her tongue, feeling the nipples tense and pucker up beneath her caresses as she gave her attention to each one in turn until they stood up as hard and brown as little acorns.

Then she took each of them into her mouth, sucking deeply, nibbling them with her teeth until Lisa shivered and ground her sex against her. 'I want you up me,' she murmured into Jarvis's ear.

Jarvis slid her hand down over Lisa's warm, flat belly, feeling the luxuriant pubic hair against the palm of her hand. She knew what the other woman wanted, three or four fingers that would give her the feeling of a nice big cock in there, but handled with the sensitivity that only one woman could show to another. Jarvis might have liked a cock too, at that moment, but Lisa's tongue and fingers would have to do instead. Later, perhaps . . . She wriggled her hips expectantly.

Still sucking Lisa's breast, Jarvis slid her hand into the warm, wet cleft and was surprised at how wet Lisa was already. There was an urgency about her now that had been lacking in the seductive languor of their lunchtime conversation. She knew what was expected of her. She pushed one, then two fingers into her lover's welcoming sheath, feeling its walls closing around them, deliciously slippery with the secretions that slowly seeped from her innermost chamber.

Lisa gasped, brushed her hands over Jarvis's breasts and kissed her passionately on the lips. At the same time, Jarvis slipped a third and then a fourth finger into her, the ball of her hand rubbing against the clitoris that stood out as firm and hard as a little nut. When she got close to orgasm, Lisa became a noisy lover. She gasped

171

and moaned and whimpered, and Jarvis knew she was soon going to shipwreck herself on the reef of her desires.

'Get it up me,' she almost hissed, quite red in the face beneath her summer tan, the words enunciated with surprising clarity.

Jarvis withdrew her index finger, rubbed it against the hard button of Lisa's clitoris and then, twisting her wrist around, managed to insert its tip into Lisa's tight little bum.

'Oh, that's it,' murmured the lawyer. 'Just give it to me there.'

Afraid that her long nails might hurt Lisa, Jarvis merely stroked the outer rim of that second little hole. But it had the desired effect on her lover. Along with the three fingers tight inside her vagina – Jarvis could almost pinch her fingers together through the thin membrane dividing vagina and anus – it quickly brought Lisa to a short, shuddering orgasm. Their tongues played little twisting games with each other, their breath coming in ragged gasps until they were still.

After that, Jarvis lay down on the cool, flat sheets of the bed and Lisa lay down on top of her. They rubbed their pubic mounds together, aping heterosexual intercourse. Jarvis wrapped her long, elegant legs around Lisa and, with her heels, she urged their bodies closer together. She wished, in her heart of hearts, that it was a man who was on top of her now, a woman to lick and caress her, perhaps, but also a man to penetrate her deeply, a man with a long, thick cock that would fill her to the hilt. A woman like Lisa, though, was fine enough for the moment.

Their bodies undulated gently against each other for some while, thigh against thigh, breast against breast, lips against lips. Slowly their movements became more urgent. The grass they had smoked ensured that their skins were becoming one flowing receptive surface that

172

told of pleasures given and experienced, the sheets a cool, smooth and pleasurable sensation against their flesh. Above them they could hear the drone of a passing aircraft. But here, in the apartment, they were living in a separate world dedicated solely to the senses of touch and taste, smell and sound.

They opened their eyes and looked at each other. One of Lisa's hands stole down into the wetness between Jarvis's legs, and then traced its way back up her belly and between her breasts.

'Do me again, down there,' Jarvis murmured, without breaking her gaze.

'Want me to tongue you?' said the lawyer. Jarvis nodded.

Her loins were as warm as the day. Lisa's tongue flicked out again and sought Jarvis's labia, opened up before her like an oyster revealing its treasure. It felt good, the way Lisa played with her. The woman certainly knew what to do. She had a finesse and delicacy about her that was extraordinary.

Jarvis parted her long, colt-like legs to make it easier for her, and to bring more of her body into contact with Lisa's probing tongue. Again she lay back and relaxed, letting her feelings flow through her, her thoughts and urges merging into one delicious stream of desire. The effect of the grass was beginning to wear off, and she was feeling warm and drowsy.

Her hips moved in a slow, easy rhythm, mimicking the movements of Lisa's tongue. Jarvis looked down at her, crouched at the foot of the bed, noting the way her firm pear-shaped breasts hung down like luscious fruits ripe for the plucking. She looked like she enjoyed having men and women nuzzle and suck them, sometimes both of her men together perhaps, Bob sucking one and Nick the other.

The three of them, she later told Jarvis, would sleep together maybe a couple of times a week. Other nights she might sleep with one, or the other, or neither. It had got so they organised it to tie in with their schedules. Bob was an obstetrician, Nick a screenwriter. Sometimes, for a change, there would be casual pick-ups. Lisa liked women and she also liked men, sometimes both together. Anything that gave her pleasure was fine by her. In her present mood Jarvis, it seemed, felt pretty much the same. She was glad they had found each other. She didn't want to go back to DC to face Stone again. And Hannah was a permanent irritation to her, like a pebble in her shoe. Why couldn't he be more the kind of guy that Bob and Nick seemed to be?

Jarvis was aware of her own large, rosy-pink nipples, of how hard and firm they were. She ran her fingers over them; they were aching for the touch of Lisa's tongue and teeth. She took each of them in turn between finger and thumb and pinched them, quite hard. The sensation of exquisite feeling, half-pleasure, half-pain, served only to enhance the urgings of her loins, made her push her mons up against Lisa's mouth, until she felt her lover's tongue pass along the furrow of her labia and gently insert itself into her vagina. She raised her head so she could see Lisa, who lay with her hair spilling out onto Jarvis's naked thighs.

They lay there on the bed, languid and peaceful, for most of the afternoon, sometimes changing or reversing position so that Jarvis could lick her friend's pussy, or Lisa could do the same again for Jarvis, or either of them could tongue the other's breasts and nipples. It was a delightful feeling, the warmth of the afternoon, the infinite tenderness of touch.

Later, Jarvis was rolling the lawyer's firm, brownish nipples between her lips while she enjoyed the synchronous movements of Lisa's hands between her thighs, manipulating her clitoris with practised ease. Then, quite suddenly, Jarvis felt herself aware of a butterfly fluttering deep within her stomach and knew that she was about to climax.

'Lick me out, darling,' she murmured. 'I want to come in your face.'

Lisa disentangled herself and slid down the bed. Jarvis opened her legs for her, aware of how wet her pussy was. She felt the now-familiar, expert tongue run along the furrow of her labia, probing and cherishing, seeking out those secret spots that gave her so much pleasure.

'Harder,' she urged, and Lisa, who knew a woman's needs, pressed her tongue into her with renewed urgency. It was like a weapon now, a penis, something with which to penetrate her fully. Jarvis wanted Lisa's tongue up her, wanted to put her own tongue into Lisa, to taste her salty essences and feel the reality of her pubic bush against her face. And then the flutterings grew imperceptibly into a tremor and Jarvis felt herself going over the edge, almost in slow motion, her nipples now absolutely rigid between her knowing fingers, her body arched and expectant as the first wave of orgasm hit her with the impact of a gale-driven sea.

They lay together in each other's arms, sated at last. Finally Lisa rose and put on a simple towelling robe.

'You're wasting your time with Sleep,' she said as she disappeared into the bathroom. 'You'll never get anything on him that will stick.'

It was the first misjudgement the lawyer had made, Jarvis felt.

TWENTY-NINE

The first night after Willie Odum moved into the trailer, which stood alone and derelict on a vacant lot at the edge of town, there had been an electrical storm of such ferocity that he thought the world must have come to an end. There were hailstones beating on the tin roof like the machine guns in Vietnam and the whole place felt like it was about to come apart.

In the morning he had gone outside. It was a sea of mud out there, with channels carved and scarred into the soft ground where the rainwater had run off. No wonder this site had never been built on – it held water like a sponge. Everywhere there was soggy trash but what caught Willie's eye were the little dull-green stones that were scattered about, dozens of them. He picked one up and looked at it. At first he thought it was just ordinary aggregate like you might find on any landfill site but it looked kind of molten, like it had been seared in a fierce heat.

They'd not been there the day before, he was sure of it, because he'd dropped his cigarette lighter out there and had spent a good half an hour crawling around on his hands and knees before he finally found it. They must have come down in the storm, he figured, swept up by the vortex. These things happened – twisters sprang up and deposited debris all over the place, sometimes a

176

hell of a long way from where it was picked up. One time, when he'd been living up in Oregon, a sudden storm had left everything coated in sand – cars, buildings, streets. People said it had been blown up from the Mojave desert, hundreds of miles away.

Willie had picked up a handful of the dull green stones and taken them inside. They were still there a week later, lined up by the sink. He'd forgotten about them because he had other things on his mind. One thing was to score some horse – Willie had a two-hundred-dollar habit – and another was to get him a woman, because Willie was feeling incredibly horny.

He hadn't felt like that for a long, long time, this urge to plunge into a woman's body. Maybe it had been the change of air, ever since he'd been discharged from Highwood and had made his way out here to High Plains. Some con he'd met in the joint had told him about the trailer, and the key that was under the back wheel, where the spare gas cylinder was. The guy had said the owner was a personal friend of his, but to Willie it was just somewhere to live until he decided it was time to move on somewhere else. It could have been a week, it could have been a year. Willie Odum didn't have any roots as such. So he caught the bus to High Plains and moved in.

He'd found a whole stash of pornographic magazines under the fold-down bed and that had kept him amused for some little while, but what had really got him going was the early-morning scene right opposite. A little after eight, right at the time when Willie would normally be sleeping off his last hit or still scouring the streets looking for it, a gaggle of schoolkids from the housing project opposite would gather to wait for the bus. They'd be there for ten minutes or so every weekday until the big yellow bus came by, and Willie had got to know them pretty well, if only by sight.

He had made a point of being at home and awake to

177

watch them because there was one particular girl Willie really had the hots for. She wasn't much more than medium height but she had long, straight blonde hair and a pretty face that still showed traces of puppy-fat. She must have been about sixteen or seventeen. In the hot spell they were experiencing she was wearing real short skirts – Willie wondered how the school principal allowed it – and once when she knelt down to get something out of her school bag Willie had got a glimpse of her tight white panties.

That really set him off, excited him no end. He spent most of the morning, after jacking up, hunched over his flying fist, jacking off. He felt so horny, it didn't seem to matter how many times he came off, it didn't quell the flow of sap that was rising within him. When he went out to steal a few items from the downtown stores to feed his habit, his hands were shaking and he almost dropped the CD player that he lifted from A&P Electrical. He sure was lonesome for some company.

He couldn't afford to have both a habit and a hooker, but the following day he resumed his acquaintance with Barbarella. Barbarella had big blonde hair and stupendous breasts and a mouth that was wide and inviting, like a bathtub plughole that had been rimmed with red lipstick. He had been with Barbarella many times, on and off, over the past few months since he first encountered her in Denver, Colorado. True, her pink plastic skin was a little grubby now and there was a cigarette burn mark on her left buttock, but she served her purpose. His cycle pump had been stolen in Branches Fork, Colorado, so he had to inflate her by blowing hard into the stiff rubber teat that stuck out of the top of her head, which damn near killed him. There were a couple of punctures in her abdomen that had been repaired with band-aids but on the whole she was pretty air-tight.

The next time he went out, he stole an alarm clock and set it for seven-forty-five, which would give him plenty of time to fix himself and get Barbarella ready. When the queue for the school bus started to form, Willie was feeling pretty good. As soon as the blonde girl arrived, Barbarella took him in her mouth and blew him so that he was practically fucking her deep and welcoming throat.

In his passion, great lumps and tufts of nylon hair were torn out of her scalp, but Willie's attention was on the blonde-haired girl waiting so demurely across the road. She was chatting to her friends, explaining a point. She made a gesture, a quick flurry of hands and arms, and Willie just loved the way it made her breasts jiggle. She obviously wasn't wearing a brassiere. He wondered what it would be like to have her suck him, to feel those rosebud lips closing over his huge stiff dick. Did she suck? he wondered. Would she be as good as Barbarella? Sure, all them girls these days were into that kind of thing. It wasn't how it had been when Willie was younger.

Willie was thirty-six but looked ten years older. Willie had been – still was – a good-looking guy and would look better still if he took a shave and got rid of his welfare clothes. But his habit had always taken precedence over other things. It had always gotten in the way of forming relationships and for many years past he had taken his ease with hookers or with fellow users who were too out of it to notice or care what he looked like or expect anything much of him. Barbarella had been a good friend to him. He called her his old lady and wouldn't let anyone else share her, though he had no compunctions about sharing his works.

But this girl, how he wished he could ravish her, could feel those soft young breasts, touch her pussy fur, slip a finger or five inside that velvety moistness between her legs, stick his tongue inside her mouth and feel hers intertwine around his.

He saw the way the morning sunlight caught her hair

and outlined her white T-shirt. She half-turned towards him and in that moment he saw, perfectly outlined in gold on white, the unmistakable shape of an erect nipple pressing against the soft cotton, and then the other one, both of them full and ripe and hugely succulent. His tongue flickered snake-like against his lips and in that same instant his seed came boiling up and filled Barbarella's ever-open and ever-willing mouth.

THIRTY

'What do you think?' asked Hannah.

'Not a great deal,' replied Jarvis. They were sitting down in the Dead Files department at the Bureau. It was the only place you could go to think – and to talk without being overheard, above the mysterious clunk and knock of the heating pipes. There were stories that closed-circuit monitors were to have been installed down here, like they were everywhere else in the building, but the budget had run out. If ever Hannah got to crack his colleague in work time, he had often fantasised, it would have to be down here.

Upstairs it was a different story. Pretty well everything was bugged, logged, generally accounted for. You couldn't blow off a quiet fart without a little counter clicking over somewhere. The amount of blank tape that was used was staggering.

'Why is he dropping Sleep all of a sudden?'

'I don't know. I don't think even Stone knows. He's just following orders.'

'You really think it came from Pepper?'

'Of course. That's what Stone told you. Why should he lie?'

There seemed no answer to that one.

'What about all that data we accumulated? What do we do about that?'

181

'Forget it. Dump it in the trash. Store it down here if you must. We've got work to do now.'

'You really want to go to Alaska?' He could sense the note of disappointment in her voice. He could tell, through having worked with her in the past, that she was starting to make connections. He was too. But now, it seemed, Stone wanted to rip all the jackplugs out of their sockets. It was a crying shame.

Of course, something was going on down there in Texas. Everyone knew that. But now, it appeared, they just had to let it go on without them.

That evening Hannah took Clemency out for a meal. He felt he had a debt to her, that he owed her something for all the time he had been taking away from her to devote to the Sleep case. Deep down, he felt guilty about the women he'd been with. Hannah wasn't the monogamous type but he felt closer to his red-haired lover than he did to any of the women he'd been screwing.

He picked her up at her apartment. It was a tough kind of place, her neighbourhood, where you might expect whimpers in a stairwell, a knife in the shadows. The doors to the apartments in her building were industrial strength.

Clemmie was waiting. She looked really good, in a short skirt and a big floppy T-shirt that emphasised rather than hid those eminently suckable tits. He fancied her there and then.

'Hi,' he said. 'Do you want to go and get something to eat? I'm starving.'

They went to a Japanese restaurant, Divine Wind, not long open. Hannah wanted to try it. It had been in the weekend magazines, very designerish, with sleek low tables and unobtrusive decor. The menu prices were astronomical. Hannah wondered if he had enough on any of his cards to cover a meal there.

It wasn't very busy, just a few well-heeled tourists and

a group of suits who could have been lobbyists or aides, not at all his kind. It wasn't his kind of place either. He felt awkward and ill at ease with the formality of it all. He'd have been happier at Mr Pizzaman but he wanted to make a statement to Clemmie. She'd been to Japan, said she admired its traditions. He thought a Japanese meal would be a way to connect with her.

They ate without really talking. Hannah felt a ball of nervousness in his stomach, like he'd done the wrong thing.

'Hey,' she said, and then she reached out and took his hand. 'Just relax, OK? Don't worry. Everything'll be fine.'

It was almost preternatural, the way she could read his mind. So he did make a big effort to relax and after that he felt fine.

'Are we going to the Deep Nine after?' asked Clemmie. The Deep Nine was a gay disco, very fashionable among DC's small artistic community but the kind of place the average Bureau agent wouldn't be seen dead in.

'Might as well. Nothing much else to do.'

'I know some people who might be there tonight. It might help you come out of yourself.'

He wanted to tell her about the case, about the things that were really bothering him, but there were agreements and contracts that had to be honoured. He felt pleasantly tired, relaxing with saki and this beautiful girl. They played footsie under the table. It turned him on, he didn't know why, perhaps the way she was smiling at him. They took their time over the food. It was a bit on the peppery side but it made you appreciate the saki.

The waiters in their black silk jackets were over at the far end of the room. On an impulse, Hannah leaned forward and took Clemmie's hand.

'I'm feeling OK now, you know what I mean?'

'I'm glad to hear it.'

183

'I'm sorry I was kind of uptight earlier.'

'Sure. I understand. You want to stay with me tonight?'

'I'd love to. But I have things to do. I have to fly out Monday, maybe be gone a week or more. I could take you in my arms right now, just like in a movie.'

'Now? What kind of movies do you watch?'

A waiter came over, asked if everything was all right. Hannah didn't tell her the kind of movies he and Jarvis watched to earn their paycheques. He'd told her almost nothing about his work. She thought he was something in public relations for the government health program.

'I feel like I wanna ball right this minute. How about you?'

'Sure, but not right now.'

'Later, then. Back at your place? It's not far. Let's skip the Deep Nine.'

'OK. Whatever turns you on.'

'What turns me on is having you for dessert, once we've finished this.' He indicated the plates with their traces of exquisite sauces, the almost empty saki glasses.

'But where? Are you taking me to the washroom? I did that with a guy once, you know.'

'Hell, no,' said Hannah. 'But maybe we could find us somewhere.'

He had in mind the back seat of his car in its stall at the underground parking garage. There was never anyone around at that time of night. Or the park, maybe. Besides, they'd done it before in the open-air darkness; Clemmie liked to do wild things like that. There were plenty of places you could find to ball in the city if you put your mind to it.

'I'll have to think about it, won't I?' she said, but he could tell by the smile playing around her eyes that she was game. She was also ripped to the tits on coke.

She felt his hand on her knee, under the crisp white tablecloth that stood out with a startling geometric effect

184

against the black table. Christ, she thought, he wants to have me in the middle of Divine Wind, the most fashionable Japanese restaurant in DC.

Hannah turned and leaned towards her. She parted her legs to make it easier for him. His hand slid up her thighs, on to the tops of her bare legs, noticing how soft and cool she felt despite the heat. Clemmie looked up anxiously, but the waiters were still at the other end of the room. Besides, there was a big pillar blocking them from the view of the other diners.

For a couple of minutes or more his fingers delicately brushed across her skin. He knew it was making her tingle, making her long for him. He knew she wanted his fingers there, his tongue, his penis. Both of them were temporarily lost for conversation.

His fingertips moved higher. She glanced anxiously around the room again. No one could possibly see them, unless they knelt down on the floor and looked up. She felt reassured, and was able to relax. She parted her legs a little more, moved forward in her seat so that his fingers brushed against her sex.

He stroked her delicately, between her legs. He was looking straight into her eyes.

Despite the short skirt she had on, she wasn't wearing any underwear. He felt delightedly surprised. She'd done it specially for him, she said later. It made her feel deliciously vulnerable.

Now his fingers slid underneath, against the moist lips of her sex, the palm of his hand cupping her pubic mound. She had to push herself almost off the edge of the chair to let him reach her, so she was leaning right back. She glanced up and saw people coming and going at the other end of the restaurant, paying their bills, ordering extra courses. She poured the last of the wine into their glasses, trying to look nonchalant. She realised her hands were shaking and she nearly dropped the bottle.

Hannah's middle finger roved around her labia, probing between the folds, finding the entrance and slipping inside her. She had not been particularly wet before but now her juices were beginning to flow, easing the passage of another finger and then another, until he had three fingers buried in her, there at their table in Divine Wind, with people stuffing noodles and sushi into their faces only a few yards away.

'Come on, Hannah, someone might see,' she heard herself say for form's sake but he could tell she wanted him to go on, to push on into her, to push her over the edge. With the ball of his thumb he found her clitoris and massaged it with infinite gentleness, his fingers all the while twisting and sliding and turning inside her. Already she was pushing out to meet him, trying to force herself onto him, ready to be penetrated.

She didn't reach a climax, though she was close to it – she felt too inhibited by the other people in the restaurant and the waiters hovering around the place. She quietly whimpered and moaned and sighed enough to make Hannah think he had brought her off. He withdrew his hand. As he brushed back a lock of his hair he could smell her musky pussy smell on his fingers, strong and exciting.

'Maybe we should spend the night together after all,' she said. He agreed without argument.

Hannah paid their bill and they made their way out into the night. It was almost dark outside, just a faint trace of colour in the sky, not a great deal of car traffic about. The air was warm and the stars were incredibly bright, high up there between the buildings. They held hands as they walked through the night-time throng.

He decided he wanted to fuck her against a column in the underground parking garage. It was kind of weird down there, with the big concrete columns festooned with graffiti and the overpowering smell of stale water and gasoline, the distant sound of a car moving along the ramps. She hoiked her top up and immediately he was sucking hungrily at her tits, lovely and round and fleshy with nice plump nipples.

Her pussy felt like it was on fire. 'Come on, Hannah,' she whispered, stroking his hair as he nuzzled her.

He pressed her against one of the columns, cold and surprisingly rough against naked flesh. Her short skirt was up around her hips and Hannah was busy with his belt. For a second or two they looked at each other in the near-darkness, the security lights bathing them in an eerie glow. They were barely able to see each other in the gloom.

And then she stood up high on her toes and parted her legs and he was pushing inside her, hot and eager. She came almost immediately, tonguing him like mad, and then again as he pumped his strong, masculine backside up and down, up and down, his cock seeming to fill her completely until she was oblivious to everything else. When he came into her, it was like a big shuddering spasm for both of them. It seemed to go on and on until finally the feeling subsided and she realised her legs were getting stiff standing like that, and then Hannah withdrew and she wiped herself quickly and discreetly with a tissue from her bag.

'Let's get going,' said Hannah at length. 'We've got a date, remember? I've gotta show you my etchings, wasn't that what you said?'

THIRTY-ONE

Jarvis was working late. She wouldn't be officially sec-
onded to the Alaska project until the following morning,
which meant she was still technically assigned to the
Sleep investigation. She was determined to do all she
could in the time that was available to her.

She had stayed up almost the whole of the previous
night transferring data into an accessible format that she
could run through the Kray-2s. Anything remotely relevant she identified and keyed in – names, addresses,
personal details, dates, places. Any kind of information
that might be important she ran a big electronic pink
highlighter over. The program she was running had
taxed to the full the memory of her home PC, but she'd
condensed as much as she could onto disk so she could
boot it through the Bureau's systems.

Stone had hung around until long after eight, no
doubt trying to sniff out what Jarvis was up to. She ran a
few games programs on her terminal, trying to put him
off the scent. Once she'd got this lot loaded, she could
effectively lose it but first she had to get everything set
up. That was the tricky part.

Eventually Stone gave up and went home. Now there
were just a couple of nightbirds at the far end of the
office, bathed in the pale blue glow of their screens.
Someone had a tape playing somewhere, it sounded like

Billie Holiday. Otherwise the only noise on that whole floor was the occasional clacking of a keyboard, or the softly rasping buzz of a printer.

Jarvis slipped her disc into the drive and found the application she wanted. It was asking a lot of the system to try to analyse all that disparate information and come up with effective correlations. The national network had something similar but it was a hell of a lot simpler to administer than the kind of co-efficients Jarvis was trying to find. It was almost as if she were asking the Bureau's computers to think intuitively.

'Hi, there. How ya doing?'

The voice made her jump. She turned round and there was Richie Robennack, the Bureau's Jerk of the Year for the past decade. Robennack was a grade A pain in the butt and Jarvis bitterly regretted the moment of human weakness that had once led her to establish a closer kind of dialogue with him. She could no longer recall the exact circumstances but it was like she had taken pity on him or something.

Robennack was one of those people everyone meets at one time or another from childhood on, the dedicated climber whose ambitions probably outweigh their abilities but who know how to get where they want to be. Within the Bureau, Robennack got up everyone's nose faster than a line of best Colombian. He cajoled, he wheedled and he gave people the creeps. The trouble was he was a fucking good analyst and he almost always came up with the goods.

He also fancied himself a womaniser.

'Hi, Richie,' she said as evenly as she could.

'What you doing here so late?' he said, parking his butt on the edge of her desk. She could feel the vibes coming off him and she didn't like it.

'I might ask you the same question.'

'Sure, but I asked first.'

'Oh, I'm just looking into a few things. I was off sick a

couple of weeks back and I'm still trying to catch up. How about you?'

'Something just came up and I had to look into it. I'm almost finished now, just waiting for a hard copy to come through. Why does it take so long to print anything in this place?'

'It just does,' said Jarvis, non-commital as always.

'Maybe I should see if I can get something done. I have a meeting with Stone tomorrow.'

'Right,' said Jarvis, looking intently at her screen. 'You do that.'

He sat there for a while, looking over her shoulder. Now the screen was scrolling through some stuff she'd done weeks ago. The real work was being done about five layers down.

'I was wondering,' he said in a dead even voice, 'if maybe you'd like to have a drink with me when you're through.'

She didn't answer for a few moments, working the keyboard instead.

'I don't think so, Richie,' she said at length. 'I've got a lot of work to get through here.'

'I've got time. Maybe I can help you.'

'No, it's something I need to keep control of.'

'You're like that, aren't you?'

'Like what?'

'You like to keep control.'

'Doesn't everyone? And what of it?'

She hoped he picked up on the note of exasperation in her voice.

She realised he was looking at the screen too.

'What's this you're going through?' He always had been a nosy bastard, made it his business to know other people's business.

'Oh, nothing. Just some machine code.'

'Looks like a funny kind of machine code to me. I'd say you were looking at map co-ordinates.'

190

'Would you now?'

'Yes, I would. Why are they mostly in the South?'

He couldn't have been able to study what was on the screen for more than three or four seconds at the most and yet in that time he'd been able to scan forty triple-column lines of figures and make sense of them. The Bureau ran courses to help its agents develop such skills. There were people who could read *Moby Dick* in under fifteen minutes and then answer a whole raft of detailed questions, even quote entire passages word perfect. People like Robennack.

'It's nothing you need bother yourself about, Richie.'

'Nothing, nothing. It's just an observation, that's all.'

'OK, well, maybe you should keep them to yourself, you know what I mean?'

'Hey, you look great when you start getting angry.'

She bit her lip. She wanted to tell the guy to fuck off but he was two and a half grades higher than her and had influence on several key committees that she was anxious to keep on the right side of.

She saved what she'd been doing and sighed, turning round in her chair. The nighthawks had gone to drink coffee from the machine, like they did every hour on the hour. They'd be gone another ten minutes.

'Listen, Richie,' she began, 'are you trying to tell me something?'

'Me? Tell you something? What would I want to tell you?'

'I don't know. But something sure seems to be itching you.'

'I love a girl who reacts, you know that? And you're reacting just beautiful, Agent Jarvis.'

'Drop it, will you? I'm telling you, I've got a lot of work to do. I start a new assignment tomorrow and I haven't wrapped up the one I'm working on yet.'

'Have dinner with me.'

'No.'

'Next week, maybe?'

'I told you, no.'

'OK, skip the dinner. Let's just go to bed and ball.'

She looked him straight in the eye.

'Whatever do you think gives you the right to speak to me like that, Agent Robennack?'

'I've got a big march on you status-wise and I've also got eight and a half inches I could give you on top of that. What more could a girl want?'

'I don't need this,' she said. 'From you or anyone.'

'But I'm not just anyone. I'm me. And I'm putting a proposition your way.'

'That's harassment.'

'Who says?' He looked around the big, empty office. 'I didn't hear any harassment.'

'Get out of here, will you?'

He stood up, but he wasn't finished with her yet.

'You know what they say about you, Agent Jarvis?'

'Forget it, will you? I tell you, I don't need this. You're annoying me and demeaning yourself.'

He appeared not to hear her.

'People think you're the Ice Lady, you know what I mean? They think you've got as much desire in you as a block of ice. But they think you'll ball just the same. People say you're balling Agent Hannah right now.'

'That's ridiculous.'

'Hey, hey. Don't get so hot now, Ice Lady. You might melt.'

'Piss off, will you? Or do I have to call night security?'

Robennack stood up, shot his cuffs. He prided himself on being a snappy dresser. He would often criticise Hannah behind his back for dressing like a slob.

'Well, I'd better go, then,' he said, his mouth fixed in a perfect smile. 'I can see you're not in the party mood right now. But just remember what I said, right?'

He leaned down and kissed her quickly on her cheek, before she had time to turn away. His hand squeezed her breast. She felt revolted by it. Compared with Robennack, Hannah was a perfect gentleman.

THIRTY-TWO

Hannah wasn't acting like a perfect gentleman at that moment. He was acting like the meanest, most sex-crazed bastard who ever walked this earth and Clemmie was loving every last lewd second of it. If anything, she was acting even crazier than he was.

His senses seemed to be on fire. It was as if Clemmie held him in her thrall and he felt he was ready for anything. It must have been the coke she'd given him.

Another thing he liked about going out with Clemmie was that he got to drive her sleek black Mustang.

'Let's go now,' she said as she got into the car beside him. 'Let's go and do something exciting. Something we might regret. I want to be dangerous, Hannah.'

His desire for her, already inflamed, was further fuelled by this sense of recklessness she instilled in him. He wanted to do her bidding, anything she wanted. Instead of him giving her the orders, he wanted it to be the other way round for a change. He wanted to give her the opportunity to express herself.

He gunned the engine and drove up the ramps, out into the streets. He flipped on the air conditioning. After the gasoline smell of the underground garage, the air smelled fresh and invigorating. It helped clear Hannah's head a little.

His hands were trembling so much he found it

194

difficult to work the gear shift. It might have been easier if she had an automatic like everyone else did.

'Shall we go back to my apartment?' he asked when they hit a red light, but she said no.

'Let's drive around a while,' she said. 'Let's see what we can find.'

She turned to face him, kissed him on the cheek. Then, as he drove away from the light, she suddenly pulled her top off over her head and slipped off her skirt.

It felt as if someone had punched him in the solar plexus. He couldn't believe this. He was driving round DC at night with this broad who was wearing only a tight black lace brassiere and nothing else.

'What the hell?' he began, but she didn't let him finish.

'I know what you're thinking,' she said. 'I just love doing this kind of thing, right? Sometimes I do it even when I'm on my own, just drive around at night in garter belt and stockings.'

She leaned over and unzipped his pants, got his cock out and started to suck him. If he hadn't shot his wad not ten minutes earlier, Hannah might have come off there and then, in the middle of the late-night city. Thank God, thought Hannah, there was very little traffic at that time of night. And yet, deep down inside his psyche, he wanted to be seen, wanted other guys to see that he was the kind who could drive an expensive car and have a beautiful, exotic woman fellate him anytime, anywhere.

Not really knowing where he was going, he drove around the almost deserted streets. Clemmie stopped sucking him, took his hand and guided it between her legs. He could feel the silky folds of her labia, could feel she was very wet, her juices running out all over the custom leather upholstery. His cock felt like a rod of iron.

She lay back in her seat, stroking her nipples as

195

Hannah's fingers worked their magic on her clit. As they passed under the street lights, anyone who chanced to look in the car would have seen her. Driving with one hand on the wheel, Hannah somehow insinuated two fingers of his right hand into her vagina. Her clitoris stood out like a little nut. She came almost immediately, as they waited at an intersection.

He wanted desperately to park in the nearest side street and have her right there, but she seemed to have other ideas.

'Drive on,' she said, and he did as he was told.

'Anywhere in particular?' he asked, but she didn't respond.

'Let's see if we can pick someone up,' she said, and laughed. 'A guy or a girl, it doesn't bother me. You can fuck her, I can fuck him. The first one we find, right? You'd like that, wouldn't you?'

Being honest with her, he was forced to agree. He wasn't the jealous type.

'Come on,' she said. 'Don't you ever wish your fantasies could come true?'

'Sure. How about you?'

'I got lots of them.'

'Such as what?'

'I'd like to watch you with another woman,' she said. 'Would you like to see me? Having it with other men?'

'I'd never thought about it.'

'Liar.' She reached across and squeezed his cock, which was still sticking out of his open flies. 'You love the idea, don't you?'

He had to agree.

'I knew I was right,' she said simply.

The idea thrilled him unaccountably. He wanted to go along with anything she might suggest. There was danger in the air but he felt no fear, just a crazed desire to explore the possibilities.

He noticed she was looking at pedestrians as they

196

drove slowly around quiet residential streets. Finally she tapped the steering wheel.

'Stop,' she said. 'He'll do.'

In a pool of light outside a now deserted bar a man was leaning against a wall. He was young, not more than twenty, long hair in a ponytail and clean-shaven. Hannah quickly zipped himself up as Clemmie called out to him.

As he bent down and looked in the window Clemmie gave him the full benefit of her exquisite breasts and long, colt-like legs. Hannah registered the surprise on the young man's face as he took in the unmistakable fact of her nakedness apart from that stark black brassiere.

'Do you want to fuck me?' she said in a rapid undertone. 'I'd like your cock up my cunt in the back of the car.'

The man was speechless for a few seconds. He gulped, looked up and down the street. It was deserted, and no lights were showing in the buildings.

'I'll suck your cock for you, if you like,' Clemmie said. 'With or without a rubber.'

Hannah felt his head reeling, not just from the coke and the wine they'd drunk in the restaurant. He wondered what the other guy made of it.

'All right, my ride won't be here for a while yet,' said the young guy. His eyes showed he scarcely believed his good fortune. It clearly wasn't every day that he got propositioned in the street at half-past midnight. Hannah wondered what he was thinking – are these people crazy, or what? They could have been a couple of serial killers, for all he knew. But, like most men, he let his dick rule his head.

197

THIRTY-THREE

WASHINGTON, DC. JUNE 30TH. 11.06 PM.

The data Jarvis wanted would be waiting for her when she got back to her apartment. Long before midnight, she'd grown sick of staring at a computer screen. By the time she had inputted as much of the data as she could, and programmed the co-ordinates, she was beat.

And she was sick of men, too, Richie Robennack in particular. What gave him the right to think he could come round to her desk and start importuning her? There were statutes in place to deal with that kind of thing but, as with the government's no-smoking policy, the Bureau somehow seemed to feel it was above all that.

She wasn't going to hang around while the computer searched the Bureau's data files for connections. She'd have it downloaded to her PC at home instead. She got out of the building as fast as she could, found her car in the deserted lot that was reserved for people who worked in her building.

Normally she would have driven straight home, but she knew it would be at least an hour and perhaps two before the machines got anywhere with her files. So she drove around, not really aware of where she was going or what the time was. Maybe this was how guys felt when they went prowling around in the dead hours looking for hookers.

She found herself in a residential area she'd not been

in before. Everything was deserted. Very few lights showed in any of the houses. All around her people were asleep, dreaming perhaps of a secure world where Mom and Pop would make everything OK. She wished it were so, to the bottom of her heart.

She stopped the car, flipped off the engine. She needed to think, without any distractions. If she went home she would find something to do. She sat there, hardly noticing as the minutes went by and the heat drained out of the car.

Her mind kept going back over her work on the Sleep project, trying to race the Bureau's immensely powerful computer systems in an attempt to analyse just what the hell was going on in all these little places in the South and West. She would obey orders implicitly and yet she couldn't follow Stone's embargo. This wasn't a case that she could let slide. Why were people acting the way they did? Was it something in the air? Something in the water? That was what she'd asked the computer – what were the common factors that could influence people's behaviour at those specific times and in those specific places?

Facts started rolling through her head again, as they had done ever since she and Hannah had been put on the case. Names, dates, times, places – it was like she was making a map inside her head. Sleep, she was now sure, was only marginal. This had been going on since he was still a small-town businessman with a regional monopoly on peanuts.

Of course it was only happening in the South and West, but why was it only happening there? Or maybe it was more the case that people were only noticing that it was happening in the those places? They didn't have any reports that she knew of from Minnesota. Sleep didn't own any papers north of the Mason-Dixon line.

It couldn't just be that people got more uptight the

further north you went and it couldn't be any kind of social trend. Changing patterns in behaviour, she knew, may have spread slowly but they still spread. This one seemed to stay put in its burrow. She couldn't figure it at all.

A tap on the driver's-side window broke her concentration. She had a .38 standard issue clipped under the dash but she wouldn't have been fast enough. She looked in the rearview mirror – she hadn't even noticed the prowl car that had come up silently behind her. Then she caught a glimpse of a cop jacket and she knew it was OK.

Down came the window.

'Everything all right, lady?' said the cop, peering round the inside of the car. There was nothing in there that gave a clue to her identity, nothing even worth stealing apart from a cassette tape of Monteverdi's Vespers and her bag.

'Sure, officer,' she said. 'I just—'

She couldn't think of any way of ending the sentence, although she wanted to tell this big strong guy about her work, her problem with Robennack, the hundred and one other things that were weighing on her like lead and that had brought her, exhausted, to this quiet residential street at two in the morning.

'Got any ID?'

She reached for her bag behind the driver's seat, aware of the cop's eyes on her legs as her skirt rode up. She never kept any kind of bag or case – not even the grocery shopping – beside her on the passenger seat, not since the time some bilko artist had reached in through the window when she was stopped at a red light and tried to snatch her briefcase. Instead, she'd snatched his wrist and had damn near broken it for him with a quick but powerful twist one way and then the other, just as they'd shown her in special operations training.

She knew to open her bag slowly and deliberately, so

200

he could see she didn't have some kind of a weapon in there. He'd have recognised the body language in that gesture alone but she still took out her Bureau card, held it out to him. He took one glance at the crest and that was enough.

'Sorry I disturbed you, Agent Jarvis,' he said. 'Only we normally know when you guys are operating around here.'

'I understand,' she said ambiguously. 'This is kind of, you know—'

'Better leave you alone, then,' he said and made his way back to the prowl car with exaggerated caution.

When the cops had gone, Jarvis got out of her car and walked around the empty middle-income streets. Here, amid tree-lined avenues, was the America she was paid to protect, a world of front lawns with built-in sprinkler systems and a station wagon parked on the drive, cable TV and a tree house out back for the kids. It seemed so silent and serene, so very far away from the scenarios of bizarre sexual behaviour that made up the Sex Files. But Jarvis was obsessed with her cases. Much as she longed for the peace of these quiet streets, she felt she could never escape the world she knew best.

She turned a corner, passing by a convenience store and a bar. She was surprised by the expensive black car she saw slewed over the side of the road. For a second she wondered if there'd been some kind of accident but then, silhouetted by the street lights, she saw figures moving inside the car, someone getting into or getting out of the back seat. The indicator light was still flashing on one side – maybe they were just dropping someone off after a dinner or a party somewhere, or picking them up even. She could even see the lights on the dash, the engine was still running. She walked on.

Suddenly her heart skipped a beat. What the hell was going on in there? The car windows were starting to mist up but there was a woman there in the back seat and she was in her underwear, black on white flesh. She stopped dead in her tracks and instinct took over. She froze and looked more closely, aware of the dryness in her throat. Was this a rape or something? Where was that prowl car? She wished she had her .38 with her.

But another moment's observation showed her that this woman wasn't being raped. She was on top of a guy in the back seat and was obviously balling him. Hell, that was a $40,000 automobile – these weren't kids with nowhere to go.

Then she realised there were three people in the car, the two in the back and a guy behind the wheel. He was obviously watching what was going on. From his body language, it was happening with his full consent. She could see him leaning over the seat to get a better view. She could see his outline against the dash lights. What kind of perverts could they be?

She heard a car approaching. Hope rose in her breast. It wasn't the prowl car though, just a sleek navy Porsche. It swung into a driveway a couple of houses down the street and as it did so its headlights swept the parked car. The driver of the latter hastily ducked down but not before Jarvis had a clear glimpse of his features.

The guy was Hannah, of that she was sure. All the same, Jarvis couldn't believe the evidence of her eyes. Him as well? Half the people of the Southern States seemed to be infected by some kind of sex-crazy virus – had it now affected Hannah too?

She remembered Agent Robennack's remarks. 'Why are they mostly in the South?' So now it wasn't just the South then? Or maybe it never had been.

Hannah – what a jerk-off. She knew he had a wild girlfriend but this was like something from the Sex Files. But the people she documented were statistics, numbers on a computer screen. Hannah was different. She knew him. He was another agent – a close colleague. What the hell did he think he was doing?

Jarvis was in a state of shock as she made her way back to her own car. All thoughts of the data she had collected had vanished from her mind. She drove home like a robot.

THIRTY-FOUR

Hannah watched as Clemmie and the stranger writhed around the back seat together. Apart from her brassiere and her wickedly high-heeled shoes, Clemmie was naked in the guy's arms; the atmosphere was crazy with forbidden lust. The man tried to kiss her but she ducked down and deftly unbuttoned his trousers and felt for his penis. Hannah noticed how large it was, larger than his own, and already hugely erect. Despite himself, he felt a stab of jealousy above the racing excitement that inflamed his imagination.

She had a condom in her hand, he noticed. She slipped it over him and then she took the stranger's cock in her mouth, sucking it deep into her throat. The guy sat there rigid as a plank, looking wildly around him, wondering how this could be happening to him. This was an expensive car and she was an expensive woman. It must have seemed like something out of a dream. Hannah wished he could have dreams like this.

And then Clemmie was climbing on top of the guy, pushing her nipples out for him to suck, reaching down to guide him into her. Hannah found the scent of her secretions almost overpowering in the confined space of the car. He badly wanted to masturbate but was embarrassed in the other man's presence.

204

Clemmie spread her legs wide, pressing her hips down onto the stranger.

'Oh God, he's big,' she called out. 'He's right up me. I'm full up.'

'Fuck him hard,' Hannah found himself urging her. 'Let's see what kind of stuff he's made of.'

He turned round to watch them. The stranger made to ask some kind of question but Clemmie cut him short, squashing her heavily scented breasts against his face. As she leaned forward Hannah could see not just her tight, wrinkled little bum-hole but also the way her vagina seemed to cup his penis like a thin-lipped mouth. The guy's balls lay bulkily between his legs, his shorts and denim jeans around his knees.

Still moving up and down on top of him, Clemmie reached into her bag, pulled out a tissue and a little glass ampoule.

Oh shit, thought Hannah, she's doing poppers now. What if the cops come? He would be out on his ear, busted for public indecency and drugs violations. The car was even parked illegally, slewed over to the side of the avenue by a convenience store with the motor still running.

He could smell the sharp, acidic smell of the amyl nitrate as Clemmie cracked open the little ampoule inside the tissue. She inhaled it deeply, pressed it to the guy's face and he took a big hit too. It worked immediately – this stuff, Hannah recalled, was designed to get cardiac victims pumping again. If your heart was beating normally, it was like the lift-off of a moon rocket.

Now Clemmie bobbed up and down with something approaching frenzy, gasping out her desire. The guy in the back called out too as he came inside her and it seemed to send her into a spasm, her backside circling his enclosed prick for thirty seconds or more until a series of rippling shudders visibly passed through her.

She sank down, head bowed, her legs spread wide on the leather seat.

There was a silence like there is immediately after an automobile crash. Hannah turned round. He heard Clemmie say something to the guy, didn't catch his muttered reply. There was the rustle of clothing and then he got out of the car. Hannah didn't bother looking round. He heard the man's footsteps on the pavement. It had started to rain outside. Hannah hadn't even noticed. He felt like he was absolutely out of his head.

Clemmie was slumped in the back seat. He turned on the radio, an all-night soul station, felt glad of the distraction. He heard her laugh.

'God, that was wild,' she exclaimed. She reached for her bag, took out a cigarette and lit it. He heard the match flare. For a split second the interior of the car was lit up, all polished wood and leather. She let down the window and breathed smoke out into the cold night air.

'I wonder what he made of it?' Hannah said. His voice was strangely hoarse.

'He must have thought Christmas had come early,' said Clemmie. 'I bet he tells his friends. He had a nice cock but I wouldn't let him kiss me.'

She was elated. He felt like everything had happened too fast for him.

'Did you see everything?' she asked excitedly. 'I bet it looked good. Did you see his cock in my pussy?'

'Sure,' said Hannah, feeling weird. He drove off slowly, his cock uncomfortable and stiff inside his pants. A prowl car came round the corner and drove towards them, two officers in it. Had the cops started their night rounds five minutes earlier, heaven knows what trouble he might have been in. He wouldn't have needed to go to Alaska, that was sure.

He'd be on the breadline instead.

THIRTY-FIVE

WASHINGTON, DC. JULY 1ST. 00.34 AM.

Jarvis let herself into her apartment and fixed herself a drink. She didn't even bother with ice, just drank the scotch straight down. She was so tired she felt like falling down and yet her mind was racing all the same, like a caffeine high or the first sex after a long time.

Robennack and then Hannah in the car – what kind of a night was this going to turn into?

The drink hit her stomach and helped clear her head. She made herself another, took it through into her study. The message she had expected was waiting for her. She printed it out. It should have done so automatically but something wasn't working properly. Her fingers were unsteady as she hit the familiar instructions on the keypad.

Still with her drink in her hand, she took the printed pages into the living room and sank into the welcoming warmth of her sofa. At least something would go right tonight, she thought, as she scanned the data sheets. Now she would find out just what had got into all those people.

She wanted to know if they all ate high-fibre diets, or took vitamin pills, or read more pornography than average, or had a low incidence of sickle-cell anaemia. Or maybe there might have been something more start-ling, like they were all on performance-enhancing drugs

207

or something. Whatever the outcome, she wanted to find something that understandably might have a definite cause-and-effect correlation with wild or off-the-wall sexual behaviour.

But the computer could tell her nothing she didn't know already. The only common factors among the majority of cases that she had analysed was that the incidents tended to take place when there was a general rise in soybean prices, the New York Knickerbockers were having a winning spell and the mean temperature was slightly above the seasonal average. The majority of the subjects listed were Caucasian males and females in their thirties and early forties, of middle-income status, but proportionally similar effects were recorded among blacks, Hispanics and other groups. The incidents, therefore, were not gender-specific and had nothing to do with race or ethnic group. As she read through the data with a trained eye, she realised that they weren't specific to anything identifiable from the available information.

Whatever it was that had hit Hannah and more than a thousand other people over a period of nearly forty years didn't have any preferences. It could happen to anyone, even herself. The figures tallied almost exactly with the laws of probability, applied to random subjects. Sure, there were exceptions but there was nothing significant there. For every possible explanation, there was something else that flatly contradicted it.

Jarvis felt crushed. She was no further along than when she started. One of the most powerful computers in the United States, put to work on a vast data bank of information of all kinds, could tell her nothing.

Pepper was right, then. There was nothing in this.

Alaska beckoned

Shit, thought Jarvis. She kicked off her shoes and fell asleep, exhausted, right there and then on her sofa.

She dreamed she was walking past the White House in

a procession. She was naked, the only one among hundreds if not thousands of people and Stone and Hannah were there beside her, dressed normally. Richie Robennack came by on a bicycle, shouting lewd remarks at her through a bullhorn. The procession reached the Potomac River and everyone waded in. Jarvis tried to stop, to fight her way free, but was carried along by the pressure of the crowd. The water was surprisingly warm. Everyone was trying to reach a sailing ship that was moored downriver.

THIRTY-SIX

Jarvis awoke, feeling hot and flustered. She turned to the clock beside the bed. It said 3.35. She hadn't been asleep more than an hour.

Her dreams had been of an almost hallucinatory vividness. She had been floating in space, deep in the asteroid belt, all around her the black vault of the heavens. And yet she hadn't felt in the least bit afraid, even though she wasn't wearing an astronaut suit, just her normal clothes, one of her linen suits in fact.

It wasn't unusual that she should recall so much – Jarvis's precision and attention to detail extended into her subconscious.

Even on waking, the sense of being at one with the universe was overwhelming. And there was the recollection of a flood of stars that looked at first like the Milky Way and then, suddenly, became an avalanche of paper, speeding past her at an incredible rate. She could see faxes, photocopies, all kinds of documents. She had learned enough in Psychology Module 3 to know that the substance of her dreams was not entirely coincidental. It had to mean something.

But why deep space? And why that extraordinary sense of peacefulness?

For the last few days she had thought of little but her failure to make headway in analysing the data she and

210

Hannah had brought back from Texas. Even though she was now, like Hannah, assigned to a different project, she couldn't drop it. She had felt frustrated, unable to make headway, working on her own at home with her laptop, not daring to open Bureau files in case she were detected.

She had felt more and more uptight and yet in the dream she had been satisfied, fulfilled. What was the significance of it all?

Lying there in the darkness, she tried to reason it through. There was a sexual element, sure enough, like there was in many of her dreams – that feeling of a deep inner satisfaction could have no other origin, the release that she had so frustratingly sought for so long.

But the stars and the planets, where was the connection there? Dreams were never literal, she knew that. But what did they symbolise?

She felt too tired to think about it in any great depth. Right now, all she needed to do was sleep. Slowly, warm under her covers, she felt herself drifting off into oblivion.

She had just reached the edge when it came to her. Calvin Caughey. Calvin, Calvin, it had to be Calvin.

Instantly she was wide awake again. Calvin was an analyst at NASA's Johnson Space Center, had worked on the Mariner projects. She and Calvin had had a thing going years back, very sexual, very strange too. They had never been very close emotionally but, with Calvin, she had often felt that sexual experience was taking her further out of her body than she had ever known before. He was one of the few lovers – male or female – who had ever brought her to the ecstatic state she had experienced in her dream.

Calvin – she didn't think of him from one month to the next. And now, all of a sudden, she had an overwhelming desire to talk to him, to connect.

It had to be about Calvin. There could be no other

explanation, even though she had been quite alone, the way she had dreamed it. But what did Calvin have to do with the work she'd been doing, that was symbolised by that endless shower of paper?

She'd have to ring him and find out. Even at 3.35 in the morning.

Calvin Caughey had always been a night bird. Often he wouldn't show up for work until gone mid-day, but would then work right through until the following morning, when normally oriented people were just starting to show up.

She had to ring him, right now.

She put on the light, dragged the phone into her bed with her. Her mouth felt dry and her heart was fluttering as she reached for her address book – his number was no longer on one of the memory keys of her home phone.

She got a brusque answerphone message when she rang his home number. On a hunch, she tried his direct line at Johnson Center.

'Calvin Caughey.' It was a real voice, not a machine.

'Calvin. It's Bonny Jarvis. How are you?'

'How am I? I'm fine. How are you?'

'I'm fine too. Listen, I'm sorry to call you at this hour.'

'No problem. I was just finishing off some work. You know me – I never see daylight.'

'What are you working on?'

He told her something about number-crunching quasars but she couldn't understand much of it. She never had been able to understand a lot of the work he did. Truth to tell, there were maybe only a dozen or so people in the whole wide world who really understood the significance of what Calvin Caughey could do with a line of statistics. But what he did would have echoes that reverberated throughout space science, into that mysterious borderland where mathematics and logic and physics and many other disciplines came together.

'But you didn't ring me just to hear me talk about coefficients, did you?' he said when he was through.

'Not really,' she said. 'I've got a problem of my own.'

She explained – without going into much specific detail – about the data she and Hannah had collected, and the difficulties she'd experienced in analysing it.

'You want me to run through it, right?'

'Well, it would be a great help.'

'How about security?'

'There's no problem. Everything's in the public domain – names, dates, places, that kind of thing. All I want to do is to find out if there's any connection. We think there's a link in there but I don't know enough about such procedures to find it.'

He told her how and in what format to send him the data. He couldn't do it immediately but certainly within the week. In fact, he had to be in DC on Friday for a conference. Maybe they could meet, have dinner or something. She got the impression he was glad to help her, wanted to give something back to her. She knew that what had gone on between them had never really died.

'What kind of thing is it exactly that you're looking at?'

She took a deep breath and told him.

After a while, inevitably, they began to talk about more personal things. He'd been living with someone for the past year but that had kind of petered out a while back. Now he was on his own again, alone in the night once more.

They made a date to eat at Quaglino's the following Friday, at eight. She would have the data by then. This was to be a purely social meeting.

'There is one other thing, though,' said Calvin when they'd made their arrangements.

'What's that?'

'Talking to you, just hearing your voice, gives me the

most incredible hard-on. And not just because of some of those stories you were telling me.'

Jarvis felt like she'd just dropped out of a window fifteen floors up. Her arms and legs suddenly seemed very prickly.

'Is that right?' she said, hoping he would mistake her breathlessness for something else.

'Sure. I mean, I just keep going back over that afternoon in the Catskills, you know, when we went to that restaurant and then back to our room at the hotel.'

'Sure,' she said. 'I remember that. I was wearing a long burgundy dress, wasn't I?'

'I keep thinking about you bending over the bed, you know, and me pulling your dress up. I wish I could lick you, down there, you know.'

'Yes I know. I know what you mean.' Oh Christ, she thought. She could feel herself beginning to lose control as waves of memory swept over her.

'Would you like that? Would you like me licking you down there?'

'Yes, sure. Tell me what you'd like to do.'

'I'd like to kneel down behind you and lick your pussy. Lick your ass, too, all over. What are you wearing now? In bed, I mean. Are you naked?'

'A silk nightdress,' she replied quickly. 'A long silk nightdress, with lace panels. Oyster, with coffee-coloured lace.' Actually, she was wearing a white cotton T-shirt and matching panties, but she didn't want to spoil his fun. Besides, she was rather enjoying this.

'Why don't you put your hand inside your nightdress?' he suggested. She had been doodling on the pad by the telephone, but now she stopped and listened to what he said.

'Yes,' she said. 'That feels nice. What are you doing?'

'I'm holding my cock. Jesus, it feels big, you know, hard and stiff.'

'I know. Your cock's really big, Calvin. So big I can hardly get it up me.'

'Think of the Catskills, Bonny. Think that I'm kneeling down behind you with this incredible hard-on and licking you out. God, I can really smell your pussy. It smells good, your pussy. Does my cock smell good to you?'

'A nice clean cock always smells good.'

'Now I want you to pull your nightdress up, all the way. Can you feel the silk sliding over your thighs? Do you dare guess what I'm going to do?'

No, she thought, but I've an idea you're going to tell me.

'When I've finished licking your cunt I'm going to make you rub your nightdress all over my cock. And then I want you to suck me, while you're rubbing that creamy silk against me – against my balls, against my backside. And I want my cock right deep down in your throat. You still like doing that, don't you? I know you can do it right, Bonny. You're the type who likes a cock deep down in the back of your throat, aren't you?'

'Sure I am,' she said. 'A nice big one. With lots of come for me to suck.'

'How's your pussy feel, Bonny?'

'Hot and juicy. I like the way you talk. I always did.'

'I'm glad you called me. It's good to talk, isn't it? So we know what we want.'

'Sure it is. But I wish you were here, Calvin, with your big thick cock right next to me. What do you want me to do now?'

'I want you to bend over, like you did over the bed that time. Then I want to shove it right up you, really hard. Can you feel me moving inside you?'

'Yes, I can. You really know what you're doing, Calvin. Are you holding your cock right now?'

'Damn right I am. But I'm imagining it's in your pussy, and it's moving in and out, in and out. That's how it goes, isn't it? In and out, in and out.'

'Yes – in and out, up and down, in and out.'

'You can feel the rhythm, now, can't you, Bonny? You can feel my big dick right up you. And I can see your bare ass, 'cause you aren't wearing pants any more, are you? And I can smell cunt, I can smell you – sexy and sweet, and nice to lick.'

She always found it a turn-on to taste her own juices, with or without a lover. Her fingers were expertly busy between her legs.

'I'm licking it now, while you talk to me,' she breathed. 'Tasting it, every little drop. Mmm, my fingers are all sticky.'

'I bet they are. I wish I was licking them too. And I'm thrusting into you all the time, really hard now, and there's your ass, and I'm going to slap it for you, even while I'm fucking you. You like that, don't you?'

'Yes – slap my bum. Slap me hard. But keep fucking me. Don't stop. Keep your cock up me.'

'God, yes, I'm so big, I just wish I could see you, see my cock going in and out of you from behind, right up there now. Christ, it's so wet, and there's your ass there and—'

'And what?'

'And now I'm up your ass.'

'Oh God, yes. Fuck my ass, Cal. But be gentle with me.'

'Easy now, oh, that's tight. That's just so tight, Bonny. I'm squeezing my cock now, just like it's up your ass. Just a little push now, I don't want to hurt you. Just a push, and another push, and—'

'Oh, do it to me, Cal. Just fuck my ass, nice and gentle. Oh, God, I can really feel you all the way into me now, so big, so strong . . .'

She heard grunts and gasps as Calvin came and then there was nothing, only a brief silence over which she could hear the static on the line.

'Was that good?' she said softly after a few moments.

'Really good. You give good phone sex, Bonny. But it's better still face to face.'

'Maybe we can fix something for Friday.'

'I think we should.'

'I look forward to it.'

They spoke for a little while longer, inconsequentially. She felt warm and drowsy, satisfied for the first time in a long time. When he rang off she got her vibro out and gently pleasured herself with it until she fell asleep.

THIRTY-SEVEN

Quaglino's was one of Jarvis's favourite restaurants in DC. It was quiet, it was discreet and the food was sensational. Old-fashioned and highly traditional, it was a favourite haunt of journalists and lobbyists. People from the Bureau never went there. Herbie's Pizza was about their limit.

In deference to the correct way of doing things, Jarvis wore a simple dress of cream linen with matching jacket and a row of red beads that went perfectly with her lipstick. She and Cal were tucked away by themselves in a small alcove or booth, one of a line that filled either side of the basement room.

She looked up, past the slowly rotating fan blades. Through an area window, they could see hurrying footsteps above them but of their fellow-diners, there was no sign. Though other people were eating barely a few feet away, all they were aware of was the discreet hum of conversation and the occasional clink of glasses. Securing a table here was never easy, even a week in advance – Cal must have moved mountains to get a booking at such short notice.

He was wearing a tweed jacket with a blue open-necked shirt. His hair had thinned slightly since she'd last seen him and he now wore rimless glasses.

They sipped wine, a Montrachet. He had always been

218

good with a wine list. She took his advice on the menu too. She felt safe in his hands.

The starter was a salmon mousse. 'How is it?' asked Cal.

'Delicious,' replied Jarvis between mouthfuls. 'I've never tasted nicer.'

They ate in pleasurable silence for a while, then Cal put his fork down.

He took an envelope out of his pocket, passed it across the table to her. She could see the outline of a computer disk.

'What did you find?' she said. It had been a week-long build-up to this moment and she felt nervous.

'It's all on there,' he said, nodding at the disk.

'Just tell me.'

'It's not as simple as that.'

'Just try. I'm not so dumb.'

'How's your astrophysics?'

'What's astrophysics got to do with it? I thought we were dealing with statistics here, the laws of probability.'

He smiled, cracked his fingers. He always did that when he was about to translate something for the benefit of the hard thinking. Jarvis didn't like being labelled a dummy but realised she had little choice.

'Initially I thought that's all we were doing. By the way, your co-ordinates were all wrong. You could never have extracted anything from this data the way you'd presented it.'

She winced. But she knew he wasn't trying to score points.

'So once I'd done a little rearranging,' he went on, 'I ran it through my systems.'

'And what did you find?'

Her heart was beating fast now. She took another sip of wine.

'Sunspots. Not only were you looking the wrong way, but you weren't even anywhere near the right place.'

'What do sunspots have to do with people suddenly going sex-crazy?'

'Maybe nothing directly. But what I found was that, in almost every case, these changes in personality or whatever you want to call them were preceded by enhanced solar activity. It happened too often to be anything other than a meaningful coincidence.'

'You mean the sun starts flaring up and instantly people start taking their clothes off?'

'No.'

'Well, what do you mean?'

'There were no other corresponding factors that we could analyse satisfactorily so it just had to be sunspots. But that doesn't mean it has to be sunspots in themselves.'

'Explain.'

'Like I said, how's your astrophysics?'

'Entry level. But try me all the same.'

He talked to her most of the way through the main course, pheasant on a bed of wild mushrooms with a green salad. She didn't understand more than about one tenth of one per cent of a lot of it.

'So what you're saying is,' she began as the waiter came to clear away their plates, 'that this increased sunspot activity may trigger other events in the solar system which may in turn affect the way people act on Earth.'

'That's it,' he said. 'But we don't know what the key event might be. Sunspots affect the weather, they cause meteor showers, they even influence the performance of magnetic instruments. It could be any one of a hundred things. All I'm saying is that, if you look back through your records, over a forty-year period each period of increased sexual activity has been preceded by these changes in the sun's behaviour.'

'And that's provable?'

He tapped the disc again.

'It's all on there. You could even predict when people's behaviour is going to change.'

'How?'

'Because there's a pattern there. The scenario repeats itself quite regularly. It's all in the mathematics.'

'Everything is numbers, is that what you're saying?'

'Deep down, about ten layers deep, that's right. Study the numbers and you get the answers.'

'So when is this likely to happen again, this repeated scenario, all these people suddenly starting to fall into bed together?'

'Any time now. Our telescopes have been monitoring increased sunspot activity for the past week. You should see the results of that pretty quickly. I think maybe you should tip off the condom people.'

He laughed quietly. Jarvis looked at him as he spoke with the waiter who came to take their order for dessert. How uncannily like Hannah he is, she found herself thinking – and not for the first time. The same kind of eyes, a similar sort of hair, similar facial features even. Cal's features, though, were more elegantly balanced – Hannah's face had an appealing lop-sidedness, the two halves almost but not quite matching, as though two portraits of the same man by different artists had been spliced together.

Cal ordered lemon sorbets for them both, and coffee, and a fine old French brandy. It was with no great surprise, at this point, that she felt his ankle against hers. At first it seemed accidental, but then it happened again. And again. So what, she found herself thinking. I like him. He is very good-looking. I am a woman who knows her own mind.

She was somewhat surprised when he offered her a cigarette. She'd forgotten he smoked. 'Not for me,' she said. 'But go ahead. I kind of like the smell of fresh tobacco smoke.'

He took out a big old Zippo. Impulsively she took it

from him, flipped the wheel over and held it out for him. His hand brushed hers as he inhaled. They looked at each other, a questioning glance. The glow was there, all right. The go-ahead.

They had more coffee, another cognac. And then she felt his hand under the table, on her knee, moving up her thigh.

She looked at him. 'Ought we to be doing this? Here?'

'I think we should,' he replied with effortless charm.

She sipped her brandy. Now his hand was under the hem of her dress, feeling the soft flesh of her legs, gliding slowly and smoothly back and forth but moving inexorably towards the sensitive skin of her upper thighs.

'It's a bit public, don't you think?' she murmured, fear of discovery rising in her conscience.

'All the more exciting for us,' said Cal. 'Besides, the waiter won't be back until we're ready to leave.'

He certainly has magic fingers, Jarvis thought to herself. She sensed her breasts swelling and the nipples hardening with desire. She wanted to go to the restroom, but she didn't feel she could break off.

His hand was at the top of her thighs, brushing against her pants. Half of her wanted him to stop, the other half to go on. The urge to pee was becoming stronger with her growing arousal. His fingers caressed her sex gently through the cream silk, catching and stroking a stray wisp of pubic hair, outlining the unseen shape of her lips. She was aware of a growing dampness in her crotch.

She moved slightly on her chair and allowed his finger to enter her vagina. She couldn't, at this stage, look at him directly. He was talking about the Jupiter probe, or at least she thought he was talking about Jupiter. She saw his other hand resting on the table cloth, the cigarette smoke curling upwards. She didn't know why she always felt so guilty at times like this. She wasn't in a relationship and neither was he, and she didn't feel she was being unfaithful in any way. Both of them were above the age of consent and they had their freedom, after all, even if old George Washington might have frowned at two of the country's salaried employees getting fresh with each other while, a couple of booths down, the chief financial columnist of the *Washington Post* was talking futures with an executive of General Motors. But it was getting late now, and there were few other diners in the basement room.

He had three fingers in her vagina now, and she felt full and stretched. The pressure against her bladder was becoming almost unbearable. And yet despite herself she parted her legs more to accommodate him, leaned backwards in the chair, thrusting out her pelvis. *I just hope I don't wet myself*, she thought.

She was surprised when he suddenly crushed out his cigarette and withdrew his fingers. He held them up to his face, wet and glistening with her secretions, inhaling deeply and appreciatively. He licked the tip of his index finger, the one that had been doing all the work on her clitoris. Then he offered the finger to her. She licked it too, tentatively at first and then drawing it deeper into her mouth, holding his palm as she did so. It tasted salty and musky, a bit like the anchovies with which her pheasant had been stuffed. They stopped the flesh drying out while it was cooking, Cal had explained.

The General Motors man and the columnist got up and left their table, joking with one another. Now Cal and Jarvis were alone in their booth on that side of the room. Jarvis felt a recklessness beginning to sweep over her.

He stood up and drew her to him. But instead of the anticipated kiss he turned her round, pushing her face forwards onto the table. Solidly built from fifty-year-old New England oak, it scarcely trembled. He drew her dress up around her hips and his hands caressed the silken globes of her buttocks. There was a pause, a hesitancy – was someone coming? she wondered with a stab of alarm.

'It's OK,' he said. 'I can see where everyone is. And I asked the waiter not to disturb us for a few minutes.'

And then he was inside her, pushing and thrusting, forcing her down until her breasts were crushed flat against the tablecloth. His penis felt big within her sheath but she knew that she was not yet fully aroused, that her vagina was still tight and tense. She caught a whiff of Cal's expensive cologne, subtle and unobtrusive, and saw smoke rising from his crushed cigarette as it lay in the ashtray.

Her own passion smouldered and caught fire. She felt no guilt about what she was doing. It was that smell of cologne that triggered her subconscious lusts, and she thought of Cal's own distinctive body aroma, clean and fresh, and of Cal himself, his muscles and his mind, and what they had meant to each other in the past. And now it was Cal who was inside her, Cal's balls brushing against the backs of her thighs, Cal's hips pressed against her backside. She closed her eyes and in a moment she was miles away, back in their hotel room in the Catskills, in a forest, giving him oral sex in the bathtub, in his car, in his bed. All the dozens of fragmented memories went spinning round in her mind like a carousel and she came, quietly but powerfully, a woman in control of her body and her mind, and she felt Cal's cock pulsing its pleasure deep inside her.

As discreetly as she could, she found the ladies' washroom and locked herself inside with feelings of considerable relief. When she got back to their table, it had been cleared of all the remains of their meal, and Cal was acting as though nothing at all untoward could possibly have happened. You're a cool one, she found herself thinking, as he asked her if she had ever been to Mexico City.

THIRTY-EIGHT

They were sitting down in the Dead Files department again.

'I tell you, this stuff is for real,' Jarvis was saying.

'I believe you,' said Hannah. He wasn't in any mood to argue. He'd got back from Alaska the night before and hadn't had much sleep.

Clemency had seen to that.

'The thing is, what are we going to do about it?'

'Go to Stone. Tell him everything.'

'Stone will nix it. If he doesn't, Pepper will.'

'Maybe you should make a hobby out of it, like quilt-making. Do it in the evenings, or on the weekends.'

'Don't joke with me. This is important.'

'We're supposed to be in Philadelphia next week, remember? The course? Pepper's big teamwork project, they send us there two at a time. Challis and Robennack were there on the course last week, they said they had a great time.'

'I don't think we should go to Philadelphia. I think we should go to Texas.'

Hannah stared at her, aghast.

'Are you kidding? They'll fry us for sure.'

Jarvis pulled a thick printout from her briefcase and passed it across to him. Hannah studied it intently.

'This is telling us what's going to happen, right?'

225

'This tells us what happens and what will happen. The rate of probability is close to one hundred per cent.'

'That's a hell of a lot of probability.'

'I know. So what do you think now?'

'I think we should go to Texas. Philadelphia's too crowded at this time of year.'

'And how do we square things with Stone?'

'We'll cross that bridge when we come to it.'

For the first time in a long time, Jarvis felt uncommonly close to Hannah. She no longer thought about what she'd seen in the car.

THIRTY-NINE

HIGH PLAINS, TEXAS. JULY 15TH. 10.06 AM.

Both of them knew the risks they were taking. If Stone found out where they really were, they would be in deep shit. But there was something about the way they'd been pulled from the Sleep case that aroused both their suspicions. Even though they knew this was no longer anything to do with the reclusive billionaire, they were still afraid of rattling skeletons in closets. Especially Pepper's.

But they pushed on, nevertheless, deeper into the twilight zone which they had been expressly forbidden to enter. Right now they were in the interview room of the sheriff's department of some cow town in East Texas. They were there to observe and not to intervene in any way. Hannah and Jarvis, of course, weren't officially there at all. They were supposed to be in Philadelphia. Hell only knew what would happen if Stone or someone else at the Bureau tried to contact them.

The first results Jarvis pulled in were just extraordinary. It was as if she had written the script herself. Well away from Stone's ever-vigilant ears, a covert on-line dialogue with police departments in several areas that were prone to unexplained activity patterns had trawled up a good half-dozen interesting scenarios within a matter of hours of the enhanced sunspot activity that Cal Caughey had predicted.

In the interview room with them was a tough cop named O'Brien and a ratty-looking guy by the name of Willie Odum. O'Brien had booted up his record for them – the usual kind of form that a drifter might have had, convictions for petty theft, vagrancy and public disorder, an arraignment for importuning, possession of narcotics. He had served time.

'You want to tell us again what happened?' said O'Brien. It was an order, not a question.

'Like I said before,' Willie Odum began in his Texas drawl, 'I was just having a party.'

'By yourself?'

'You can't party by yourself, officer. Don't you know that?'

'The fact that we found a rubber woman in your trailer, Willie, suggests that *you* can. So who was with you?'

'A couple of girls I knew.'

'You know their names?'

'One was called Felice and the other was Roxanna.'

'And do you know how old those girls are?'

'I reckoned they was about twenty.'

'Felice is sixteen and Roxanna is seventeen. You were aware of that?'

'Course I wasn't. You don't go around asking people how old they are, unless you're a cop. I don't know how old you are, officer.'

'So you weren't aware of their age.'

'No, I wasn't.'

'Do you know the age of consent in this state?'

'I do now, since yesterday when you told me.'

'Were you aware that what you were doing with those girls in that trailer constitutes an illegal act?'

'That's what you're charging me with, officer. Any sign of that lawyer of mine yet?'

'All in good time. You just answer my questions now so these officers can hear what you have to say.' He indicated Jarvis and Hannah with a sweep of his hand.

'Them girls weren't resisting any. They took their own clothes off.'

'Did you suggest it to them?'

'No. It just kind of happened. Like I knew it would.'

'How did you know that?'

''Cause I showed them my magic rocks. They always work.'

'You got magic rocks that make sixteen-year-old girls take their clothes off? You trying to be funny, Willie? You crack me up, you know that?'

'All the same, that's what happened.'

'You expect me to believe in these rocks?' O'Brien glanced at Hannah and Jarvis.

'I sure do.'

'Where d'you get them, then? Mars or somewhere?'

'They just fall down in the night. I heard 'em pattering on the roof of the trailer. I seen 'em in the desert too.'

O'Brien turned to Hannah and Jarvis again, raising his eyebrows as if to say this was a hoot, sure enough. The guy he was interviewing was plainly out to lunch.

Willie Odum rummaged in his pocket, brought out a pile of dirty tissues and some pocket change. They'd taken his works off him and he was getting pretty desperate for a fix.

'Here's one,' he said, and tossed it on the table.

Hannah reached forward and picked it up. It didn't seem anything special, just a dull green pebble, kind of globby looking, like melted glass. He passed it to Jarvis.

'They make people horny,' said Willie Odum with his lopsided, snaggle-tooth grin. You'd need to be pretty horny, Hannah thought, to want to hop in the sack with someone like Willie Odum. He'd been a good-looking boy once, maybe, but now he looked kind of seedy. You could tell he was an addict the minute you looked at him.

229

'So you're saying these rocks had an effect on the girls, is that right?' asked O'Brien, regaining the initiative.

'That's what I said. It wears off after a while. Then the rocks don't work no more. Like dope, you know.'

'You expect a jury to swallow that?'

'That's the God's honest truth.'

'Since when have you told the truth, Willie? You wouldn't know the truth if it bit you in the butt.'

A deputy came in and took Willie Odum back to the tank. O'Brien turned to face the agents from Washington. His face was large and he was sweating. It was a good ten degrees warmer in Texas than it was in DC.

'Guy's as nutty as a five-buck fruitcake,' he said to them, a big grin on his face.

Hannah and Jarvis exchanged yet more significant glances.

'How did you pull him in?' asked Hannah.

'There was a disturbance reported. One of the girls' fathers had found out where his daughter was. He broke down the door of the trailer and there was Felice and Roxanna in their underwear and Willie Odum buck naked. He damn near killed the guy. One of the neighbours in the trailer park called the cops.'

'Did anything illegal actually happen?' asked Jarvis. 'Did Odum demonstrably have intercourse with the girls?'

'That's what we're waiting for the lab to establish. There was reefers around and those girls were pretty well out of it. Anything could have happened.'

'What do you think happened?'

'I think he met them someplace, got them high and then took them back to his trailer. Kids that age, they think they're grown up but they're pretty suggestible even with a guy like Odum.'

'You think it was the drugs made them act like that?'

'What else could it be? It sure as hell weren't friend Willie's personal charms. Or his magic rocks either, for that matter. That's the durndest story I ever heard and I been a cop for fifteen years.'

'Mind if we take this rock away with us, all the same?' asked Jarvis, rolling it around her hand.

'Kind of a souvenir, huh? Fine by me, but I guess you shouldn't. Odum's lawyer will suggest we removed evidence for the defence, or something like that.'

'I guess you're right,' said Jarvis. 'We'll call you.'

There was a prowl car outside Odum's trailer home and there were too many neighbours poking about for Hannah and Jarvis to feel much like rooting around the place. They drove by in their rented Ford Taurus, turned and came back and decided to give it a miss. They went for drive-thru cheeseburgers and shakes instead, drove down the road a ways and parked in the shade of a clump of trees to eat them.

'What do you reckon?' asked Hannah, chewing with his mouth open as usual, which was calculated to annoy Jarvis.

'About what?'

'About the rocks.'

'I don't know.'

'It sounds crazy to me.'

'I know. It does to me too. And yet I can't help thinking there might be something to it.'

'Such as what?'

'There is a pattern there. We get increased sunspot activity and all kinds of things happen. But on different levels.'

'I know. You told me all about it on the flight. But what about the way people act?'

'Maybe something is happening that makes them act that way. If only we could find a common factor. Maybe find someone else who says the same thing. Someone else who knows about these rocks. Maybe they are affecting people but no one knows it.'

'These rocks fall to earth as a result of solar winds or something and they make people go crazy? Is that what you're saying, Jarvis?'

'I don't know.'

'That's what Willie Odum is saying, though, isn't it?'

'But he's a bum. And an addict. How do we know he wasn't out of his head at the time?'

'The guy's a few cards short of a full deck, that's for sure. Imagine what Stone would say if you brought Willie boy out as your prime witness.' Hannah laughed, crushed his empty shake carton in his fist.

'And yet, why would he make up something so patently crazy? He mustn't have thought for a moment that O'Brien would believe him.'

'We only have his word for it.'

'There ought to be a correlation. But no one else is saying anything about it, that's the maddening part. Or has said, for that matter. We've looked at hundreds of these cases and this is the first time anyone's mentioned magic rocks.'

'You think that's significant?'

'I just have this hunch that there's something there. I mean, we know these things have an energy all of their own – quartz crystals is the classic example. I just wish we could establish a link.'

'Surely you'd have found that when you were trying to analyse the data we got last time?'

'Yes, but we didn't know what we were looking for,' Jarvis sighed.

'So what's your scenario?'

'I don't have one, at least nothing plausible. I just figure we ought to try and get hold of some of these rocks, all the same. See if we can have them analysed.'

'The only sample we know of is held as police evidence. There may be others scattered around Odum's trailer, but the place is crawling with cops. Where are we going to find some more, without arousing suspicion?'

Jarvis looked around her. Texas stretched off in all directions, bleak and parched. It would be like looking for a needle in a haystack.

They filled up with gas at a little Mobil station miles from anywhere. The place looked like it hadn't changed much since James Dean was hot.

It was like a house turned into a gas station. There were curtains in the upstairs windows that flapped in the afternoon breeze. They didn't have any self-service pumps and there was no one in the battered tarpaper-covered repair shop when Hannah went to look.

He sounded the horn but nothing moved. He opened the door to the office and shouted. He could see the cash register. He could have had that drawer open in seconds and been down the road a mile before anyone realised.

He went back to the car, leaned in the open window. 'Guess there's no one around,' he said laconically. 'Maybe we should just drive on.'

A noise made him turn round. A guy was standing in the office doorway, tucking his shirt into his pants.

'You want something?'

'We want some gas.'

'Sure. That's what we're here for. Sorry, I was kind of busy, didn't hear your car.'

As the guy worked the pump he whistled to himself, as though he was mighty pleased about something. Jarvis glanced at the house and caught a glimpse of a woman's face at the window, and a naked body. Then she was gone.

'You two not from around here, then?' the guy asked.

'No, we're just passing through. Admiring the scenery.'

'We had a big meteor shower a couple of nights back, you see that?'

'No, we didn't.'

'Durndest thing I ever seen. Like sparks flying through the skies.'

233

'Really?'

'Sure thing. I was out watching it. I reckon something must have hit over there.'

He pointed in the direction of a prominent butte that stood out against the skyline.

'I could see this flash and then a big glow in the sky for maybe four, five seconds.'

'Must have been spectacular. You take Amex?'

'I'd prefer cash if you got it, buddy. But I'll give you a receipt.'

Jarvis was poring over the map. 'It must have been around here,' she said, stabbing with her finger at the contour lines.

They could see the butte, maybe ten miles distant. There was a country road leading right past it, out into the desert. There was nothing else for another fifty miles, across the Pecos River and clean on into New Mexico.

It sure as hell looked different from Philadelphia.

'What are you saying?' asked Hannah as the car bumped along the rough dirt road. 'We're going to get out there and find this place littered with green rocks glowing with lust?'

'I don't know what we're going to find,' said Jarvis. 'That's why we're going there. And keep your eyes on the road, please.'

Her skirt had ridden up over her thighs. She was getting more and more of these signs from Hannah. Ever since she'd caught sight of him in the car parked in that suburban avenue, she had realised he was worse than an animal.

The terrain around them was bleak and inhospitable and yet it had an undeniable beauty. It was a landscape familiar from a hundred movies and Jarvis half-expected to see a man appear out of nowhere at the side of the road, waving a gun. She felt her own life was like something out of a movie right now, as they moved deeper and deeper into this forbidden zone – she and Hannah were supposed to be in Philadelphia. Why were they doing this, risking their necks in more senses than one to drive out into this Godforsaken country, with only telephone wires and a few scrawny-looking buzzards for company?

'I reckon here's as good a place as any,' said Hannah.

Jarvis couldn't see that this particular stretch was any better or worse than any other piece of land they'd driven through. It was just boulders and scrub and parched, crumbly soil under a brilliant sun.

It was hot, too – the hottest day of the year so far. She noticed it as soon as she got out of the car, wished she had a hat or something. She took off her jacket, tossed it on the back seat of the rented Ford.

'What do you think we should do?' she asked.

'Start looking,' said Hannah, and he set off in a westerly direction.

She walked across those barren, baking lands for upwards of an hour. Her neck ached from keeping her eyes fixed to the ground. Every now and then she would look around her to keep her bearings, to see the car parked up on the side of the butte, windshield glistening in the noon sun. She could see Hannah in the distance, dust trailing behind him.

She was trying to pace out the land, a hundred steps this way, a hundred steps that. Her shoes would be ruined – she should have had hiking boots with her for this kind of work.

She saw all kinds of things out there in the semi-desert, pebbles and ring-pulls and fragments of old bottles, soft drink cans and candy wrappers, and every now and then the bones of some bird or animal, picked clean by the wind and by scavengers, and she realised that no part of this country could ever be so truly remote that people didn't come along and litter it up with their trash.

But she didn't find any little green rocks, no matter how hard she looked.

She sat down on a boulder that was shaped like a cow lying down, felt the heat on her forehead. Ahead of her she could see maybe forty or fifty miles in the clear noontime light and there was no human being to be seen, nor the sign of any habitation.

She was hot, thirsty and hungry. She took a bottle of aerated water from her bag and sipped. The water was warm and unpleasant. She wondered what it would be like to be alone out here.

Maybe it had all been a terrible mistake, after all. Maybe they should pack it in, turn in their rented car, catch a flight and turn up for their teamwork course in Philadelphia, dirty and a little late but there all the same. She wondered just how long they would have before Stone realised they weren't where they should have been. It made her nervous.

Something made her look up. She could see Hannah maybe half a mile away, off to the north. She stood up and waved. He waved back.

Up in the sky she could see the contrails of at least three airplanes. At any minute she expected a helicopter to come skimming out from behind the butte, Stone sitting in the passenger seat, looking for her, the finger of accusation pointing, his lips already working. She didn't want to be here. She felt insecure and threatened.

She had to talk to Hannah. Either she could persuade him to go back or he would persuade her to stay. She needed some direction. The hunch that there was something in an addict's story wasn't strong enough any longer.

She got to her feet, could feel the stiffness in her neck. She struck off in a new direction, a hundred paces south, a hundred paces west. Methodically scanning the dust. She knew there wouldn't be any marks on the land

236

like a crater or anything that would give her a sign of what she was looking for.

She tried to focus her mind on what she was doing, but all kinds of random ideas kept running through her head. She thought of Cal Caughey and the crazy things they'd done in that restaurant. Sure, she'd loved every second of it but there was the fear thing too, the feeling of how much she was risking by doing such a thing.

Jarvis didn't take risks, or at least she didn't used to. Everything was plotted and co-ordinated in an attempt to reduce the element of chance to a minimum. That was what made her such a good operator, as Stone and the others had several times told her. And that was also what was messing her up right now.

She heard a cry, very faint, and looked up. For a moment she couldn't see Hannah and then she caught a glimpse of him away over in the opposite direction to where she'd last seen him moving.

He was standing on a boulder or something and frantically waving his jacket in the air. His words came drifting over the undulating scrubland like they were coming from the far side of the moon.

'Over here, over here.' She could just make out what he was saying but his gestures were enough. She broke into a stumbling run, cursing her flat loafers, trying to keep one eye on where she was going and the other on the tangled roots that lay draped over the parched earth like spilled knitting.

He was standing on the edge of a narrow gully, a watercourse of some kind. He had that smug, patronising expression on his face that she hated so much.

'I told you, you were looking in the wrong place,' he said. Someone else had said that to her recently.

'You didn't say anything of the kind,' she reminded him smartly. She had a scratch on her calf from a thorn bush and her throat was caked in dust. She wasn't in any mood for Hannah trying to get one over on her.

'Didn't I? Well, never mind. Just take a look at this.'

He pointed into the gully. She followed his finger. There was a thin scatter of the little green rocks, most of them no bigger than a pea, some a lot bigger, the size of an orange or an apple.

'Incredible,' she said. Her heart raced and she felt a warm glow swell up in her heart.

'Goddamn amazing.'

'I was trying to calculate the chances of us finding something like this. It must have been tens of thousands to one.'

'These are them, right?' said Hannah, scrambling down the sides of the gully. He didn't bother to offer her a hand. She nearly slipped in the loose dirt as she followed him.

They knelt down, looked at what they found.

'You feel any different?' asked Hannah.

'How do you mean?'

'You feel kind of raunchy or anything? That's the effect Willie Odum said these rocks had on his teen angels.'

'You're sick, Hannah.' And yet she had to admit there was something, nothing to do with these dull green pebbles but more a kind of frisson of fear to go with her elation, a sense that she had taken a step further into the unknown.

'What do you think we should do now?' Neither of them had touched any of the rocks. They had too much professional respect for the laws of evidence.

'Maybe we get a proper team in—'

'How are we going to swing that? This isn't an official investigation.'

Hannah looked stumped. 'The thing is,' he began, 'this gully is a watercourse. You get a flash flood and these rocks will just go. We can't risk leaving them here. Maybe we should just take a couple for now, then come back later.'

'Having done what?'

'Had some analysis done on them. I don't know.'

'How do you do that? You can't just go into a pharmacy and buy a test kit. You need a fully equipped laboratory.' She knew, as well as he did, that both of them had felt that the possibilities of their actually finding anything out here in the scrub were so remote that neither had considered what they should do if they did come up trumps.

'I have a friend who works for NASA,' Jarvis said after a few moments' thought. 'I think he could help. Maybe if we could get some samples to him, we might be able to do something.'

She reached down into the dust, picked up a single green pebble. It felt surprisingly light, like it was made out of plastic or something. They ended up scooping up a dozen or more of them. She put some of them in her bag and Hannah slipped the others inside a Hershey bar wrapper he found in his pocket.

'What if they're radioactive or something?' he said.

'Then we get cancer and die. You're probably going to get cancer anyway, Hannah, the way you live and the way your stress levels must be operating. I shouldn't worry about it.'

They went back to the car. The sun was hotter than hell.

FORTY

When Jarvis awoke it was three in the morning. She struggled for a while with the heavy waves that kept crashing over her head and then sat bolt upright in bed.

Almost everything of any significance seemed to happen to her at night, these days. It was as if her dreams were trying to send her a message from her subconscious. She felt feverish, as if she were coming down with something. The bedclothes tangled and her mind was racing.

She touched her skin. It felt overly sensitive, like there was something burning her up inside. And her dreams. She couldn't tell, at first, whether she had been awake or not, what was real and what wasn't. She had those dreams increasingly often these days, hyper-real, more like a visualisation than an imagining of the subconscious. Where was she? Where had she been? Why did she feel such an urgency?

She was aware of this all-embracing desire, this dream-world yearning that left her flushed and short of breath, sitting up in bed in the soft glow of the bedside light. She felt like she was someone else, and it wasn't just the strangeness of the room.

She shook her head and it cleared a little more, enough for her to begin to get her bearings, to quell

240

those insistent but irrational fears that sometimes stole up on her like this in the small hours. She switched off the light, got back under the covers again, rolled over onto her side. She'd been dreaming, just dreaming, she told herself, and yet it had all been so real, like a hallucination.

She was aware of the fact that Hannah was sleeping a few doors down, of the distant hum of traffic on the highway and of her clothes folded neatly on the chair by the foot of the bed. Everything was normal, everything was OK, she told herself, but the ache and the longing was still there like an energy source. She could feel herself drifting back into the drowsy warmth of her cocoon once more.

She felt reassured. She knew who she was, where she was, that she was in a room somewhere, that everything would be fine. She opened her eyes wider. She felt serene and yet the desire was with her still. She got out of bed, went to the window. Outside it was just starting to get light. She could see the highway, stretching from one horizon to the other, beckoning her.

Something was drawing her outside, though she didn't know what it was. She dressed quickly, brushed her hair, aware still of the palpitations in her heart, the feeling of being driven by something beyond herself.

Outside, the night air was clean and dry and cold. The stars up there were big and bright, just like it said in the song. She knew what she had to do. There was a plot to this dream, rich in metaphor.

She took in every detail of the motel, with its lobby with the big palm plants in pots and the universal beige carpeting. She drifted by in the chill morning air, looking for the night man, but the lobby was deserted. There was a truck stop just past the motel, with a dozen or more big rigs pulled up outside even at that ungodly hour of the morning. Jarvis felt like she was watching

241

herself in a movie, walking on the grass verge along the side of the road, over the smooth concrete of the lot, becoming aware of the smell of diesel.

She floated up and down the lines of trucks. There were flatbeds, tankers, box trailers. The tyres seemed huge. Chrome fenders and exhaust stacks glistened in the darkness.

A match flared, incredibly bright. She caught a glimpse of a man's face, dark hair and a plaid shirt. He looked up and their eyes met.

'Hi,' she said.

'Hi,' he replied.

Could he feel the animal heat coming off her in waves? She felt pretty sure that he could.

Cigarette smoke drifted across the parking lot, pungent in her nostrils. It smelled fresh, exciting even. She realised how much she liked the smell of fresh tobacco smoke.

Now that the moment had come, she didn't know what to say. Her head felt light and yet she was extraordinarily aware of everything that was happening to her.

The trucker was young, younger than her, certainly, with dark eyes in an almond face.

'You looking to hitch a ride or something?'

Jarvis didn't look like she was on the road. At four o'clock on a July morning she was wearing black trousers and a sweatshirt, had nothing with her by way of baggage. Her look didn't say young hitchhiker or student. It said woman in her late twenties, tall and extremely attractive and interested in only one thing.

She smiled at him. She wasn't in control of herself. She couldn't help what she was doing. And yet she wanted to, all the same.

Then she laughed, tossed back her hair. 'What's your name?' she asked.

'Lester,' he replied, kind of slow and open.

'Lester, huh?'

'Lester. What's yours?'

'I'm Ginny,' she said, quick as a flash. Lights came on in her head. Ginny, Ginny. When she was a kid, six or seven, she'd wanted to be called Ginny. She used to play games with her friends where she was always called Ginny. She'd forgotten that.

'Hi, Ginny.'

'Hi, Lester.'

There was a pause. Neither of them said anything. They just looked at each other. He seemed sure and confident, she thought. She wondered if it would have been different if she had been a man, apprehending him out there in the parking lot as dawn broke in the east. He might have been a heck of a sight safer, she reflected. She could have snapped his neck with one well-rehearsed move and he wouldn't have known a thing.

And he was so good-looking too, she thought as she took a step or two forward, right into his personal space. Instantly, the two of them were on a whole new footing. She took hold of his cigarette, drew on it and blew out smoke before handing it back to him.

'Just wanted to see what it tasted like,' she said simply. The nicotine was making her head spin.

He dropped the butt to the floor. 'That all you want?' he said, not looking up at first, but then raising his eyes very slowly till he was looking deep into her soul.

He took a step closer to her, put a finger on her breastbone. Then he drew his finger upwards, across her neck and under her chin so her head was tilted back. And all the time his eyes never left hers, even when his lips closed over her mouth and she clasped him to her with an urgency that surprised even herself.

Jarvis had never made out in the sleeper cab of a Kenworth before. Lester hastily smoothed out the bedding he had in there and then he helped her as she took

243

off her clothes. There wasn't any art to any of this but she didn't need any, she was carried along on waves of feeling such as she had never experienced before.

Even as he climbed on top of her she seemed to be on the brink of orgasm. He pushed inside her and she felt as if she were peeling herself open, raw and urgent and slick with desire. And the pleasure of it all, this feeling of abandonment that she felt, the letting go – it wasn't any kind of big cataclysmic deal for her, it was just that it all seemed so natural. Why should she feel bad or anxious or uncertain about what she was doing? At long last, her body seemed to be ruling her mind instead of the other way round.

The guy, too, was almost an irrelevance – Lester or Duke or whatever his name was, forgotten already, like so much superfluous and repetitive evidence that she could comfortably shed. All she was aware of was the wave of feeling that swept over her, the pulsing power of her own body and the tingling of her nerve ends. She felt free, lifted up and away from conscious thought. There was no specific detail in this love-making, no tongue seeking nipple, no hand on penis, no mouth upon mouth, chest upon chest. It was all there for her, of course, and yet not there. Everything was a part of something so much bigger, something that she rushed out to greet as others wanted to greet the millennium or the second coming, her arms metaphorically open wide and her legs wider still, as her truck-driver divine slammed into her body, his body slick with sweat and effort as she mauled his back and bit his shoulders and thrust her pelvis up to meet his thrusts. And then his semen was swelling up hot and urgent as though she could sense it a long way off, riding on the crest of her own shattering orgasm – an orgasm that wasn't an orgasm at all but a piercing entry into light and a new realm of being, beyond rational thought and analysis and muscle control and all the cloying instruments of consciousness from which, momentarily and majestically, she had finally managed to free herself.

She believed in the green rocks now. They were in her bag in the motel room. They worked for sure.

FORTY-ONE

As they sat at breakfast in the motel coffee shop, Hannah could hardly help but notice the abstracted behaviour of his partner. She seemed to be toying with her food, didn't really connect when he spoke to her. She was like this when she had something on her mind, but this was different somehow.

'What do you think we ought to do, then?' he said finally.

She was gazing out of the window. As far as Hannah could see, there was nothing out there that could possibly hold her attention – just a stretch of bare grass outside the motel, a highway and a truck stop. They could have been absolutely anywhere in the whole of the continental United States.

He repeated the question.

'Huh?' said Jarvis, and turned to face him.

'Have some coffee,' he suggested. 'It might wake you up a little. Then we can decide what we're going to do.'

'With what?'

'With the rocks.'

'Oh, sure, the rocks.'

'You said you had a friend at NASA, is that right?'

'That's right.'

'He can help get them analysed?'

'Not personally. That's not his department. But he'll

know someone who can. They did all the rocks they brought back from Mars.'

'And they'll do it off the record?'

'Strictly off the record. For now, at any rate. The Bureau doesn't need to know about this. Not yet, anyway.'

She seemed to be coming round, at last. As soon as he started talking about Bureau business, the mists seemed to clear. Hannah still felt he was in control, though.

'OK, then,' he said, trying to be brisk and positive. 'We send these samples off to your guy at NASA.'

'All of them?'

'What do you mean?'

'I mean, I have some in my bag and you have some in the car, right?'

'Signifying?'

'Isn't it better we keep them separate? In case anything goes wrong. Things do get lost in the mail, you know. Cheques and so forth.'

'OK, I got you. So we send a sample to your friend and hang on to the rest.'

'You think that's safe? What if Stone finds out where we are and what we have?'

'He's bound to find out sooner or later.'

'True enough. But let's try to keep him in the dark at least until we know what we're dealing with. Maybe we could rent a safe deposit box.'

'Smart thinking. Or I could mail mine to my girlfriend to keep hold of.'

'Let's do both. And then maybe we can try and locate some more samples.'

Hannah looked at her quizzically. 'You think there's something in this, right?'

'I don't know. I'd want my friend at NASA to run some checks first.'

'But what does this tell us about Sleep? That's why we're here in the first place.'

'I think Sleep's right out of the frame now.'

'Why do you say that?'

'Because it's obvious.'

'It's not obvious to me.' Hannah called the waitress over, ordered more coffee. This was clearly a three-cup conundrum.

'All that moral indignation, the public humiliations, that holier-than-thou stance, can't you see that's just a reaction?'

'A reaction to what?'

'To what's been going on at a deeper level.'

'So it's a part of a reaction, then. It's a chain.'

'OK, let's take it from the start. Maybe what we're saying is that these rocks somehow alter people's patterns of behaviour.'

He raised his hand, to try to bring up an objection. It came out a little too bluntly. 'You thought that was bullshit.'

'I never said that.'

'But I could tell that's what you thought, right after we saw Willie Odum.'

'Maybe I've reconsidered.'

'OK,' he said quickly. 'Look, I agree with you. We don't know for certain, but just suppose that's the case. That these rocks make people loosen up in a certain way so that they forget their inhibitions and start to go partying, you know what I mean.'

'This had better be good, Hannah.'

'And this is what's been happening all along, right back through all those newspaper records that Siz gave us. All those press reports and things, it's happened often enough to become a matter of public record.'

'Most of what we found is strictly off the record. Censored.'

'Sure, but you know what I mean. So all the while these people have been acting the way they do because they're under the influence of something we don't yet understand. Maybe it's some kind of magnetism, maybe the rocks set up a vibration just like quartz does, except that it's on a frequency that makes people start ripping their clothes off.'

'That sounds crazy, Hannah. But it just might be true.'

He looked at her in astonishment. 'That's what I've been thinking too, these last few days. And that's why Sleep comes into it.'

'How do you mean?'

'He's a part of the reaction to the rock behaviour, rather than a catalyst in his own right. He – or rather his organisation – has become aware of the phenomena, but without understanding it. They see the change in people and they think it's the devil at work, or something. They don't see that it's organic.'

'Why does he register it now and make such a big deal of it? I mean, this guy is building up a whole television empire on the back of it. If what Stone says is true, the next thing is he'll be building a political career as well.'

'Exactly. That's his whole strategy.'

'No one's done that before, in quite the same way.'

'So now he controls the flow of information.'

'Right. It's like Hearst all over again, the Citizen Kane thing, only it's working for Sleep because of the way he gets his information. Only now, with electronic news-gathering and the Web and helicopter news journalists and everything, have people like him started to put two and two together. Before, it's all been hushed up at a very local level, it's never really reached the big organi-sations, the movers and shakers. Until now. These people at the Salvation Channel know almost as much about what's happening as we do, Hannah. That's why we have to work so damn hard to keep one step ahead of them.'

They sat in silence for a while. The waitress brought

Hannah's coffee. He noticed Jarvis was still looking out across the parking lot.

'One thing puzzles me, though,' he said.

'Just one thing?'

'You know what I mean. How do these things get to Earth?'

'Do you know much about meteorites?'

'I have a feeling I soon will.'

'There's all kinds of things hurtling around in space. Bits of asteroid, fragments of interplanetary rock, they're falling through into the Earth's atmosphere all the time.'

'I know that. That's what shooting stars are, right? And meteor showers.'

'Did you know we've found bits of Mars on Earth?'

'That's true. I read about it in *Scientific American*.'

'It was in *Nature* first. And then there were the meteorites with the DNA fragments, the ones that started the "life on Mars" stories.'

'So what's happening?'

'Do you understand Newtonian physics?'

'No.'

'Let's make it simple, then,' she said. 'It's all about force and reaction. A big lump of rock, I mean like a really big one, hits another one and it causes a reaction. Bits fly everywhere. If it hits hard enough, bits of the planet or whatever it is that's been hit, they just fly up into the air.'

'And come down again.'

'Usually. But just suppose the impact is forceful enough to propel material out of the planet's gravitational field. It can happen, you know. And then that material either goes into orbit or it breaks free entirely. That's why we got bits of Mars landing on Earth. Maybe there are bits of Earth on Mars, who knows? Maybe there are bits of Neptune or Pluto or something out there in the parking lot.'

'So our green rocks come from Mars, eh?'

'Who knows where they come from? They could have been zapping around in space for millions of years.'

'Jesus,' said Hannah. 'And I've got a whole bagful of them in my glove compartment.'

They checked out of the motel. They figured it wasn't wise to stay in the same place for too long. At any moment they might be missed. Privately, Hannah gave the two of them forty-eight hours at the most before they were discovered. In the forbidden zone, they needed to be on the move constantly.

They drove into town, bought some packaging material. In the parking lot in the of the A&P supermarket they made up one parcel for Calvin Caughey at NASA and another for Clemmie. They found a dispatch company and made arrangements for delivery.

Next they found a company that rented storage space in an old warehouse. For $150 plus taxes they got a three-month rental – the minimum they could take – on a ten-foot square wire mesh box in a secure compound. They filled it with a load of empty cartons from the A&P, in one of which was a small Styrofoam box – a piece of packaging that Hannah found in a trashcan – that contained five small fragments of green rock.

Then they set off to look for some more samples.

FORTY-TWO

BURNT OAK, TEXAS. JULY 17TH. 10.38 AM.

Hannah didn't know much about the laptop that Jarvis carried everywhere with her, but it sure as hell wasn't the kind of thing you might pick up at Radio Shack.

Right now she had it hooked onto a public-access terminal in the Burnt Oak town library and was downloading data just as fast as she could.

'Look at this,' she said, and turned the screen to face him.

'STREAKERS NIX TOWN FEST' read the headline, lifted from the printer of that week's Burnt Oak *Clarion*, which wouldn't be on sale until the following morning. And under it: 'ROSE BOWL PARADE DISRUPTED BY NUDE INVASION.'

It was familiar stuff to both of them, the sudden outburst of irrational behaviour. After the print works, Jarvis accessed the account-handling section of a cable TV company's soft-porn channel and found a fifty to sixty per cent increase in demand over the three evenings prior to the meteor activity. Everything seemed to point to the same conclusion.

'So we see what people are doing,' said Hannah, who was beginning to get the hang of things. 'I think we might even know why they're doing it. So can that thing of yours tell us *where* they're doing it?'

'Why do you need to know?'

'I just have a hunch, you know, that we ought to get hold of some more of that stuff. Something that came from a different place, a different time. It might make more of a case. The more we can put in front of Stone that proves we're really onto something, the better chance we'll stand when the shit hits the fan.'

Inside two minutes they had a map of Texas and the other states of the South and West up on-screen with the relevant data. Instances of unusual behaviour in the last three days – as recorded by fax, phone, IDS and e-mail – were marked in pronounced clusters of red dots. Jarvis patched this onto data freely available from NASA and other government agencies regarding meteorite activity over the corresponding period. The correlations were difficult to ignore.

The catch was, pretty nearly everything was in an urban area, which made it useless for any kind of ground search. Jarvis blew up the maps and all they could see was streets and houses. There was one area, though, that remained a blank. According to the satellite reports, a whole parcel of Arizona had been subjected to meteorite bombardment over the past couple of nights and yet there was just one on-site report – a patrolman radioing in a report of spectacular meteorite activity, the exact details available only via high-security cop networks. Cops were always touchy about these things. Too many cops had seen UFOs and they knew they had to be careful.

Jarvis clicked the spot. It was about as remote a place as they could ever hope to find and search, without arousing suspicion.

'You want to guess why that piece of real estate is so remote?' asked Hannah.

'Does that mean you know?'

'Tenth grade American history tells me why. That's Indian country, out there. The biggest and least populated reservation in the West. That's where we've got to look.'

FORTY-THREE

BROKEN LANCE, ARIZONA. JULY 18TH.
10.00 AM.

Weary from driving through the night, Hannah called
Clemmie's number from a pay phone at the first gas station
they'd encountered in a hundred miles of loneliness.

She sounded wide awake. He'd forgotten about the
time zones in his sleepless state, figured she'd be half-
past dead just like he was.

'Did you get a package today?' he asked her. He didn't
have much time and he had to remember she too
thought he was in Philadelphia.

'Sure did. I haven't opened it yet, though.'

'Don't open it just yet, will you?'

'Whatever you say. When are you coming back?'

'Soon, honey. I figure we're on to something.'

She ignored him. 'I sure wish you were here with me.
It gets pretty lonesome all by myself.'

'I know the feeling.'

'In fact, I'm feeling real horny right now.'

Hannah wiped his finger inside the collar of his shirt.
It must have been well over a hundred inside that phone
booth. And Clemmie was making him feel hotter still.

'You try and hang on to that, till I get back.'

'I'm not sure I can wait that long, honey. I need a
man right now. Maybe the pizza delivery boy or
something . . .'

254

He wasn't entirely sure she was joking. Maybe the green fragments were working on her too. Everything seemed to tally and yet Jarvis had spent the night before last with a bagful of them beside her bed and they apparently hadn't had the slightest effect on her. Well, they wouldn't on *her*, would they?

'Oh, and some guy from the Bureau's been calling the last couple of days. I told him you were in Philadelphia. Then last night someone came around looking for you, but I wouldn't open the door. He looked Bureau material too. Tall, shaven head, rimless glasses.'

That's got to be Stone, thought Hannah. Or one of his minions. Of course they were looking for him now. It was his – and Jarvis's – turn to be the hunted animal. He wondered just how long they had. If there was one thing the Bureau could do well, it was finding people.

He rang off. Jarvis was studying a large-scale map of the area, one finger rolling the trackball of her computer.

She stabbed at a point among a lot of tightly packed contour lines.

'This is where the cop car was. They'd been on duty most of the night here – waiting for some dope dealers or something. They didn't move from that one spot until the radio picked up what they were doing.'

'Which was when?'

'At two-thirty in the morning. A little before one, we have reports of meteor showers in the area. They even reported it themselves over the car radio. I could get hold of the controller's log if we needed to.'

'How far is it from here?'

'Sixty miles, maybe more. It's on reservation land so we'd better be careful.'

'They don't scalp white men any more, you know. Or rape our women.'

She looked at him with distaste.

'There are other sensibilities, Hannah,' she said.

'That's Native American land. The Bureau doesn't set up operations on their reservations without obeying the protocols.'

'This isn't Bureau business. We're doing this on our own, Jarvis.'

FORTY-FOUR

DRY GULCH, ARIZONA. JULY 18TH. 4.17 PM.

The heat was beyond belief but the Arizona landscape was something else, like nothing Hannah had seen outside the pages of *National Geographic*. Everything was just form, colour, outline – sculpture in the raw, the bare jagged hills that stretched as far as the eye could see, through three hundred and sixty degrees. He'd seen pictures of the mountains on the moon that looked more homely.

They found the cop car's hideaway pretty easily. It was a natural place to lurk in wait for any drunk drivers or late-night dope dealers who might happen along – a little ridge above a stretch of open ground, with plenty of scrubby bushes to hide suspicious outlines. There were tyre tracks in the barren, dusty soil that suggested the place was used a lot.

Hannah got out of their rented Taurus, shielding his eyes from the glare. He had a feeling he was not alone and yet, though he could see for maybe ten miles in each direction, he couldn't see a single sign of human habitation beyond a straggling line of telephone cables. All around him, he knew, snakes and gophers and jackrabbits and suchlike were watching him, trying to figure out his next move.

'Are you sure this is the place?' said Jarvis, smoothing the creases in her skirt.

'It has to be. We have all the co-ordinates and the map reference.'

She indicated the laptop, sitting on the back seat like an honoured guest.

'I could get us a satellite fix if you like.'

'No, this has to be the place. Where else around here could you hide a cop car? Let's go for a walk, see what we can find.'

Secure behind their Ray-Bans, they set off across the boulder-strewn landscape. It was, Hannah knew, a million to one chance that they would find anything – but they had to take it. That time they had found something before, in the gully, that was just pure luck. But the laws of probability didn't stop him hoping they'd get lucky again.

And Jarvis, too, the cool one. She wouldn't be out here if she didn't think they had more than a snowball in hell's chance of finding something.

He felt very focused and at the same time hyper-anxious, the more they pushed on into the wilderness. It was that same old fear of going beyond the bounds of duty, of a Bureau run according to systems that he'd dared to break. But he was safe out here, he tried to tell himself. And yet another voice told him he'd taken the law into his own hands and some day Stone was going to exact vengeance – if he and Jarvis didn't get a result.

All the while his eyes methodically scanned the ground. A couple of times he thought he might have found something but it wasn't, just a piece of sand-blasted glass or a pebble. He picked a few things up that he thought Clemmie might find interesting – a piece of bone, bleached white by the sun, a feather that he couldn't identify. He knew there were eagles around here and he longed to see one, having served under its image for so long.

His mind went back over the last few weeks, trying to find the connections that Jarvis – with her scientific mind – seemed to believe he could make almost intuitively. But his grey matter wasn't working too well this afternoon.

They had seemed to be forever on the brink of discovering something, of working out just what it was that had driven so many people over so many years to act the way they did. He was sure, now, that it was these amazing rocks that lay behind it. At first it had seemed like one science-fiction story too many, these little green fragments from outer space that had real power over people. Bullshit, he kept telling himself, but now he knew it just had to be true. There could be no other explanation. The only irrational thing was the process of explanation.

He'd always thought that major scientific discoveries were made by severe-looking people in white coats working in laboratories, or else pioneered by ageing longhairs who'd forsaken their Grateful Dead records for supercomputers. Things like this – a rock that influenced behaviour – weren't, as a rule, identified by a couple of middle-ranking Bureau agents who were supposed to be pushing paperwork around and making phone calls instead of scuffling around in the dust in a lunar landscape. He felt a strange kind of pride in the very oddity of their situation, their uniqueness.

'I think I got something here,' said Jarvis, breaking into his reverie. But when he had stumbled over to where she was looking, she was shaking her head.

'No, it's just a piece of quartz or something,' she said, tossing it back to the ground. 'You find anything?'

'Nothing. Nothing at all.'

'Maybe we should go back, towards the car. Maybe this stuff only operates over close range. Maybe some fell right by the cop car.'

'What are all these maybes?'

'Life is full of maybes. Maybe we need to be more rational about where we're looking. We need to be looking in open ground, not close to these hills.'

She was right, as she usually was. And yet he had again that sensation of being watched, as if someone knew where he was.

They turned and began to retrace their steps. As they did so, Hannah caught sight of the Indian, standing on a little ridge away to his left. He had been looking right at the spot only a minute ago and no one was there.

For a second or two their eyes met. He must have been in his fifties at least, possibly much older, but as he made his way down the slope towards them he moved with the grace and agility of a man half his age. He was tall, dressed in loose jeans and a T-shirt, sandal-shod, and around his neck wore an elaborate beadwork chest piece that would easily have fetched two thousand dollars or more in a craft shop.

They exchanged greetings. Hannah remembered what Jarvis had said, about treating their presence on Indian land with circumspection. They might not have bothered.

'Is this what you're looking for?' asked the Indian. He held out his hand. It contained maybe a half-dozen pieces of a dull green mineral.

Hannah and Jarvis exchanged glances. They weren't used to being second-guessed like this.

'Do you know what it is?' Jarvis countered, evading the question.

'We call them love rocks,' said the Indian.

Hannah's heart almost stopped beating. 'You know anything about them?'

'We find them out here sometimes. They fall from the sky. Some rocks rise to the surface from down below but these come from above.'

The Indian waved his hands towards the heavens. It probably has more significance to him than it does to me, thought Hannah. 'And you collect them?' he asked. 'Why do you do that?'

'I could ask you the same question, my friend. Come and talk with me a while.'

He turned on his heel and led them towards a narrow ravine. A pick-up truck was parked in the shadow of an outcrop of rock. Hannah had passed this way not ten minutes earlier and hadn't seen a thing.

Afterwards, Hannah never did quite figure out how the Indian came to get so much information out of them without giving them in return much more than his name, Walter Passing Cloud, and little bit of history of the Nanina Indians. He knew who they were, what they were doing and why they were there and, although he had never heard of Eugene Sleep or seen a laptop computer in his life, he was on their wavelength like an automatic tracking station.

He took them to his pueblo home, remote among the high rocks. Inside it was cool and surprisingly spacious. There was a young woman there, whom he introduced as his wife, and a much older couple who were his parents and a whole parcel of kids who could have been anybody's. There were other pueblos around, all along the canyon. Outside most of them were pick-up trucks and beat-up station wagons.

They drank something that might have been tea and ate something that might have been meat, and then some extraordinary little cakes made with maize flour or something and it really was like taking tea with the Queen of England. After a while the old people and the young ones left and it was just Hannah and Jarvis talking to Walter Passing Cloud.

Finally he told them what they wanted to know.

He talked to them quite openly about the dull green meteorite fragments and their powers. Sure, the Indians knew a surprising amount about astronomy – they had devised calendars that were phenomenally accurate over hundreds of years, predicting eclipses of the sun and moon, all kinds of things. Some of his tribe even

261

believed they knew which planet the fragments came from – he gave them the Indian name for it, but it was almost unpronounceable and besides, the Nanina didn't use a formal written language. But he, Walter Passing Cloud, didn't believe any of that. It was as much a mystery to him as it was to the two Bureau agents and in that mystery lay the magic of the stones. He didn't want to break the magic and Hannah could respect him for that.

For centuries they had been a part of Indian ritual – there was even a fertility dance, last performed in 1910, that was associated with them. They were also used therapeutically by some branches of the Nanina, almost like a modern anti-depressant, but very few people had the wisdom to work with them nowadays. Prozac from Mars, Hannah murmured, but Jarvis cut him dead.

'It's good energy for some people but bad energy for others,' the Indian explained when he came to talk about its uses. 'You have to know how to handle it. Indians have used peyote and all kinds of things like that as a part of their rituals for centuries. I guess the stones have a similar kind of place in our culture.'

The words of Walter Passing Cloud made Hannah think of Willie Odum, the drifter with the rotten teeth and the penchant for young girls. He thought of some of the other people they'd encountered in the course of their investigations, the inadequates who couldn't handle the power of the stones, like a high-school kid with his first bottle of hard liquor. They were the ones who'd ended up beating up on their wives, or going on panty-snatch raids on the neighbours' washing lines, or exposing themselves in public, their minds and bodies reeling with unaccustomed desires.

And then there were people like Carmen Fisher, the art teacher he'd met in Hastie, Colorado. It seemed like an aeon ago, and yet it was barely two weeks. They were good energy people, the ones who could handle it, who could use it to enhance the quality of their lives.

But where could you draw the line between the two? Who was to say who would be OK with the love rocks and who would go ape? Everyone knew that hard drugs ought to be legalised – it was the only way to guarantee purity of supply, because it was never smack or cocaine or whatever that killed anyone, it was the shit it was mixed with – but who was the man or woman in the White House or in Congress who would publicly stand up and say what they were all agreed on in private? It would be exactly the same dilemma with the love rocks, the liberals against the control freaks. And liberal, in the United States of today, was a dirty word, far worse than faggot or bastard or even commie.

They listened to Walter Passing Cloud as he told them about rituals and belief systems. Hannah couldn't believe that the information had remained exclusively with the Nanina for so long.

'It hasn't,' said the Indian. 'But so few people believe in these things any longer; they're not open to the possibilities any more.'

'Do you make use of the rocks yourself?' asked Jarvis.

Walter Passing Cloud glanced at his young wife, who was standing near the doorway, framed by the brilliant sunlight outside. A smile crossed his bronzed face.

'Sure,' he said. 'Why not? It's free and it doesn't harm anyone.'

'In itself,' Jarvis quietly added. Hannah knew she was going to say something like that.

Later, Walter Passing Cloud took them to the store of rocks that he kept in a silver box in a remote cave. He must have had a couple of hundred of them, at least, some no bigger than a seed and others the size of a pea. There was one, wrapped in leaves, as big as a golf ball. He handed it to Jarvis.

'My father found that forty years ago,' he said. 'It's still active.'

'These things have a life?'

'We think so. We think that direct sunlight destroys their energy. It's at its most intense when the rocks have just fallen but if you keep them in darkness, you can preserve it, at least for a little while. The bigger they are, the longer they last. But forty years is unusual.'

'How do you know they're still active?' asked Hannah. 'I mean, do they glow in the dark or something?'

Walter Passing Cloud laughed. 'No. It's just something you feel. You can be in a room with them and you will feel a presence. Not directly, like you might be aware of heat or bright light, but in the way it makes you feel. It doesn't work with everyone, either. They say people who live near power lines have things happen to them too, only not so good. We don't have power lines around here. These rocks give us all the energy we need.'

'I think I know what you mean,' said Jarvis. 'I had a few pieces in my bag, from the ones we found in Texas. I was aware of an effect.'

Hannah looked at her, momentarily taken aback. She hadn't said anything about it to him and yet Walter Passing Cloud seemed the kind of person you could trust with such confidences. He would have made a superb counsellor but the Indians had that kind of thing built into their culture. They didn't need psychotherapists because they were all psychotherapists, in their own way.

Walter didn't make any comment, merely nodded, and his eyes glowed a little. 'Here,' he said, and took out a couple of the ball-bearing sized stones. 'Take these with you. My gift.'

Hannah was on the verge of saying they already had a whole boxful of them in the lab at NASA but he heeded Jarvis's caution. The guy wouldn't like to know that his culture was being taken apart and analysed and besides, he was probably telepathic anyway and knew exactly what both of them were thinking.

He could sense they were afraid of something, at any rate. 'Are you hiding from something?' he said as they made their way back to the pueblo. 'Or someone?'

'Sort of,' said Jarvis, who seemed to have opened up completely. 'It's just that we're not really supposed to be here, if you know what I mean.'

'I understand,' said Walter Passing Cloud. 'Where should you be?'

'We're supposed to be in Philadelphia.'

'That's not what I meant.'

Outside it was starting to get dark and the air was suddenly much cooler.

'You'd better stay the night here with us and in the morning I'll drive you back to your car.'

'What if someone steals it? It's not our car, it's a rented car. A Ford.'

'What kind of use is a car like that out here?' said the Indian. 'No one will steal it. There's no one to sell it to, anyway. Everyone wants four-wheel drive these days.'

FORTY-FIVE

NEHI APAHANA RESERVATION, ARIZONA.
JULY 19TH. 2.36 AM.

He was lying on the bed, naked, his legs apart. He
couldn't remember the last time he had had his cock
sucked with such finesse, such obvious relish. She was
the best he had ever known. He lay back with his eyes
closed, savouring the moment. He wanted to banish all
sensation other than that of her tongue, lips and hands.

She was using just the tip of her tongue to coax little
jagged shards of electricity from him. The physical
pleasure made him melt, made his mind go shooting off
somewhere into the ether. She licked the tip of his penis
as though it were a species of exotic fruit, reassuringly
expensive, to be savoured slowly, one sip at a time.

He couldn't see her face in the darkness. Somehow he
preferred it that way. That made things too specific,
being able to see who he was with.

They lay thus for many long minutes, her tongue
washing over him. At times she seemed to be trying to
probe down into the little oval-shaped hole with its
supremely sensitive skin. She didn't seem to want him to
do anything, just lie there and roam free through the
realm of his senses.

Gradually she drew all of him into her mouth. He was
conscious only of his stiffness and of how her ministra-
tions seemed to soothe and seduce him. He was alive

purely for the moment, and felt no need to push her onto her back, force her legs apart, take her in haste and excitement. Only what was *now* was of any importance and what was now was all-absorbing.

Her lips closed over the ridge of his glans as if she were sucking a plum. Her teeth – those small, white, infinitely perfect teeth that he had contemplated so often – nipped him lightly and deliberately, but it served only to enhance rather than interrupt his consciousness of the moment. He moaned gently. He didn't want her to stop. He wanted this moment to go on forever.

Then she was moving her mouth down the thick stalk of his penis, pursing her lips to take him all in. He could feel her tongue swirling against him and the soft pressure of her lips. He seemed to penetrate deeper and deeper inside her, until he could feel her nose against his thick pubic bush.

She was gently bobbing her head up and down now, and involuntarily he found himself responding to her rhythm. He made to move his hips up to meet her thrusts but she seemed to try to stop him, to make some cautionary noise from the back of her cock-filled throat. He settled back on the soft bed and touched her lightly on the shoulders in acknowledgement of her wishes.

The bobbing movements became as regular and hypnotic as the surging of waves, one following another as surely as the motion of the moon. He found himself breathing in and breathing out with infinite slowness, trying to match to perfection the movements of her mouth. Soon he could no longer tell when one breath ended and the new one began; it had all become an endless loop, like watching the breathing of a patient etherised on an operating table.

He opened his eyes and he realised she wasn't there any more. Had he fallen asleep? No, he was far too conscious of his bodily sensations for that to have happened. He had, he realised, simply floated away into an ecstasy where the barriers between what was her body and what was his had simply ceased to be relevant any longer.

His tongue sought hers. She sucked in his lower lip and nibbled it, nipping it gently with her teeth.

She was feeling more aroused than she ever had before, despite the roughness of the bedding and the cold night air that enveloped them both like a mist. She pushed her hips up against him, meeting him thrust for thrust, willing him to move deeper inside her. She arched her back, surprised at her own strength as she lifted herself against the weight of his heavy body, and almost immediately he came inside her in short, rhythmic pulses.

He lay his head down on her shoulders and she ran her fingers through his thick, tangled hair. His chin felt scratchy against her skin – she had not lain with a man in the early hours for so long that she had forgotten how the texture of their bodies changed in such a short while.

He rolled over onto his back. She could feel his penis trail across her thighs, damp and sticky with their mingled juices. She pressed her leg against him, took his hand and squeezed it gently.

Then she led it towards the warm moist place between her thighs.

He rolled over once more until he was face to face with her. The bedding rustled. She wondered what kind of material it was. He kissed her on the tip of her nose – earlier, while words had still not given way to actions, he had said it was one of the things he liked most about her.

His hands roamed up and down her body, stroking the sensitive flesh of her upper arms and the delicate nape of her neck. It felt good. The palms of his hands were strong and confident but in his fingertips he had magic. She liked just to lie there and let the subtle little waves of pleasure wash over her. Once, a long time ago, she had lain down on a beach at the water's edge and let the incoming tide lick around her, becoming stronger as it climbed the sand, inch by shingling inch. Making love often reminded her of that moment.

They were in no hurry, they had no end-point to reach. His penis lay snugly against her leg, warm and limp. Gradually consciousness of the room and the cold night air began to slip away from her. His fingers began to draw little patterns around her breasts, hardly touching them, but just getting near enough to make her nipples pucker up in anticipation. She sighed and moved closer to him, feeling his breath against her neck. The sensation of being held back became almost maddening after a while. She started to want him to take her.

Now he was pushing his palms against her breasts and she felt almost embarrassed by how erect her nipples had become. Her vagina, too, seemed exceptionally moist and succulent, the lips engorged with the blood that hammered through her from her pounding heart.

'Suck my tits,' she breathed, urging him into action. She liked that.

And he needed no second bidding. His tongue flicked down around her bosom, across each soft white breast in turn, lingering tenderly at her nipples. She pushed herself against him, holding her breasts up for him, offering them. Her nipples were as hard and swollen as rosehips.

He sucked as much of her right breast into his mouth as he was able – it was an extraordinary feeling, the sensation of his tongue crammed against her wet nipple, the level of suction he was able to exert. Then he turned his attention to the other breast, drawing that in, his hand between her thighs now, seeking her wet places as she gladly parted her legs.

He slid down her body, his tongue tracing a line down across her firm, flat belly. She knew her own body and had always delighted in it, had always explored its secrets and discovered its pleasures. Her breasts were

269

just large enough for her to reach and suck for herself, but for now she merely played with them, delicately pinching her nipples between forefinger and thumb as her lover's probing tongue found her clitoris at the first attempt.

She pushed him away. It was too soon, there were other things to do first. He understood her movement's meaning and instead planted soft, butterfly kisses against her pudenda, stroking her thighs, reaching out for her hand.

Minutes went by that seemed like hours. She seemed to swirl away into another level of consciousness and then come back, refreshed and eager, as though she had been away for years instead of seconds.

She focused all her attention on her lover and the waves of pleasure that were flowing through her. It had taken them so long to find the right path, for the gap between them to close. She had stood apart from him for too long.

She came as he tongued the slick, widening gap between her legs, the pulsing eddies of pleasure becoming almost unbearable at the end, as if she were being tormented rather than pleasured by him. She had to make him stop, or he would have carried on all night, making love to her in that fashion . . .

She lay back on the lumpy mattress, eyes closed, aware of nothing but the moment. An aeon flowed by. Oh, but he knew how to bring joy to a woman, she thought to herself when consciousness finally returned. There was so much they had to say to each other, so much that had remained unspoken for so long.

But now was not the time to talk of such things. Aware again of her role, she took hold of his penis once more and guided it to her mouth. She seemed possessed of an irresistible energy and so was he. And there was a levity now in their love-making, a joy that had not been there before, until their bodily lusts had hurled themselves against each other and exhausted themselves. Rawness and fire were being replaced by tenderness and warmth.

She was sitting half-upright on the bed and he was kneeling up to let her suck him. She frigged his shaft a few times and then her tongue flickered out and she teased the tender nerve-endings of his glans, gliding over its spongy surface, nibbling with her teeth.

She had surprised herself by how much she liked to suck his dick. She took it deep into her mouth, tasting his saltiness and the mixture of their juices, her own tang as well as the flavour of his come. She bobbed her head up and down, swirling her tongue around the sensitive tip, nipping him playfully so that he winced and laughed and protested. She knew he liked it the way she did it. She would have been happy to suck him all night if he'd wanted her to.

With his glans just inside her mouth, she formed her lips into a tight ring and managed to insinuate the tip of her tongue into the little dark slit at the end of his cock. As her lips massaged the ridge around his penis she stroked his shaft with a firm, regular rhythm. He moved backwards a little, perhaps rocking back and forth slightly on his heels, gently fucking her in her mouth, inserting and withdrawing his cock no more than an inch or two at a time.

She could hear him moan but she didn't look up, concentrating instead on her task. When he came she would have almost choked had she not taken a deep breath when she felt his balls contracting, so great was the rush of semen into her mouth, but she swallowed most of it down – men, she knew, placed a great value on their sperm and felt insulted if you spat it out.

FORTY-SIX

The meeting with Stone was short, sharp and explosive.

'You disappear off the face of the earth for the best part of a week, you disobey my orders, you fail to attend a course you've been nominated for, you violate your code of conduct and now you come to me and say you've found some meteorite that's going to change the world. Just what in the hell do you think you're doing? Auditioning for Star Trek?'

The veins on his forehead stood out like the plumbing on the outside of a house. His face had turned a deep red colour and his hands were shaking. His bald head shone like an angry beacon and those rimless glasses seemed to be magnifying the rage that was in his eyes.

Hannah and Jarvis were standing in front of his desk. They hadn't been invited to sit down.

'No, sir—' Hannah began but Stone wasn't in the mood to listen.

'I've had Pepper on my case all week. I told you to stay well clear of Sleep and you go wading in like the Marine Corps.'

'It wasn't Sleep, sir—'

'I don't care.'

'Sleep has nothing to do with it—'

'Shut the fuck up. You disobeyed orders and that's bad news.'

272

'We were told to stay clear of Sleep and we did. This is something else entirely.'

'Has all that jacking-off made you go deaf, Hannah? I said shut the fuck up and listen to me. I can get you thrown out of the Bureau for insubordination, do you realise that? Have you any idea how much bargaining I've had to do with Pepper, how many brownie points I've lost? I don't like to suck ass but that's what I've had to do on behalf of you guys. You got that?'

'Sir—'

'Don't sir me.' He launched into another tirade. His dome-like head positively glowed with fury.

As discreetly as possible, Jarvis opened her briefcase and took out a slim folder and an ordinary PC disc. She placed them respectfully on Stone's huge and empty desk. She waited for a pause in the onslaught.

'Everything's in here, sir,' she said as respectfully as she could. Her eyes were downcast, avoiding contact. Her training told her how to handle these situations. It didn't do to be confrontational. 'This is the preliminary report from NASA.'

'Oh my good fucking God! NASA! What in the hell have you got NASA involved for?'

She'd set him off all over again, spinning and twisting like a malevolent clockwork toy. His eyes burned a hole in the yellow brick wall opposite.

'I don't need this,' he said finally, exasperation pervading every vowel and consonant.

There was a long, long silence.

'I really don't need this,' Stone repeated, turning round to face them. His eyes lit on the disc on his desk. 'What did you say this is?'

'It explains the preliminary findings. It's provisional, but the rocks we found do appear to have a powerful energy source.'

'Does anyone else know about this?'

'No. Unless you count Willie Odum.'

'Who the fuck's he?'

'He's a drifter the cops pulled in. He had some rocks in his pocket. He said they turned him on. Girls too. They found him in bed with two high-school girls.'

Stone turned to face the window again.

'I have two of my top agents saying they've found an aphrodisiac rock,' he said, calmness slowly beginning to return to that rich chocolate voice. 'For corroborative evidence they cite a bum the cops threw in the drunk tank.'

'He's not a drunk,' said Hannah. 'He's a junkie.'

Stone was silent and still. What could he say?

Hannah and Jarvis looked at each other, a question in the eyes of each of them. When ten or fifteen seconds had ticked by, they knew the meeting was over.

Hannah closed the door quietly behind them. In the corridor, he realised how much his heart was racing.

FORTY-SEVEN

WASHINGTON, DC. JULY 25TH. 10.15 AM.

Hannah and Jarvis went back to normal duties. They saw neither hide nor hair of Stone but every time either of their internal phones rang, they jumped.

Finally they got the call they had been dreading. Stone wanted to see them both down in Dead Files, in three minutes.

When they got there he was sitting on the edge of a desk. It didn't look any too secure and neither did their job prospects.

'I looked at that material you gave me,' he said. He had the disc in his hand, the same one Jarvis had placed on his desk. He waved it at them. There was a computer on the desk beside him but the screen was blank, like Stone's face.

Hannah and Jarvis nodded.

'Anything NASA might have said at that point in time was largely conjectural, you knew that?'

They nodded again.

'They say it would take at least another couple of years' work to produce any conclusive findings. That would cost anything from two to three billion dollars, minimum. What would the point of it be, do you think? What are we trying to prove?'

'Well,' began Hannah, 'for a start it's an amazing discovery. Surely we have a duty to investigate such things?'

'We don't have a cure for cancer,' said Stone. 'Welfare is a joke. We cut the budget drastically on the Space Program. The Bureau is ten per cent down on funding in real terms. All these things are relative.'

'If this stuff works like we think it works,' ventured Jarvis, 'it might have uses.'

'You mean, like some kind of quack love potion? Give me a break, will you? The Government can't associate itself with things like that.'

'They sold War Bonds,' said Hannah, but Stone shot him a look that made him shut up fast.

'No, it's not like that at all,' Jarvis cut in. 'To be honest, I don't really know how it might be put to use. I think the applications of this knowledge would suggest themselves in the course of research.'

'You can't research something without an end-point in sight,' said Stone quickly. 'That's what science is all about. You should know that. You're qualified.'

'OK, but sometimes, I think, we should be open-minded. I think we shouldn't rush in to condemn just because we don't understand something. I think that's what this is about, in part. From what we can gather, this is all about people opening up. This force, call it what you will, makes people open up, makes them more themselves. Their true selves.'

'It's also about people taking their clothes off in shopping malls. It's about couples screwing among the avocados in their local Safeway. Bums fucking teenage girls in trailer homes.'

'That's because some people can't handle it,' Hannah objected. 'But if people knew better how to use it, to make it work to their advantage, it would be different.'

'How?'

'I don't know how. That's what we need to find out.'

'You got three billion dollars, Hannah? These days, you don't look like you've got three hundred in your chequeing account.'

'That's peanuts compared with how much it took to develop Prozac,' Jarvis said quietly.

'You saying this stuff could be used like Prozac?'

'It seems a sight more natural,' Jarvis continued. 'What we do know is that it makes some people feel a whole lot better. And that's one good reason to start doing something.'

'That's a damn good reason to forget all about it,' said a voice behind her. She spun round. She hadn't heard anyone come into the room.

'Those pharmaceutical companies have got billions invested in drug treatments. How d'you think they're going to react if we announce that you can pick rocks right off the ground that do the same thing for free?'

The voice came from a small man standing near the door. He didn't announce himself. Neither Hannah nor Jarvis had ever seen him before.

He came closer. His clothes smelled heavily of cigarette smoke.

'No, we can't rock their boat,' he went on. 'And even if we did the research ourselves, can you imagine what the press would say? Have you any idea of what the Moral Majority would make of it? Can you see the headlines? "US Government pumps billions into love-rock research". Can you imagine the anti-Government stories that would come out? They'd see it as a licence for people to start balling in the streets.'

'Maybe Eugene Sleep would see it like that,' countered Hannah. 'But there are some decent people out there too. You can't always hide from the truth.'

'Don't mention Sleep's name,' the newcomer said quickly and quietly. 'He stays out of this issue.'

'Sorry,' Hannah said. He hadn't a clue who the guy was and Stone sure as hell wasn't making any introductions. He continued to sit on the edge of the desk, tapping the side of his nose with Jarvis's disc.

'Whatever the proven benefits of this thing of yours

277

might be,' the short man went on, 'there's a multi-billion dollar industry out there thriving on people's frustrations and unhappiness – from pharmaceutical giants to psychotherapists. If people could get better just by picking up meteor fragments in the desert, the Government would lose millions each year in taxation, not to mention the campaign contributions that the big companies would no longer make.'

'But we're talking about two or three years' work. We'll be on the edge of the millennium by then. Think of what an announcement this would make, the scientific discovery of the next thousand years. Surely the Government ought to look into this, even if the multinationals won't.'

'Sure. But look at it this way. The law-and-order brigade would have a field day. The President can't take that kind of risk if he wants to be re-elected for a fresh term.'

'I just can't believe nobody's got wind of this before,' said Hannah, the frustration rising in his voice. 'I just don't believe we're the first.'

'You're not,' Stone said quietly.

Hannah spun round.

'There have been covert teams working in this area since the thirties.'

Hannah and Jarvis looked stunned. One door opens, another one closes.

'Why all the fuss now, then?' asked Hannah.

Stone fielded that one. 'Various things had led us to believe that some of the work might start to leak out. Late last year, with a Presidential campaign about to peak. We were afraid the story was going to break in some way and it wouldn't have been convenient, not now, not in 2000, not ever. We couldn't take that risk. We might have lost an element of control.'

'How come?'

'You don't need to know that,' said the little guy. Who

278

the fuck was he? Hannah wondered.

'We needed to deflect attention when these stories started to come out,' Stone went on. 'So we set up some counter-intelligence, a little disinformation. We let some of the stories come through. But the only people they were leaked to were the moral rearmament people, the fundamentalist press, the evangelical TV channels. That was the way to regain the initiative.'

There was a pause while Hannah and Jarvis considered the implications. Stone rolled the disc around between his fingers, turning one edge at a time like a card-sharper.

'So the Bureau deliberately fed them the stories?'

'We're not saying that.' The little guy, again.

'We didn't tell them anything you don't know,' said Stone. 'And nothing whatever about those fragments. We gave them nothing specific, just a line of thought. That was enough.'

'But you were the ones who set us up to look into them in the first place,' Hannah protested.

'We just needed to know they were doing their job, however unwittingly. They were serving us, remember, even if they didn't know it at the time. And hopefully never will.'

'Just what, excuse me asking, is the point of all this?'

'Because if you can build up a chorus of disapproval in Middle America, then you make the world a safer place.'

'Disapproval of what?'

'Disapproval of anything we don't like. Communism, drugs, employees' rights, Iran, Iraq, you name it. You've got to admit, the policy works. If you can control the media, you can control everything. How do you think we've kept the big UFO stories quiet all these years? The policy sees to that.'

'But what policy? We seem to have stumbled on some game that everyone else has been playing all along, and we don't know the rules.'

'There aren't any rules,' said the little guy. 'We make 'em up as we go along. And there isn't any policy either. That, ultimately, *is* the policy. And that's why you two can keep your jobs.'

He turned and went out through the door.

'Who was that?' asked Jarvis. The smell of cigarette smoke lingered in the air.

'I didn't see anyone,' said Stone. His hands were dancing over the computer's keypad. He was using just his index finger, like someone who'd learned to type on a manual.

'That little guy.'

Stone affected not to hear. He put Jarvis's disc into the external drive of the computer and booted it.

'Let me show you something,' he said as he double-clicked the icons.

They looked closely as he opened up the folder. They could see the names on the files that Jarvis had assigned. Cases. Individuals. History. Statistics. Technical information. Summary.

And then, one by one, Stone dragged each of the files over to the wastebasket and clicked on the delete function. Did he want to continue? the dialogue box asked. To do so would erase all information in the files on the disc.

Stone clicked again.

The window repeated the erase message and told him the trash held sixteen items, 4.2 megabytes in all.

Stone double-clicked, and then there were none.

Scandal in Paradise

A CHRONICLE OF OUTRAGEOUS LECHERY

ANONYMOUS

Playtime in Paradise

Amanda Redfern may be blonde and busty but when it comes to finance she's no booby. This former escort-girl and owner of the Paradise Country Club is not usually taken in by men. Flattered and fondled, stroked and willingly seduced, yes. But diddled – in the business sense – definitely no.

Then comes demon debaucher, Roger Vennings, a man who can roger like a stallion and sweet-talk the knickers off a nun. In his hands Amanda is putty, so how can she resist his latest scheme? Which is to use the Country Club as a base for his sex rejuvenation clinic. Unfortunately for Amanda, Roger's business plans all have their shady side. And this one has a shady lady to boot – a redheaded dominatrix with a cupboard full of sex toys . . .

FICTION / EROTICA 0 7472 4398 0